Ed Thomas was born in Aber
founder member of Y Cwmni
Factory where he has worked a
producer. Since 1988 he has w
House of America, Adar heb A
Michael Roderick, Flowers of th
From the Gantry, Hiraeth/Stra

G000145440

Envy, Song From a Forgotten City and *Gas Station
Angel*. They have toured widely in the UK, Europe
and Australia and been translated into eight
languages. His work in theatre, film and TV has
earned numerous awards including Time Out/01
For London, BBC Wales Writer of the Year, Arts
Foundation Fellowship Award, Celtic Film Festival
and BAFTA Cymru Awards for *Silent Village, Fallen
Sons, House of America* and *Satellite City*.
He lives in Cardiff.

PARTHIAN BOOKS

Russ Gomer *Mountain Man*   *photograph linton lowe*

'95-'98 selected work,

Song from a Forgotten City
House of America
Gas Station Angel

Ed Thomas

PARTHIAN

Parthian
The Old Surgery
Napier Street
Cardigan
SA43 1ED
www.parthianbooks.co.uk

ISBN 1-902638-24-7
Typeset in Galliard by NW

Printed and bound by Dinefwr Press, Llandybie
With support from the Parthian Collective

The publishers would like to thank the Arts Council of Wales for
support in the publication of this volume

A cataloguing record for this book is available from the British
Library

Cover Design: Marc Jennings

Cover Photographs: Mark Tillie (Family Portrait, *House of
America*), Brian Tarr (Bell Boy, *Song from a Forgotten City*),
Pau Ros (The Roof, A Man Alone, *Gas Station Angel*).
Author Photograph: Jo Mazelis

Fiction Factory at
Chapter, Market Road, Canton Cardiff CF5 1QE
post@fictionfactoryfilms.com
www.fictionfactoryfilms.com

1995-1998

Iddyn nhw
Wrtho fe
You know who you are
Success and failure
Up and down
Alive and dead
Just to say
Diolch
good as gold
mad as Hell
no Harley
No helmet
Dim fuss
Double Armani
I don't pitch that shit

Then
Now
Whenever
Whatever
Innit
Skin's grown back
And the whites of our eyes
Returned from a long holiday
in off yellow
(Don't take the family)
Too much time on the bar willie

Fishing for trout in strange rivers
While o'dd y
Plastig pipes yn rhedeg
yn y cwt ffowls
So long
Ta ta
Where to
Somewhere good
Good be buggered
Rugby be buggered
But where are all the Roos?
Cer am rol ar y green
Wyngalcha twll dy din
What's the point in being welsh
if we can't be insincere?
Diolch
Thanks
O galon
Memories…huh
You know who you are
X

June 2002

Dorien Thomas *Carlyle*   photograph: Brian Tarr

SONG FROM A FORGOTTEN CITY

"a post-modern theatrical car crash, a mind blowing evening, a fierce elaborate brilliant stream of consciousness. This strange and powerful piece of theatre manages to say more in two hours than many writers manage in a lifetime; and it is also at the same time extremely funny. The actors give great performances - unforgettable, witty, funny, heroic, right on the edge of theatre and its possibilities."

Scotland on Sunday

SONG FROM A FORGOTTEN CITY *premiered at Chapter Arts Centre, Cardiff on February 14th 1995. It toured Wales and the UK before opening in June at the Royal Court Theatre in London as a Barclays New Stages Award winner.*

Original Cast

Carlyle	:	*Dorien Thomas*
Benny/Bellboy	:	*Richard Lynch*
Jojo/Night Porter	:	*Russell Gomer*
Director	:	*Ed Thomas*
Lighting	:	*Nick MacLiammoir*
Designer	:	*Jane Linz Roberts*
Production Manager:		*Ian Buchanan*
Stage Manager	:	*Alison Davies*
Sound	:	*Mike Beer/Barney Freeman*
Music	:	*John Hardy*

Patrick Brennan, Jack James and Andrew Howard also appeared in productions during the tour .

Tour History 1995/1996:

UK tour: Royal Lyceum, Edinburgh. The Royal Court, Barclays New Stages, London. The British Theatre Festival, Bucharest, Romania. The Donmar Warehouse, London. Bonne Biennale Festival, Bonn, Germany. The Melbourne International Festival, Australia.

Translations:

German, Catalan.

ACT 1

Fade up the dub of a metropolis - we see a full moon on one side and a neon light of 'The Angel' on the other. A door smashes open and the NIGHT-PORTER and BELLBOY stare in dismay at the apparently dead CARLYLE.

>   NIGHT-PORTER
>   The little bastard.

>   BELLBOY
>   The twat.

>   NIGHT-PORTER
>   Exactly, Bellboy, exactly.

They examine the body.

>   BELLBOY
>   Is he dead or alive?

>   NIGHT-PORTER
>   What do you think?

>   BELLBOY
>   I wouldn't have asked if I'd known.

>   NIGHT-PORTER
>   Is your head made of FUCKING RUBBER?
>   HE'S DEAD YOU STUPID BASTARD.
>   SHOT. WHAT YOU THINK THIS IS, A
>   FUCKING FICTION?

>   BELLBOY
>   I only asked for Christ sake, no need to chop off

my head. *(PAUSE)* Can I go and get my
camera?

NIGHT-PORTER
No. Go down to the desk and phone the police.

BELLBOY
Can't I just...

NIGHT-PORTER
GO AND PHONE THE POLICE.

BELLBOY
Jesus, I don't know, one of these days.

The BELLBOY exits.

*The NIGHT-PORTER notices a cassette player still playing. He
rewinds it and plays.*

DEAD CARLYLE'S VOICE
'Binoculars' said my father. 'Whatever you do don't
let him have the binoculars.'

NIGHT-PORTER
Is that it?

Fade in Iggy Pop's "Passenger".

We see the caption:

SONG FROM A FORGOTTEN CITY

followed by second caption:

FEBRUARY IN THE CITY. EVENING.
INTERNATIONAL DAY.

The BELLBOY enters to answer a ringing phone.

> BELLBOY
>
>> Good evening, Angel Hotel. Bellboy speaking.
>> I'll check for you now sir. *(Looks at register)*
>> Sorry sir, nobody under that name. Alright.
>> Bye. *(Puts down the phone)* Twat.

NIGHT-PORTER enters distraught.

> NIGHT-PORTER
>> Christ.

> BELLBOY
>> I know.

> NIGHT-PORTER
>> 16:14.

> BELLBOY
>> It's a bastard, did you see it?

> NIGHT-PORTER
>> I heard it.

> BELLBOY
>> Where?

> NIGHT-PORTER
>> A bog. Hayes Island cubicle three, frosted glass
>> looking up at the street.

BELLBOY
  Alone?

NIGHT-PORTER
  Mostly.

BELLBOY
  With a can?.

NIGHT-PORTER
  A four-pack, a spliff and some liquorice allsorts.

BELLBOY
  Ssshhhiiitttt.

NIGHT-PORTER
  Silence for eighty minutes *(PAUSE)* Then shouts.
  Footsteps. Heavy footsteps. Language. Tears. The
  crowd leaves the ground. Sixty thousand capacity. I
  estimate at least ten thousand walked above me with
  the heavy tread of defeat.

BELLBOY
  Ten thousand?

NIGHT-PORTER
  At least.

BELLBOY
  In boots?

NIGHT-PORTER
  In boots, in shoes, in sneakers, in daps, in
  pumps, in wellies. IN SENSIBLE
  FOOTWEAR!

BELLBOY
>In defeat.

NIGHT-PORTER
>In defeat.

BELLBOY
>In Defeat.

They both look at their feet.

NIGHT-PORTER
>I knew we'd been crushed from the weight of boot
>on pavement. One man stopped and looked down at
>me. Couldn't see him clearly. Frosty glass. 'There's a
>bloke down there' he says to his mate. 'See him?'
>'Yeah' says his mate. What's the score and where you
>from I shout. 'He wants to know where we're from'
>says the bloke. 'From?' says his mate. 'From' says the
>bloke. 'Tell him we're from Pyle'. 'Pyle' says the
>bloke. Pyle I say. 'Pyle' he says. 'We're part of a
>coachload from Pyle near Bridgend. Coach leaves at
>six, but we're going early by train.' Why? I shout.
>'Cos we lost' he says. 'We were stuffed' he says.
>'Annihilated' says his mate. 'Crushed to fuck' says the
>bloke. 'We don't like to hang about after a crushing,
>the crack's too bad, and the fighting fierce. You
>alright down there?' No, I shout. 'So long then' says
>the bloke. 'Dull fucker' says his mate. 'Let's get on
>the five past four' says the bloke, 'we'll be in the club
>by six'. *(PAUSE)* So long, I say. I'm alright. Thanks
>for asking. Do you like my hat? *(PAUSE)* I crush an
>allsort, pink in colour knowing it's my last. *(PAUSE)*
>You?

BELLBOY
> Down on the river.

NIGHT-PORTER
> The Taff?

BELLBOY
> Where else?

NIGHT-PORTER
> Walking?

BELLBOY
> The very. I passed a bloke fishing with the radio on.
> Can I listen to it I say. 'Alright' he says. 'Sit down' he
> says. I sit. Never threw his line in once. Why I asked
> when they were five-nil up? 'The fish are fucked' he
> said. 'Poisoned. Chemicals from the valley. Washed
> down in water, not so black now that the mines are
> shut, but the chemical content's high as fuck'. What's
> that? 'A try'. To us? 'To them. Jesus fuck. 10-nil.'
> Who'd have said ten years ago. Or five or three. THE
> WHOLE FUCKING WORLD IS BEATING US
> AT OUR OWN GAME. Who'd have said? No-one.
> Nobody. No-fucker. England, Ireland, Scotland,
> New Zealand, Australia, France, Canada, Western
> Samoa, England again. Beating us. Laughing at us.
> The laughing stock. Us. 10-nil honest to fuck. Turn
> if off. Click. Flies buzz on the river. A trout, drugged
> up to the hilt, 'bout a pound in weight wriggles its
> tail. Come in here shouts the trout, the chemicals are
> lovely. I'm tempted. In his bag he pulls out a doll.
> Cindy, I say. 'Cindy' he says. 'She's lovely. My
> comfort and joy. My ideal woman.' I look him in the
> eye. 'No crack, no muff and tits made of plastic' he

says. 'But she's mine. Not Ken's. K/
He puts his hand on dolly's thigh.
have a look up her skirt buster?' l
he kicked the conversion I say. 'You
'Cos if you're queer, I got Ken in the car. K
shag anyone. Ken's a shagger. Cindy's mine.' Click.
listen to the second half. He pulls himself off in front
of me. Burying his Welsh face in platinum blonde
dolly hair. *(PAUSE)* 'I'm fucked in the head' he says
when he's finished. 'I'm Welsh and I'm fucked in the
head. We're losing.' He left me the dolly. *(PAUSE)*

THE BELLBOY hands the NIGHT-PORTER a dolly. He looks at it watched by CARLYLE from the shadows. CARLYLE rings the desk bell. Lights change.

CARLYLE
Alright?

NIGHT-PORTER
Alright?

BELLBOY
Alright?

CARLYLE
Have you got a room?

(PAUSE)

NIGHT-PORTER
We certainly have sir, in fact it's a special offer.

BELLBOY
£49.99 including VAT and breakfast.

NIGHT-PORTER
>Always a special rate on International days.

CARLYLE
>Is there a discount for losing?

NIGHT-PORTER
>I'm afraid not.

CARLYLE
>Pity.

BELLBOY
>Did you see the match?

CARLYLE
>I saw it on T.V. On the Taff Embankment. The river Taff separated me from the ground. I was on one side, the ground on the other. When the match ended, I felt like a sing. But there was no singing. I went to the Albert. There was a crowd but they weren't singing.

NIGHT-PORTER
>A silent crowd.

CARLYLE
>A silent Welsh crowd.

CARLYLE
>Wales was quiet. *(PAUSE)* I thought I knew the words. The words to the songs. I opened my mouth to sing but fuck all came out. I looked around for some other fucker to start something but they couldn't either. We all

stood there quiet. Silent... Silent as fuck.
(PAUSE) So we drank. And we drank. And we
drank til the barman said 'fuck it.' *(PAUSE)*
'Fuck it' he said.

NIGHT-PORTER
Fuck it.

BELLBOY
Fuck it.

CARLYLE
He rung his bell. He got everybody's attention and
then he jumped onto the bar. 'WHAT THE
FUCK'S THIS?' he said. And no-one said nothing.
'Forty years I been behind this bar' he said. 'Forty
years. And in all that time there hasn't been one
Saturday night that's gone by after an international
match that there hasn't been singing in here. Not
one. What the fuck is the matter with you? DO YOU
WANT THEM TO THINK WE CAN'T SING
ANYMORE? Do you? 'No' they said. 'So sing you
fuckers, SING!' 'We don't know what to sing' they
said. 'You sing the old songs that's what you sing', he
said. 'How do they go?' they asked. 'Go? They go
like they always gone. Nobody's changed the tune
have they? Have they? Same tunes. Same songs.
Nothing new, no new tune, no worries, not to worry,
forty years of bitter top, half a lager, Campari coming
up, look you, fuck off, don't butt in. *(PAUSE)* I've
listened. Forty years I've listened and sung. I aint
going to the grave voiceless. Singless. Without a
sing', he said. 'No way. No how. My name is Bill.
I'm Barman Bill. Sing me a song. *(PAUSE)* Sing me
a fucking song. *(PAUSE)* Sing.' *(PAUSE)* He said.

Bill did... 'Sing... *(PAUSE)* SIIINNGGGG...'

Silence.

I couldn't bear the fucking silence man. We all
stood in the bar looking at the barman then
looking at each other then looking at the floor.
Ninety per cent of the people in that bar have
that carpet pattern imprinted on their brain.
Pink and red it was. Part worn where I was
standing. Nobody said a thing. The barman sat
on the bar, he started crying, a grown man, a
soldier. He took off his tie and threw it. Then
he picked up a glass. And he threw it. Then he
threw another and another and another. He
smashed up the bar. We watched him smash up
the bar. All of it. *(PAUSE)* Then he put a glass
in his wrist. He bled. Nobody stopped him. He
bled and he bled. Somebody called the
ambulance. But it never came. We watched him
die. We never sang. *(PAUSE)* Then somebody
switched on the TV. To watch the highlights.
In the Welsh language. A bloke with a
moustache. 'Anelu at y pissed' said the
commentator. Don't know what the fuck it
meant. We all watched the highlights in a
language we don't understand. But the score
was the same. It didn't change the score. It was
still 16-14. *(PAUSE)* People drifted away. By
the time I looked round there was just me and
the barman. Me standing and him lying dead
on the floor. *(PAUSE)* I starting walking. I
stopped a taxi. I got in. 'Where to?' he said.
Take me somewhere good I said. 'Are you real
he said... fuck off out of my car.' So I came here

to The Angel. To sing. Can you sing?

NIGHT-PORTER
No.

BELLBOY
No.

CARLYLE
(BEAT) Where the fuck are the golden years now
boys?

CARLYLE
In the shops.

BELLBOY
On video.

NIGHT-PORTER
To watch with a can.

CARLYLE
With a spliff.

NIGHT-PORTER
Nice.

BELLBOY
With a leek.

NIGHT-PORTER
Leeks. Yeah.

BELLBOY
The golden era.

NIGHT-PORTER
The golden bollocks.

CARLYLE
Winning.

BELLBOY
At rugby.

NIGHT-PORTER
At the Arms Park.

CARLYLE
The fortress.

BELLBOY
You never beaten Taffy til the final whistle.

NIGHT-PORTER
Every fucker respected us.

CARLYLE
Respect.

BELLBOY
Knew not to fuck with us.

NIGHT-PORTER
Taffy knew his rugby they said.

CARLYLE
All you needed to get into a team anywhere in
the world was to say you were...

ALL
>Welsh.

BELLBOY
>From Wales.

NIGHT-PORTER
>Could kick the ball with either foot.

CARLYLE
>From the hand.

NIGHT-PORTER
>Or the foot.

BELLBOY
>Forty fucking yards or more.

CARLYLE
>Between the posts.

NIGHT-PORTER
>Regular occurrence.

BELLBOY
>Like clockwork.

CARLYLE
>The red devils.

NIGHT-PORTER
>Unbeatable.

BELLBOY
>Invincible.

CARLYLE
The boys you couldn't fuck with.

NIGHT-PORTER
I was part of a nation that was fucking good at
something.

BELLBOY
Anything.

CARLYLE
Something...

NIGHT-PORTER
Not... not...

BELLBOY
Fucking hell...

ALL
16-14.

The phone rings. Sounds of the city.

NIGHT-PORTER
Good evening. Nightporter speaking. I'm sorry
about that Mr Jones, I'll see to it immediately.

Puts phone down.

NIGHT-PORTER
Twat.

NIGHT-PORTER *(To BELLBOY)*
> Fuck off and fix the radiator in room 228
> there's a good lad.

BELLBOY
> I already fixed it.

NIGHT-PORTER
> Fix it again.

BELLBOY
> I...

NIGHT-PORTER
> FUCKING FIX IT!

BELLBOY
> Fucking hell, Night-Porter, one of these
> days.

Moves to exit.

NIGHT-PORTER
> Oh, and Bellboy...

BELLBOY
> What?

NIGHT-PORTER
> Be careful up there.

BELLBOY
> I will.

The BELLBOY exits.

NIGHT-PORTER
Sorry about that sir... his father's from the
disturbed districts.

CARLYLE
I...

NIGHT-PORTER
He's got no social graces, no manners, unlike me.

CARLYLE
Oh?

NIGHT-PORTER
Yes. I once met the queen.

CARLYLE
Really?

NIGHT-PORTER
I shook her hand when she came to open the bypass.

CARLYLE
Which bypass?

NIGHT-PORTER
She cut the ribbon with a scissors. She taught
me the social skills. She wore a pink hat and a
pink dress with brown tights and shoes. She
took the scissors from her handbag, cut the
ribbon and declared the bypass which fucked up
the town open.

CARLYLE
It fucked up the town?

NIGHT-PORTER
> Fucked it completely... it became a bypassed
> town, a bypassed South Walian one horse Welsh
> Western town.

CARLYLE
> Who owned the horse?

NIGHT-PORTER
> I meant the business was fucked.

CARLYLE
> The horse business?

NIGHT-PORTER
> All business sir - the whole place shut down.

CARLYLE
> The horse was shot?

NIGHT-PORTER
> Shot to smithereens, it's a fucking crime. Do you like
> the monarchy Mr...

CARLYLE
> Carlyle... Austin Carlyle, and no... I don't.

NIGHT-PORTER
> Nor me either... I fuckin' hate the monarchy
> me. What the fuck has the monarchy ever done
> for us?

CARLYLE
> Waved clean palms in our direction on

International days.

NIGHT-PORTER
Tell me about it.

CARLYLE
What is there to tell... we lost.

NIGHT-PORTER
No, no.

CARLYLE
Yes, yes.

(PAUSE)

NIGHT-PORTER
No, no. I think you got the wrong end of the stick there see Mr Carlyle. When I said tell me about it, I didn't mean for you to tell me about it because I know all about what you're saying, you got me?

CARLYLE
I'm sorry?

NIGHT-PORTER
When I said 'tell me about it', I just meant as a saying.

CARLYLE
A saying?

NIGHT-PORTER
Like a fucking colloquialism... a slang saying.

CARLYLE
'Tell me about it' is a slang saying?

NIGHT-PORTER
Yeh, it means you don't need telling about it.

CARLYLE
So what's the point in saying it?

NIGHT-PORTER
No point Mr Carlyle, but all kinds of people use
it man. It's common... you'll hear any fucker
using it, dentist, lawyer, bus conductor,
everybody....it's slang man.

CARLYLE
Slang?

NIGHT-PORTER
Yeh... slang.

(PAUSE)

CARLYLE
Slang means we're connected?

NIGHT-PORTER
Yeh.

CARLYLE
Connected right through society.

NIGHT-PORTER
Yeh.

CARLYLE
Part of something?

NIGHT-PORTER
Yeh.

CARLYLE
Something good?

NIGHT-PORTER
Yeh... good if you...

CARLYLE
We're connected then... connected by the way
we speak? We speak the same language as
dentists man.

NIGHT-PORTER
We do Mr Carlyle.

CARLYLE
Next time I see a dentist man, I'm going to feel
a connection... me and him are going to be
connected, he's going to say 'your tooth is
rotten Carlyle' and I'm going to turn round
and say tell me about it.

NIGHT-PORTER
That's it.

CARLYLE
World could do with more dentists man... don't
you think so?.

NIGHT-PORTER
>   Dentists are only good for teeth Mr Carlyle, they're
>   not experts on the whole body man.

CARLYLE
>   I wish I'd been a dentist man, giving injections
>   to take out the rotten without hurting no
>   fucker and saying tell me about it whenever I
>   want man... making connections. (*PAUSE*) You
>   know what I'm saying man?

NIGHT-PORTER
>   I know what you're saying Mr Carlyle.

CARLYLE
>   I should have gone into dentistry Night-Porter...
>   maybe stayed on at school... done exams... gone a
>   different path... I could have sorted out your teeth
>   man....

NIGHT-PORTER
>   My teeth are fucked.

CARLYLE
>   Let me see.

NIGHT-PORTER opens his mouth and the roar of the metropolis comes out. CARLYLE reels back as shocked as the NIGHT-PORTER is.

CARLYLE
>   Fucking hell man!

NIGHT-PORTER
>   Wha? Wha?

CARLYLE
Your teeth are bad.

NIGHT-PORTER
(DEFENSIVE) My teeth are fucked Mr Carlyle,
I never said I had good teeth.

CARLYLE
With teeth like that man you're liable to get
toothache.

NIGHT-PORTER
I ain't liable Mr Carlyle... I already got toothache.

CARLYLE
You got toothache now?

NIGHT-PORTER
Not now, but I do have toothache.

CARLYLE
You do?

NIGHT-PORTER
I get toothache all over my mouth.

CARLYLE
You go to the dentist?

NIGHT-PORTER
Not me Mr Carlyle. I won't go to the dentist
after what they did to the Bellboy.

CARLYLE
The Bellboy?

NIGHT-PORTER

The Bellboy had an abscess. But the dentist made a
botch-job man... when the Bellboy came back from
the dentist he was in agony... I never seen a man in so
much pain. He was holding the one side of his face
like I've never seen anyone hold their face. He
scrunched his face up like a ball. He had a ball face.
His face swelled up and distorted like a balloon. He
had an elephant face. It was really bad Mr Carlyle.

CARLYLE

What was the dentist's name?

NIGHT-PORTER

Pigott I think... Lester Pigott.

CARLYLE

The jockey?

NIGHT-PORTER

The dentist.

CARLYLE

You sure?

NIGHT-PORTER

I'm sure... it's Lester Pigott with one gee.

CARLYLE

One 'g'?

NIGHT-PORTER

Not two gees.

CARLYLE
As in 'giggees'.

NIGHT-PORTER
No.

CARLYLE
He aint a giggee, never.

NIGHT-PORTER
No, he's a fucking dentist... Lester Piggott the jockey's got two gees in Piggott.

CARLYLE
You sure?

NIGHT-PORTER
I seen his name so many times I'd never forget it.

CARLYLE
You gambled?

NIGHT-PORTER
I was a gambler... I took regular tips from an anonymous tipster named O'Reilly but he died and my luck changed.

CARLYLE
Never trust to luck.

NIGHT-PORTER
I don't... not no more... that's why I never got a phone installed at home.

CARLYLE

A phone can be handy.

NIGHT-PORTER

Too handy Mr Carlyle... a phone can get you
into all kinds of trouble if you're a gambler. It
can ring any time - day or night - you answer it
and it's a tipster. An anonymous tipster. A
tipster who won't leave his name when you ask
him.

CARLYLE

That's bad.

NIGHT-PORTER

I know you pick up the phone and say hello
(Picking up a carrot) and the bloke says
'Florence Dancer in the 3.15' and before you
get time to answer, he puts down the phone.

CARLYLE

That happened to you?

NIGHT-PORTER

No, but it would have happened if we'd had a
phone *(He bites the carrot, spits it out)* Fucking
hell.

CARLYLE

What, what?

NIGHT-PORTER

It's a carrot.

CARLYLE
So?

NIGHT-PORTER
I thought it was a banana.

CARLYLE
You don't like carrots?

NIGHT-PORTER
I fucking hate carrots... what the fuck is a carrot
doing in a fruit bowl. DOESN'T THE
MANAGEMENT IN THIS PLACE KNOW
THAT A BANANA MAKES A BETTER
IMAGINARY PHONE THAN A CARROT?

CARLYLE
Obviously not.

NIGHT-PORTER
It's not the right kind of shape.

CARLYLE
The bend.

NIGHT-PORTER
That's why I picked it up!

CARLYLE
You can never fault a banana.

NIGHT-PORTER
Do you think I'd have picked it up if I'd seen it
was a carrot?

CARLYLE
    Never.

NIGHT-PORTER
    Exactly.

CARLYLE
    But there again... it never rang.

NIGHT-PORTER
    No.

CARLYLE
    Cos it's not a phone.

NIGHT-PORTER
    No.

CARLYLE
    Is this a phone?

CARLYLE points to the phone at the reception desk.

NIGHT-PORTER
    That is a hotel phone.

NIGHT-PORTER freezes. Lights change, sound of dub. CARLYLE picks up the phone in a dream sequence.

CARLYLE
    Benny? I never meant to hurt him Benny. Amos was my butty. He called Yvonne a slag. I loved Yvonne man. She was no slag Benny. We went out for a walk, me and Amos. He used to go through shoes like no-one's business, he left a

paper trail from St Mary Street to the West Canal. The paper was pink. I think it was the Financial Times. *(PAUSE)* I don't know what the fuck Amos was doing with the Financial Times in his shoe. He aint got no business interest. He called me a slag. He called Yvonne and me slags. She was no slag and neither am I Benny. We only rented our arses to live man. She only did tricks to survive man, she only rented her arse for money. Yvonne had class Benny. Yvonne was a waitress. Where else do you think I was getting the cash for the Chinese take-aways I brought back for us... for you Benny... me and Yvonne fucked for them... men... most of them had wives. *(PAUSE)* Some of them just wouldn't stop talking... some of them I reckon just got off on talking... I told them I wasn't a talker but they'd just keep on talking... some of them had thick band Welsh gold wedding rings Benny, and all they did was talk... I wanted to tell you man... I'd watch you crunch the prawn crackers and the ribs and the fried rice... and all the time I wanted to tell you Benny... but I just couldn't... I just couldn't. I never meant to hurt him. Benny? Benny?

Music fades. Lights change back.

NIGHT-PORTER
Everything alright Mr Carlyle?

CARLYLE
I think so, Night-Porter.

NIGHT-PORTER
You think so?

CARLYLE
Yes. I think I just had a dream sequence.

NIGHT-PORTER
A dream sequence?

CARLYLE
I just dreamt I talked to Benny...

NIGHT-PORTER
Who's Benny?

CARLYLE
Benny's my friend, we're connected by cars but I think he fucked my woman behind my back.

NIGHT-PORTER
That's bad.

CARLYLE
It is. I'm a writer and a dreamer and I think I killed a man.

NIGHT-PORTER
Good Christ!

CARLYLE
Not necessarily in that order.

NIGHT-PORTER
Does the order really matter?

CARLYLE
It does to me.

NIGHT-PORTER
Why?

CARLYLE
Because I'm a writer Night-Porter.

NIGHT-PORTER
So?

CARLYLE
I'm the writer of this fiction.

NIGHT-PORTER
What fiction?

CARLYLE
This fiction.

NIGHT-PORTER
This aint a fiction.

CARLYLE
Says who?

NIGHT-PORTER
Says me.

CARLYLE
And who are you?

NIGHT-PORTER
> I'm the Night-Porter of the Angel Hotel
> goddamit.

CARLYLE
> Exactly.

NIGHT-PORTER
> Exactly what?

CARLYLE
> With no name.

NIGHT-PORTER
> Excuse me?

CARLYLE
> I bet you haven't got a name.

NIGHT-PORTER
> What the fuck do I want a name for, I'm the
> Night-Porter, I hold a responsible job.

CARLYLE
> A minor character.

NIGHT-PORTER
> Excuse me?

CARLYLE
> You ever seen a Welsh Night-Porter of a
> downtown hotel play a hero before ?

NIGHT-PORTER
> This aint no downtown hotel.

CARLYLE

The voice of the Welsh Night-Porter is invisible
in the pan national world of fiction, he and
many of his ilk will be consigned to the dustbin
of the insignificant forever.

NIGHT-PORTER

I am not insignificant.

CARLYLE

I know that and you know that but who else in
this world cares Night-Porter?

NIGHT-PORTER

I care.

CARLYLE

And I care too, my job is to give a voice to the
voiceless, the dispossessed, the fuck all squareds
who come from fuck all and who got fuck all.

NIGHT-PORTER

Just cos I got fuck all don't mean that...

CARLYLE

Our voices must be heard Night-Porter, we
must play our part on the world stage. We've
got to show that the way we live, love and die
means something, that we are part of the world,
not unique but similar, universal, like small
countries all over the world! You're a minor
character Night-Porter.

NIGHT-PORTER

Well fuck me, there was me thinking I was real.

CARLYLE

Anyone can make a mistake.

NIGHT-PORTER

So you're a major character then?

CARLYLE

I am. I'm a writer trying to escape the corridors
of the invisible who has come to the Angel to
sing.

NIGHT-PORTER

Sing?

CARLYLE

Tell my story Night-Porter, in my own way.

NIGHT-PORTER

So what's your story?

CARLYLE

I've been lied to... I've been lied to since the
beginning. My name is Carlyle. Austin Carlyle. My
father who wasn't my real father said my name was
Carlyle and my mother who wasn't my real mother
told me he called me Carlyle because that's where
they went on honeymoon. Carlisle. But that was a lie.
They'd never been to Carlisle. They never even went
on honeymoon cos he was working man and
couldn't get the time off. And when he did get time
off they went not to Carlisle, but to Yarmouth. Can
you believe that? *(PAUSE)* So why did they lie to
me? I'll tell you why they lied to me. My name is
Carlyle because I was found abandoned in an Austin
Carlisle as a baby somewhere between Merthyr and

Fochriw on the A4-fucking-9 sometime in the sixties.
I was found by a passing fisherman by the name of
Butts... Michael Butts... screaming, and the name
stuck. I was never named after that North Western
town that once made the first division of the football
league at all, and I've felt cheated ever since.
(PAUSE) Do you know what it's like to feel cheated
man... like on a permanent basis? Like ever since you
can remember? Like a convention? Do you know
how long it takes to create a convention man, do
you? I do. In my case, thirty six years man. 36
YEARS. *(PAUSE)* Wouldn't you have got sick of it
after 36 years? *(PAUSE)* Do you know what I'd like
to do with convention man? I'd like to fuck
convention right in the arse and do you know why?
Convention started life as a good idea... such a good
idea that everybody loved it... loved it so much they
all took it up. Took it up for so long they forgot what
a good idea it used to be. They got stuck in a groove
and however much they tried to break free of it man,
convention kept holding on. It held on so tight that
it got right into their souls. Even made them forget
convention altogether. They imagined themselves to
be free. Thought of themselves as individuals living
the way they wanted to live, only thing that bothered
them was why from time to time did their souls
scream. They just put it down to the old screaming
soul. They called it the old screaming soul syndrome
and their souls screamed as they said it. Do you know
that some of those people can manage three
'Shredded Wheat' of a cold winter's morning? Can
you manage three 'Shredded Wheat' man, or do I
mark you down as a 'Frosties' man. A 'Frosties' man
I can tell. Spot it a mile off. Don't tell me, you love
the smell of 'Frosties' in the morning. *(BEAT)* I

came to the city in search of the metropolis and
found only Cardiff. This aint a city for dreamers man.
Sometimes I'm not sure it's a city at all, more like a
place waiting for something good to happen. Like it
hasn't been invented yet. Like it doesn't really believe
it exists. I went out walking with a man who I
shouldn't have messed with by the name of Amos.
(PAUSE) I'd been drinking and smoking all day with
Jojo. Benny asked him to look after me. Benny and
me sometimes write together... but he went out.
(PAUSE) Amos came round with Jackson. We took
some smack, we took some coke, me and Jackson got
talking, Jackson's only young man, but he's the head
shit, the chief man, he's got connections with film
people, writer's people, big people, that's the bottom
line man, he's the head shit and we got talking in the
bathroom man, me and him, he said he knew a man
who was looking for thrillers, low-budget thrillers. I
said I was a writer, I said I've got an idea for a thriller.
A psychological thriller. I was talking psychological
man, I was talking fucking ART man!

*Crash in music, dub, industries. Lights change. JACKSON enters a
bathroom with a sink full of water and lines up some coke on a mirror,
cutting it up, CARLYLE enters.*

JACKSON
I want bums on seats and eyes on stalks Carlyle,
I don't want no heavy art shit.

CARLYLE
It's a thriller Mr Jackson, a psychological
thriller.

JACKSON
> Oh yeh.

CARLYLE
> Yeh.

JACKSON
> So what's the location?

CARLYLE
> The location's the city man.

JACKSON
> What city?

CARLYLE
> An invented city, an imagined city, a mythical
> Welsh city Mr Jackson.

JACKSON
> A Welsh city... CARDIFF.

CARLYLE
> No.

JACKSON
> Swansea!

CARLYLE
> No, Mr Jackson. Swansea is smaller than Cardiff
> man.

JACKSON
> So?

CARLYLE

So the location is a Welsh metropolis, it's got to be a metropolis Mr Jackson, with 2 or 3 million people, man.

JACKSON

But the fucking country's only got 3 million.

CARLYLE

So they all live in the city now.

JACKSON

How come?

CARLYLE

Because they're sick of the country.

JACKSON

Why the fuck should they be sick of the country?

CARLYLE

Maybe because the crops failed.

JACKSON

This is Wales, Carlyle, we don't fucking have crops.

CARLYLE

We have hay Mr Jackson.

JACKSON

BUT NOT CROPS! NOT ON THE GRAND SCALE! And not everybody in the country works on the crops, dammit.

CARLYLE

So what do they do Mr Jackson?

JACKSON

They have chickens and big birds fuck you...
with eggs... they take them to shows... like
agriculture shows... in the West where the land
is good.

CARLYLE

The land is fucked Mr Jackson.

JACKSON

It aint fucking fucked.

CARLYLE

The country's fucked Mr Jackson.

JACKSON

The COUNTRY IS GOOD DAMN YOU! IN
MY HANDS!

CARLYLE

With respect, Mr Jackson, the only country
you've got is the country you got in your
head... it's just an idea sir.

JACKSON

My country aint in my head Carlyle! My
country is real... I've been there... I've been
fishing there... I've been on fishing expeditions
with the finest men and women you could meet
in your life... film and television chief
executives! I have seen spawning fish... REAL
FISH... in the mountains, there were trees and

grass and streams... I saw a man on a tractor baling hay, he gave me directions to the river where all the fish were spawning... I sat on the bank and watched them swimming... millions of them. I SAW FISH... I SAW FISH IN THE WATER, I FUCKING SAW FISH IN THE WATER!

The dub noises change to a lakeside location. JACKSON puts his hand in the water and smiles. PAUSE.

I saw fish in the water in the country... the country was good.

CARLYLE joins him.

CARLYLE
Good?

JACKSON
It was good Carlyle... it was real, it was my country, our country... it was Wales Carlyle... it was beautiful...

CARLYLE pulls a dead, poisoned, plastic fish and a hand holding a sword out of a bucket.

CARLYLE
I don't think so Mr Jackson.

JACKSON recoils in a coke-rage.

JACKSON
What the fuck do you know, you weren't even there!

CARLYLE
But I been there Mr Jackson... I...

JACKSON
Don't you Mr Jackson me, you cunt. Who the
fuck do you think you are?

CARLYLE
I aint fucking with you Mr Jackson, I'm just
telling you how I see it man.

JACKSON
Think you can fuck with the big guys just
because I got a habit.

CARLYLE
No but...

JACKSON
I don't fuck with minnows man, and you're
a minnow man.

CARLYLE
I'm a writer Mr Jackson.

JACKSON
So where's your form, where's your qualifications?

CARLYLE
I don't need no qualifications Mr...

JACKSON
A MAN HAS GOT TO HAVE
QUALIFICATIONS CARLYLE... HE'S GOT

TO HAVE THAT POTENTIAL ON THAT
PAPER. Who wrote 'Crime and Punishment'?

CARLYLE
What?

JACKSON
Who wrote it?

CARLYLE
Doyze-evsky Mr Jackson.

JACKSON
(STRUGGLING TO FIND A NAME) Who
wrote '*Zen and the Art of Motorcycle
Maintenance*'?

CARLYLE
Uh?

JACKSON
You heard.

CARLYLE
I don't...

JACKSON
Come on Carlyle, give me an answer.

CARLYLE
I don't know I said.

JACKSON
GIVE ME AN ANSWER CARLYLE!

CARLYLE

I SAID I DON'T KNOW... WHO GIVES A
FUCK... I AM A WRITER AND NO CUNT
CAN TAKE THAT AWAY FROM ME MAN,
INCLUDING YOU MR JACKSON, SO IF
ALL YOU GOING TO DO IS TAKE IT
AWAY FROM ME MAN, YOU CAN FUCK
RIGHT OFF... YOU CAN FUCK RIGHT
OFF, YOU HEAR ME?

*JACKSON stares at him... he backs off, looking for a way out. He
lights a cigarette.*

JACKSON

Take it easy man... who'd you think you're
talking to?

CARLYLE

I... I'm sorry... It's just....

JACKSON

You see this lighter? I got it from Korea. A
friend I used to know brought it back for me.
He was in the construction business. Fly-overs
and roundabouts, one job he was on finished
thirteen and a half months behind schedule.
(PAUSE) Do you think that's a long time
Carlyle?

CARLYLE

I...

JACKSON

My friend thought it was. Nearly drove him
over the edge. He said that if it wasn't for

me he'd have gone over the top. *(PAUSE)* Not often you meet a man who'll discuss a fly-over with you. *(PAUSE)* That's what he used to say to me. He's moved to Hull now. *(PAUSE)* He wasn't an ordinary bloke see Carlyle. He was out of the ordinary. Like me. I hate the ordinary me. Me and ordinary like to keep our distance, the opposite ends of the map. If ordinary is Dubrovnik and the extraordinary is the South Pole, I like to stay on the South Pole side of things... away from the ordinary. Do you get my drift Carlyle? *(PAUSE)* Good. Because you're ordinary man. You're a.... schmuck.

He moves to exit.

CARLYLE
I aint a schmuck Mr Jackson.

(PAUSE) JACKSON turns.

JACKSON
I just called you a schmuck, so you are a schmuck.

CARLYLE
I aint a schmuck.

(PAUSE)

JACKSON
Schmuck.

CARLYLE
Don't call me that.

JACKSON
Schmuck... schmuck!

CARLYLE
I'm warning you.

JACKSON
SCHMUCK, SCHMUCK, SCHMUCK,
SCHMUCK.

CARLYLE
Shut up.

JACKSON
SCHMUCK, SCHMUCK, SCHMUCK,
SCHMUCK.

CARLYLE
AAARRGHHHH.....

CARLYLE snaps and grabs JACKSON round the neck. JACKSON struggles, CARLYLE forces him down amidst a torrent of shouts and abuse and puts JACKSON's head into the toilet.

CARLYLE
No-one calls me a schmuck and gets away with
it man.

JACKSON
I'm sorry... I'm sorry *(In between duckings)*

CARLYLE
> Sorry aint fucking good enough Mr Jackson,
> sorry is shit.

JACKSON
> No... please... Amos! Jojo!

CARLYLE
> You got fuck all I want man.

JACKSON
> I'll make sure your script gets seen by the top
> brass man, the head shits, the...

CARLYLE
> Fuck off and drown.

CARLYLE holds JACKSON'S head under the water. JACKSON struggles.

CARLYLE
> Better that I find out now rather than later
> man, what do you say, before you get your
> hands on it, thriller by Jesus, you wouldn't
> know a thriller if it smacked you on the arse,
> you never been thrilled in your life, you aint got
> a clue what thrill fucking means man, you hear
> me, you're just white Welsh trash. WHITE
> WELSH TRASH MAN.

JOJO enters.

JOJO
> What the fuck?

A struggle ensues, JOJO pulls CARLYLE off the stricken JACKSON, who recovers, spluttering.

JACKSON
>Get him out of here man.

JOJO
>You okay Mr Jackson?

JACKSON
>Just get him out man... OUT.

JACKSON walks away, music. CARLYLE slumps. Music stops.

JOJO
>What the fuck you do that for, do you know who he is?

CARLYLE
>Yeh.

JOJO
>Are you fucking nuts?

CARLYLE
>He's Jackson Jojo... the top man, the head shit, no bullshit, Jackson is the bottom line, the arse, the honest arse, the honest bottom in the dark recesses of his arse lies the truth, the honest truth, the stinking truth and the stinking truth is that Jackson's full of shit, full of putrid fucking stinking shit.

JOJO
>Take it easy Carlyle.

CARLYLE

He called me ordinary Jojo... he called me a
schmuck.

JOJO

You aint no schmuck.

CARLYLE

I offered him something beautiful man... I
offered him a vision of this shit palace forgotten
country that would make people sit up and
watch, a metropolis, something good, a fucking
architecture man, a rumble of trains, an uptown
and a downtown, maybe a fucking aristocracy
driving Ferrari's getting bumped-off by the
fuck-all squareds. *(PAUSE)* I got it all in my
head man. In my mind. An imagined city. I
made it up man... in my story... not Cardiff...
not Swansea... but a metropolis. *(BEAT)* Jojo?

JOJO

Sure Carlyle.

*JOJO exits. Music fades in. CARLYLE gets up, snorts the remains of
JACKSON'S coke, looks in a mirror.*

CARLYLE

It's a metropolis man. *(PAUSE)* A place where
something good might happen. You get off a
train and you look up at the tall buildings where
the sun reflects all its windows. You hear a clock
striking twelve... you smell food from all over
the world coming at you from every angle, and
you hear ships blowing their horns as they come
into dock man. You feel throbbing in the pit of

your stomach. You feel alive. The city is yours.
You know that people from all over the world
want to come and visit it... to feel it for
themselves. They want to share your city with
you for a day... or a week... then go back home
and tell their people that they never knew such
a city existed man. Your city. Your country's
city. You aren't invisible. You hail a cab. You
get into the back of it and the driver turns
round to you and says 'where to?'... and you
say... take me somewhere good... and he says
'good?' and you say, yeh... good... 'You sure?'
he asks, you say, I'm sure man. So he smiles,
turns on the meter and pulls away. He drives
you to a place you never knew existed... a place
your head never imagined man. A place where
you aint treated like a piece of shit. A place
where you're not a fuck-all squared. A place
that counts on the scale of things. Is noted for
something good. Is not invisible. A place
anyone in the whole fucking world would want
to check out... maybe visit... stay... who knows.
(BEAT) But it aint this city. *(BEAT)* This city
aint grown up yet. It's a junior city, still on free
school milk, not on the map, the cool map, the
map of cool, any fucking map! It's other places
that are getting the fucking bubbly.

*Music changes, dub, lights come back up on reception, CARLYLE
leans on it. The NIGHT-PORTER watches. CARLYLE is groggy
and unsure.*

CARLYLE
  I'm sorry.

NIGHT-PORTER
Forget it.

CARLYLE
He called me a schmuck... It's Yiddish for penis.

NIGHT-PORTER
Ah...

CARLYLE
Do you speak Yiddish man?

NIGHT-PORTER
No. *(BEAT)*

CARLYLE
Could I have that room now?

NIGHT-PORTER
Certainly sir, single or double?

CARLYLE
Single.

NIGHT-PORTER
No problem. If you'd care to sign the book Mr
Carlyle. That'll be £49.99 exactly if you please.

CARLYLE
Can I pay tomorrow?

NIGHT-PORTER
It is a special rate Mr Carlyle.

CARLYLE
> I haven't had a chance to go to the bank.

NIGHT-PORTER
> We take plastic.

CARLYLE
> I don't carry plastic.

NIGHT-PORTER
> I shouldn't really do this, but...

CARLYLE
> I'd appreciate it.

NIGHT-PORTER
> You do realise that if you do a runner I'll have to pay the difference myself. And I'm not rich. I live in a bedsit. I might even lose my job.

CARLYLE
> I won't do a runner.

NIGHT-PORTER
> Honest?

CARLYLE
> Honest.

NIGHT-PORTER
> I'm on duty till 10.00 tomorrow morning so don't try anything.

CARLYLE
> No.

NIGHT-PORTER

> A bloke from Coity once tried a runner not so
> long ago. I doubt if he'll try it again.

CARLYLE

> Why's that?

NIGHT-PORTER

> They found him dead in the Taff with his heart
> ripped out.

CARLYLE

> Straight up?

NIGHT-PORTER

> No.

CARLYLE

> No?

NIGHT-PORTER

> I was only joking. *(PAUSE)* He's thick that's
> all, mind you, eighty per cent of everybody I
> meet these days is thick see. Violently drunk,
> violently sick or violently stupid. Sometimes all
> three. *(PAUSE)* Not worth looking in the pram
> for. *(PAUSE)* I never sit on a toilet seat see.
> Afraid of cats me - when I was little I sat on the
> seat and heard a cat purring down the bog. I
> jumped off the seat and pulled up my trousers
> and from that day on I have never sat on a toilet
> seat. Even when I broke my arm. It's not the
> germs I'm afraid of. It's the cats. *(PAUSE)* Not
> worth a rattle most of them.

CARLYLE
    Cats?

NIGHT-PORTER
    No, no. People. Not worth an egg. Not worth a
    nappy. Not worth putting your head in the
    pram for. *(PAUSE)* What you want to be when
    you grow up? I want to be a doner kebab.
    Where do you want to eat your Sunday dinner?
    I want to have a hot dog by the out of town
    DIY store where the boy next door accidentally
    cut his brother's head off with a Black and
    Decker. *(PAUSE)* His father only went in there
    for a barbeque set. A barbeque set on a trolley.
    To put hamburgers on. Frozen. And sausages.
    Frozen. To wheel about on Sundays. And oven
    ready chips. What a schmuck.. What a stupid
    fucking Welsh schmuck. *(PAUSE)*
    Are you Welsh Mr Carlyle?

CARLYLE
    I thought it was obvious.

NIGHT-PORTER
    Course it is, course it is... Well there we are then
    Mr Carlyle. Here's your room key. Room 321,
    third floor, first left, second on the right, not
    the first landing but the one after that. The lift's
    just through there.

CARLYLE
    Thanks.

NIGHT-PORTER
    Oh, and Mr Carlyle...Good writing.

CARLYLE
D'you think I could have some Bourbon?

NIGHT-PORTER
Single or double?

CARLYLE
A bottle.

NIGHT-PORTER
Certainly sir.

CARLYLE exits.

NIGHT-PORTER
Twat.

CARLYLE enters and approaches a door with 321 on the front. He goes inside, looks around and puts his suitcase on the bed. As he opens it, lights change and dub noise comes up. We see the caption:

FEBRUARY IN THE CITY. INTERNATIONAL DAY. BENNY AND JOJO'S PLACE:

BENNY and JOJO enter and stand looking out as lights fade.

END OF ACT ONE.

Patrick Brennan, Russ Gomer   photograph brian tarr

ACT TWO

Sound of docklands location, lights up on BENNY entering a scruffy squat. Syringes and whisky bottles litter the set. JOJO lies in bed.

BENNY
>Where's Carlyle?

JOJO
>*(WAKING UP)* He must have gone out.

BENNY
>Carlyle don't go out.

(PAUSE)

JOJO
>Carlyle's gone out.

BENNY
>Where?

JOJO
>He didn't say.

BENNY
>He must have said something.

JOJO
>Nothing.

BENNY
>Where were you?

JOJO
>I was asleep.

BENNY
     And he went without saying?

JOJO
     Yeh.

BENNY
     That's funny.

JOJO
     He said he wasn't well.

BENNY
     When did he say this?

JOJO
     Last night... said he was depressed.

BENNY
     Where was I?

JOJO
     You were in bed.

BENNY
     You two talked after I went to bed?

JOJO
     Yeh.

BENNY
     What you talk about?

JOJO
     This and that.

BENNY
>You talk about me?

JOJO
>No.

BENNY
>You sure?

JOJO
>Sure... why would we talk about you?

BENNY
>I don't know.

JOJO
>You were in bed. You weren't the subject.

BENNY
>No?

JOJO
>We talked about different things Benny. Like the future.

BENNY
>The future?

JOJO
>Get things working again.

BENNY
>Working, yeh...

JOJO
> Get on our feet.

BENNY
> Sounds good Jojo... sounds... really good.

JOJO
> Yeh... good.

BENNY
> You talk about me?

JOJO
> No.

BENNY
> Why not Jojo... aren't I part of the future?

JOJO
> Course you are Benny.

BENNY
> So how come you didn't talk about me?

JOJO
> We were talking generally.

BENNY
> You should have woken me up.

JOJO
> We thought we'd let you sleep.

BENNY
> I would have got up Jojo.

JOJO

I know Benny.

BENNY

I would have come out to discuss things.

JOJO

I know.

BENNY

I don't like being left out Jojo.

JOJO

Nobody's leaving you out Benny. This is Jojo you're talking to Benny. Me. I aint ever going to leave you out.

BENNY

I just don't like it when you talk late at night without me too Carlyle.

JOJO

It wasn't planned... it just happened. I was sitting here trying to get a few things down... Carlyle was standing by the window looking out and we started to talk.

BENNY

About what?

JOJO

We just talked Benny.

BENNY

What did you talk about Jojo? *(PAUSE)* Jojo?

JOJO

> We were wondering if you'd ever fucked Yvonne, Benny.

BENNY

> Yvonne was Carlyle's woman Jojo.

JOJO

> If ever there was a woman who could wear a skirt man, it was Yvonne. Did you ever fuck Yvonne, Benny?

BENNY

> I never fucked Yvonne, Jojo.

JOJO

> She told me one night she fucked you man.

BENNY

> I never fucked Yvonne.

JOJO

> She said 'I fucked Benny Jojo... I fucked him all night long.'

BENNY

> I never fucked Yvonne.

JOJO

> She said you did it behind Carlyle's back.

BENNY

> I never fucked Yvonne behind Carlyle's back.

JOJO

Yvonne said you did man.

BENNY

Yvonne was Carlyle's woman Jojo. I never
fucked Yvonne... I would never fuck my best
mate's woman man, even if I fancied her like
crazy, Jojo... it's the unwritten law man, you
look but you do not touch man, it's a question
of loyalty.

JOJO

I reckon you fucked her behind his back man.

BENNY

No.

JOJO

She said you came on to her behind Carlyle's
back... when he was on walk-about... when he
was AWOL... when he was smashed out of his
head, he never knew what day it was or what
planet he was on, man.

BENNY

Carlyle knows what planet he's on man...
Carlyle is my mate man... Carlyle only went
AWOL cos he was depressed man... he was
down... like the chemicals in his head got
mixed up... that's what they said at the
hospital.

JOJO

Yvonne said you came on to her when he was in
the hospital.

BENNY

That's a lie.

JOJO

She said you gave her eyes... looks... smiles...
she said one night you lifted up her short skirt
and put your hand on the inside of her thigh.

BENNY

I have never fucked Yvonne man.

JOJO

When Carlyle was AWOL.

BENNY

Carlyle was ill... he's still ill Jojo... he shouldn't
be walking the streets on his own man... he
needs constant looking at man...

JOJO

Carlyle's safe man.

BENNY

You know where he went?

JOJO

No need to worry about Carlyle man.

BENNY

Where the fuck is he Jojo? *(PAUSE)* Jojo?

JOJO

We took some smack man, then we smoked
some draw.

BENNY
>Fucking hell, when?

JOJO
>All day, all night.

BENNY
>Shit Jojo. Fuckin' shit man.

JOJO
>Shit Jojo or not baby, we smoked some draw...
>good draw... lovely draw... me and Carlyle.

BENNY
>Shit Jojo, I asked you to look after Carlyle man.
>I trusted you to look after him man.

JOJO
>I looked after him best I could Benny.

BENNY
>Looked after him bollocks, you got stoned and
>smacked bullshit, he don't need smack in his
>condition man, he gets shit stupid ideas into his
>head when he's on smack man.

JOJO
>Everybody got shit stupid ideas Benny, but we
>were happy man, I am still fucking happy man.
>I got the smack and the draw and we dealt it
>like we were a fucking cocktail man, we shared
>it

BENNY
>I trusted you to look after Carlyle but you let

me down man... you fucking let me down.

JOJO

Carlyle was happy man... me and Carlyle were
both happy as fucking priests man... I looked
after him man... we had a happy time looking
after each other man.

BENNY

So where the fuck is he Jojo?

JOJO

Fuck knows man. Me and him got things down
on paper man.

BENNY

What?

JOJO

We got things down on paper... we got ideas...
we started to get things down man.

BENNY

Bollocks.

JOJO

I had an idea man... like a fucking good idea...
Carlyle went for it man... we started action
writing, me and Carlyle... ideas were popping
into my head... we were like two fucking wild
poets in the city man.

BENNY

You aint a poet Jojo.

JOJO

I'm a poet man... Carlyle said I was a poet
man... a poet of the city man... that's what
Carlyle called me Benny.

BENNY

You know shit all about poetry man.

JOJO

I am a fucking poet of this city Benny. Carlyle
called me a poet of the forgotten city man... me
and him.

BENNY

Carlyle may be a poet man, but not you Jojo...
no way you're a poet man.

JOJO

I AM A FUCKING POET MAN...
CARLYLE'S CALLED ME A POET, SO
THAT MAKES ME A POET MAN.

BENNY

Bullshit.

JOJO

I can prove it man... we got paper on which we
set down the poems man... we got them here...
me and Carlyle wrote them down man.

BENNY

You aint a poet man and you can fuck your
poems.

JOJO

Here it is Benny... this is a bit of poem here,
except it aint a poem man, it's like a play
idea...me and Carlyle thought we'd start a play
man, like a play they could put on in some
room or something or a theatre or something...
Carlyle said maybe he'd write a play man, or a
film or some shit.

BENNY

Carlyle is ill Jojo... his head chemicals are mixed
up...

JOJO

You just jealous Benny, cos me and Carlyle are
poets and you aint.

BENNY

I'm a poet man, I'm as much a poet as you are
man.

JOJO

Carlyle said there's money in it, he said he could
get our stuff seen by the right people, money
people, get us out of this shit, get us known,
put us on the map.

BENNY

It's all shit talk Jojo... all draw talk... drink talk,
smack talk, it aint fucking real, it's bollocks.

JOJO

It aint bollocks man... You ask Jackson... it's a
big business... I can be a poet part-time man,
write shit.

BENNY

You aint no poet Jojo.

JOJO

I am.

BENNY

You're not.

JOJO

I fucking am man, I am... we all can be man...
Carlyle showed me a book... a book of fucking
poems. He said anyone can do it man... write
poems, plays, films and Carlyle says he's got
connections man... can get CONNECTIONS.

BENNY

Jesus Christ Jojo.

JOJO

Jesus Christ your fucking self Benny... I was
only fucking... we were happy... I am still
happy... why the fuck did you come back and
spoil it man... we got something going... we got
it going. You stopped it going Benny... you've
fucking stopped it going... you didn't have to
do that man.You given me a downer man. I feel
down. Why the fuck did you come back man...
why didn't you just stay out til tomorrow... you
could have stayed out man... you could have
stayed out. *(PAUSE)* Made me feel down
man... I was a poet. I was a street poet man.
Carlyle said. *(PAUSE)* Why'd you come back
man... why didn't you stay out. *(PAUSE)*
Fucking Yvonne or something. *(PAUSE)*

Fucking Yvonne behind Carlyle's back.

BENNY

Yvonne's dead Jojo.

JOJO

So what, Carlyle's your mate man and you went and shagged his woman behind his back.

BENNY

Shut up man.

JOJO

Lifting up her skirt slowly man... and feeling all the secret parts of her body man... through her clothes man... through her underwear... your hands on her body man... you tell her things... all the kinds of things you want to do to her man... maybe you tie her wrists to the bed man... maybe tie her legs to the bed with her silk underwear man... you touch her slowly man... with your hands... then with your tongue... *(PAUSE)* And all the while... Carlyle's on his own man, his head all fucked up... maybe his head's in a gas-cooker... maybe he's got his head in a gas-cooker man with the gas on because his best mate is fucking his woman man... maybe the gas runs out and the meter needs a fifty pence piece man... he's skint... he aint got any money... HE CAN'T EVEN KILL HIMSELF PROPERLY MAN COS HE AINT GOT THE MONEY AND ALL THE WHILE HIS BEST MATE BENNY IS FUCKING HIS WOMAN MAN, IN AND OUT, IN AND FUCKING OUT BENNY.

BENNY
(EXPLODES) AAARRGHHHH.

He pulls a gun out of his pocket, puts it right to JOJO's head as he holds him against the wall.

BENNY
One more word from you man and I'll blow
your fucking brains out.

JOJO
I... I aint... saying nothing Benny... Benny, I
aint saying nothing... put the gun down man...
put the fucking gun down...

BENNY holds the gun to JOJO's head, then slowly takes it away.

BENNY
You ever say I fucked Yvonne again and I'll kill
you Jojo.

JOJO
I won't say nothing Benny.

BENNY
I never fucked Yvonne... you understand me?

JOJO
I understand man... I fucking understand.

BENNY
So apologise.

JOJO
I apologise, Benny.

BENNY
Say you aint a poet.

JOJO
I aint a poet.

BENNY
Say you aint never going to be a poet.

JOJO
I aint never going to be a poet.

BENNY
Good... cos you need soul to be a poet, Jojo
and you got no soul... have you?

JOJO
No.

BENNY
Say you aint got no soul.

JOJO
I aint got no soul Benny.

BENNY
Good... now tell me why you aint got no soul
Jojo.
JOJO
I aint got no soul because... because... fuck, I
don't know why I got no soul Benny.

BENNY
Tell me why you aint got no soul Jojo.

JOJO

I don't know why Benny... I don't FUCKING
KNOW WHY I GOT NO SOUL.

BENNY

Shall I tell you?

JOJO

Tell me.

BENNY

No.

JOJO

TELL ME, TELL ME, TELL ME!

BENNY

Because you prey on people man... you prey on
people's heads man... you suck them dry then
you throw them in the gutter that's what you
want to do to me and to Carlyle... but you
don't fool me man, cos I can see straight into
your soul man and there is fuck all there...
FUCK ALL. DO YOU HEAR ME? You don't
fool me and you know it. But Carlyle's a
different matter altogether... Carlyle aint
himself... Carlyle's vulnerable... Carlyle can be
preyed on... Carlyle can be taken advantage of...
Carlyle maybe got some ideas... maybe Carlyle
can fucking do something with himself... maybe
Carlyle is a poet after all... maybe Carlyle can be
a poet man... a writer... maybe Carlyle can get
himself out of this shit... maybe Carlyle's the
only one of us who could be something
different man... something good... so you set

your sights on him... you get into his head...
you get yourself inside his head so that he don't
know his own head from yours... then you start
to suck Jojo, you suck and you suck... all the
good from his head man and into your own sick
one til Carlyle's empty... til Carlyle's a fucking
cabbage... a vegetable... and you Jojo, turn all
that good into shit man... you turn it into one
great heap of shithouse man... do you
understand what I'm saying? *(He pulls back the
hammer of the gun. Beat)*
Say you understand what I'm saying Jojo?

JOJO
    I understand what you're saying.

BENNY
    Good... cos it's the truth man.

(PAUSE) BENNY pulls the gun away. The tension eases.

JOJO
    It aint the truth Benny.

BENNY
    It's the truth.

JOJO
    We all done bad things man.

BENNY
    We all done bad things yeh... but you Jojo...
    you're different man... you aint any more the
    man I used to know.

JOJO

>Things change Benny... you're just afraid of change... things got to move forward man... us three are changed with it Benny, but you man, you're still stuck somewhere on a road man.

BENNY

>I aint stuck on a road.

JOJO

>Stuck in a groove man, in limbo in the middle of a nowhere road man.

BENNY

>I AM NOT IN A FUCKING NOWHERE ROAD.

PAUSE)

JOJO

>Was a time we were on the same wavelength man... when we understood each other, without having to explain.

BENNY

>Them times are gone.

JOJO

>Was a time when I knew all your habits man... your sleeping habits. I lied back in the van and watched you sleep man... with the radio on... the World Service. I used to look at your face man and think, I know that face man... that's Benny's face. I would think to myself... Benny's my friend man... he's my butty... nothing will ever come between me and Benny man, but

now... *(PAUSE)* I never thought you'd ever pull a gun on me Benny... pull a gun on me and hold it to my head man. *(PAUSE)* Never.

BENNY

I never fucked Yvonne.

JOJO

Maybe you did or maybe you didn't Benny, but you still pulled a gun on me man... and called me bad things. I won't forget that man.

BENNY

You said I fucked Yvonne and I never did... I never been disloyal behind Carlyle's back... it's the unwritten law... the code man... you said I did and I never...

JOJO

I was high on smack man. *(PAUSE)* My head was shot, I been smoking all day long man, I said them things in my draw, in my smack.

BENNY

You do too much smack Jojo.

JOJO

That's as maybe man, but I got to relax somehow Benny... we all got to relax sometime. Everybody's got to relax man... dream things'll get out of the shithouse man, even you Benny.

BENNY

I never relax.

JOJO

> Maybe that's your problem, if you'd been
> relaxed, maybe none of this would have
> happened man.

BENNY

> What happened Jojo?

JOJO

> You fucking tell me.

BENNY

> I don't like it when you take smack, smoke draw and
> wear skirts man... smoking draw and wearing skirts
> on smack don't mix... they are off the menu Jojo.

JOJO

> So what's on the menu Benny?

BENNY

> What?

JOJO

> You said draw and a skirt is off the menu.

BENNY

> Yeh.

JOJO

> So what's the menu... what was on the
> menu. *(PAUSE)* Benny?

BENNY

> Wearing a skirt when you're smashed on draw
> and smack is off the menu that's all I'm saying.

JOJO

It was Carlyle's idea man.. he saw a skirt on
the floor... he said 'Jojo, see this skirt... this
is Yvonne's skirt', and I said yeh, and he said
'yeh'... then he said 'can you imagine how
good she would look in this skirt... the way
her hips would move inside it man...' and I
said yeh... *(PAUSE)* and he said yeh... so I
put on the skirt man... and Carlyle put on a
record man... and we started to dance like
we were Carlyle and Yvonne man... we
started to dance man...

Enter CARLYLE.
Music, dub, JOJO starts to dance drunkenly, lights change,
CARLYLE joins him. BENNY exits.
Music continues as they embrace, getting more passionate, erotic, they
end up on the bed, the full dub of the metropolis takes over, lights etc. to
darkness.
Silence.

CARLYLE and JOJO are spread all over the floor. JOJO drinks and
crawls along. CARLYLE looks wasted.

CARLYLE

You aint Yvonne man. *(PAUSE)* Yvonne had
class... You aint Yvonne.

JOJO

I got class... but no man, I aint Yvonne.

JOJO laughs.

CARLYLE

You ever touch her?

JOJO
>No.

CARLYLE
>You never fucked her?

JOJO
>No man. *(PAUSE)* I shared a bed with Rosie
>man... but I never touched Yvonne.

(PAUSE)

CARLYLE
>Did Benny ever touch her? *(PAUSE)* Jojo?

JOJO
>What you asking me for?

(PAUSE)

CARLYLE
>I loved Yvonne Jojo. We could have been an
>item. I loved her and she loved me... she could
>have married class once upon a time man, but
>she picked me.

JOJO
>Yvonne's dead Carlyle and you never married her.

CARLYLE
>No, but we talked about it man. She used to
>give me extra coffee. I was on the street but she
>still gave me extra coffee. She never gave
>anyone extra coffee Jojo... no-one. She said she
>liked me Jojo. She said that everyone is capable

of being loved man, no matter how fucked up
and lost that human being is man. That's what
she said Jojo.

JOJO

Yvonne was a good woman man.

CARLYLE

She was.

JOJO

Rosie was just a ship in the night.

CARLYLE

I liked Rosie, but I never loved her man.

JOJO

Rosie was damaged.

CARLYLE

Rosie was cut-up.

JOJO

Rosie kept geraniums.

CARLYLE

Outside on her balcony. We went in... me and
you... I wore a big thick tie I found outside the
tailor's next to Greco's. Had a lion on it... I
wore a tie and a t-shirt. She said we could go
home with her. Parked the van at the foot of
her steps and went up to her room. Do you
remember her room?

JOJO
I remember her cats... big cats... the biggest,
fattest cats I have ever seen Carlyle..

CARLYLE
No furniture, except a bed settee and a
photograph of nothing. She said she had a
burglary... someone broke in and stole her
photographs.

JOJO
Nothing else to steal except the cats and who'd
steal them cats... fucking elephant cats...
dinosaur cats.

CARLYLE
Whale cats.

JOJO
Fucking whale cats.

CARLYLE
She stepped out of her corset and I saw her stomach.

JOJO
I remember.

CARLYLE
Rosie was beautiful Jojo, but why did they rip
up her stomach?

JOJO
I wouldn't have hurt her for the world Carlyle.

CARLYLE
    Nor me.

JOJO
    She could have been beautiful Carlyle.

CARLYLE
    She was still beautiful Jojo.

JOJO
    That's right.

CARLYLE
    In her red dress and corset.

JOJO
    We were young pups.

CARLYLE
    She was older... she was an older woman.

JOJO
    She'd been cut up.

CARLYLE
    Yeh.

JOJO
    By the airman.

CARLYLE
    I hate the airman Jojo.

JOJO
    Me too.

CARLYLE
You know what I reckon?

JOJO
What?

CARLYLE
I reckon if you took the air out of the man he would never fly again. *(PAUSE)* You get my drift?

JOJO
You separate the air from the man?

CARLYLE
Yeh.

JOJO
So let's do it. *(PAUSE)*

JOJO & CARLYLE
Man.

CARLYLE
Ordinary fucker.

JOJO
Ordinary... man.

CARLYLE
Over there.

JOJO
Over where?

CARLYLE

Over there by the window, looking out into the street.

JOJO

What the fuck's he doing in his flying hat Carlyle?

CARLYLE

It's the only way he can know who he is.

JOJO

What time do you reckon it is?

CARLYLE

I reckon it's nine twenty five on a Saturday night.

JOJO

In the city... the forgotten city.

CARLYLE

Yeh... foghorns can be heard out at sea... mixing with the rumble of the underground trains and Henry Mancini.

The sound of the city can be heard with Henry Mancini's 'Theme from a Summerplace'.

JOJO

Street walkers plying their trade Carlyle... looking for punters.

CARLYLE

In short skirts and stockings.

JOJO

> The Ferrari set step out of their cars in pearls
> and dickies.... going to the opera.

CARLYLE

> I aint never been to the opera man.

JOJO

> Me neither.

CARLYLE

> Fuck opera.

JOJO

> Fuck the pearls.

CARLYLE

> THOUSAND QUID A TICKET.

JOJO

> Taffy knows his singing Carlyle... Taffy is a
> fucking expert on the singing man.

CARLYLE

> Taffy is a Welshman.

JOJO

> Taffy is a thief.

CARLYLE

> Taffy is the new aristocracy man.

(PAUSE)

JOJO

> Who's Taffy?

CARLYLE
Taffy is us.

JOJO
Us?

CARLYLE
Yeh... we're stepping out to go to the opera man.

JOJO
I hate opera Carlyle and I know jack shit about singing man.

CARLYLE
So pretend.

JOJO
Yeh...
CARLYLE
Clap and say bravo when the pearls and dickies do.

JOJO
I aint never been to an opera man.

CARLYLE
Look at the costumes and the diva's cleavage.

JOJO
She got a chest on her Carlyle... she sings like a fucking mocking bird.

CARLYLE
A robin.

JOJO
> A raven.

CARLYLE
> She can bust cut glass from four hundred feet man.

Sound of breaking glass loudly.

CARLYLE
> I can see the airman man.

JOJO
> Me too.

CARLYLE
> Looking out at the rain on a Saturday night.

JOJO
> In the metropolis.

CARLYLE
> Two million people leave the country cos their crops and factories and way of life is fucked.

JOJO
> Poor bastards.

CARLYLE
> Stuffed into the city.

JOJO
> Giving it an edge.

CARLYLE
> A something.

JOJO
This city can be dangerous man.

CARLYLE
Imagine.

JOJO
I am.

CARLYLE
A Welsh metropolis with attitude.

JOJO
Fuck.

CARLYLE
An international airport with international flights from all over the world.

JOJO
A capital city Carlyle... with us in the centre.

CARLYLE
The boys from the valleys at the centre of the big city.

JOJO
Bigshots.

CARLYLE
Bigshot hipsters.

JOJO
Writers.

CARLYLE
Fucking dirty realism hipsters writers with bust up souls.

JOJO
Bred on defeat.

CARLYLE
Dull cunt romantics man with hearts of neon.

JOJO
And cocks of iron.

CARLYLE
Making up, making up, making up.

JOJO
Like crazy.

CARLYLE
Crazy making up ARTISTS.

JOJO
Fuck.

CARLYLE
Fuck.

JOJO & CARLYLE
FUUUUUUCKKK...

The noise subsides. PAUSE.

CARLYLE
Did we sleep in Rosie's bed Jojo?

JOJO

> We did Carlyle, we really did.

CARLYLE

> I know.

JOJO

> So why did you ask?

CARLYLE

> To make sure Jojo... I got to make sure of
> things sometimes man... you know what I
> mean?

JOJO

> I know what you mean.

CARLYLE

> Cos things can get fuzzy man... like blurred.

JOJO

> Got to trust your memory man.

CARLYLE

> My memory gets blurred Jojo on account of...
> my head... my smack.

JOJO

> I know.

CARLYLE

> I've told so many stories Jojo, my memory gets
> so blurred I don't know where my life ends and
> my blur begins.

JOJO

>Never underestimate the power of the blur
>Carlyle.

CARLYLE

>The blur is all I got.

JOJO

>I blur, you blur... the whole of the country
>blurs man.

CARLYLE

>Why do we blur Jojo?

JOJO

>We blur because... we blur man because... what
>sort of question's that Carlyle?

CARLYLE

>A question.

JOJO

>Some question.

CARLYLE

>Wouldn't it be good to have a pure memory... a
>pure recollection of good things that have
>happened man, that are like sweet? Like friends.
>A whole feast of friends. A giant family... a
>sparkling room where we all go to laugh...
>celebrations and successes punctuated by... by
>laughing... like a full stop to a good thing... til
>the next good thing happens. *(PAUSE)* You
>know what I'm saying?

(PAUSE)

JOJO
> Roll us a joint Carlyle.

CARLYLE
> Like something good?

JOJO
> Like a fucking trumpet Carlyle, roll it like a
> trumpet... and let it blow the cobwebs in my
> damaged fucking skull.

(PAUSE)

CARLYLE
> We're out of draw Jojo.

JOJO
> Uh?

CARLYLE
> We got no draw.

JOJO
> Never.

CARLYLE
> Drawless.

JOJO
> Fuck, what about whiskey?

CARLYLE
> Whiskey? Have we got whiskey?

JOJO searches.

> JOJO
> Looks like we're out of whiskey.

> CARLYLE
> Vodka?

> JOJO
> No.

> CARLYLE
> Gin?

> JOJO
> We're out of alcohol altogether Carlyle.

> CARLYLE
> Fucking hell. No booze, no drugs, no heating,
> no view, no imagination. Do they think that
> being original is easy? Like picking a crab apple
> off a crab apple tree? WHAT KIND OF
> FUCKING HOTEL ROOM IS THIS?

(PAUSE)

> JOJO
> It aint a hotel Carlyle.

> CARLYLE
> Uh?

> JOJO
> This aint no hotel.

CARLYLE
It is.

JOJO
It isn't.

CARLYLE
No?

JOJO
No.

(PAUSE)

CARLYLE
So where the fuck are we?

JOJO
This is my place... mine and Benny's place.

CARLYLE
Oh...

JOJO
It aint the Ritz, but it's a place and we needed a place man. *(PAUSE)* I sorted out the electric fire in here with bars, switch it once for one bar, switch it twice for two man.

CARLYLE
Will you turn it on?

JOJO
You cold man?

CARLYLE

I'm freezing Jojo... will you turn on that electric fire man!

JOJO

It's bust.

CARLYLE

I thought you said...

JOJO

It bust a while ago man... I tried to fix it but... it's just...

CARLYLE

I'm fucking freezing Jojo.

JOJO

So am I.

CARLYLE

We got to do something man... *(Pulling on clothes)*

JOJO

The only thing I can think of is water-torture man.

CARLYLE

What the fuck is water-torture?

JOJO

Four years ago I saw a man light a fire in a bin, cooking chestnuts he was in West Bute Street. Fire in the bin. He had a Russian hat on which came down over his ears. *(PAUSE)* You warm I asked. 'Freezing' he said. Never, I said. 'Straight

up' he said. How the fuck do you manage then?
'Chinese water-torture'

CARLYLE
Uh?

JOJO
They tie you to the floor under a dripping tap
Carlyle, it drips, drip, drip on to the centre of
your head above your nose til you go mad.

CARLYLE
I don't want to go mad.

JOJO
Nor me man, but I...

CARLYLE
That won't help the cold Jojo.

JOJO
It will Carlyle. He was talking adaptation man.
You will go mad if you let the drips get the
better of you he said, but if you imagine every
drip on your head to be like water to a parched
man in the desert, every drop becomes like
heaven. It aint torture at all... you just get
happier and happier with every drop... it's a
question of mind control Carlyle. Adapt or die.
Adapt or imagine.

CARLYLE
Adapt?

JOJO
>We adapt the theory we imagine.

CARLYLE
>Imagine what?

JOJO
>Imagine each shiver of cold is like a breeze on a hot summer's day.

CARLYLE
>Summer?

JOJO
>Summer Carlyle. Now you shut your eyes and imagine it's summer.

CARLYLE
>Summer.

JOJO
>And it's hot.

CARLYLE
>Hot?

JOJO
>The bees are humming above your head and you're lying down in the grass by a blue lake.

CARLYLE
>Blue lake.

Dub and music of summer.

JOJO

> You been on a bike ride. An uphill bike ride and you're sweating man. Sweating like you never sweated in your life. The sun is beating down on you man. It's one o'clock on the hottest day of the year... and you're aching for a breeze man... just a light breeze to cool you down man... you're just waiting for a breeze.
> *(PAUSE)* Did you feel that breeze Carlyle?

CARLYLE

> I feel that breeze man.

JOJO

> Was it good? *(PAUSE)* Carlyle?

CARLYLE

> *(PAUSE)* It was total shit man. I never heard the bees, I never went on an uphill bike ride, I never sweated, I never saw a lake, the sun never beat down on me and it wasn't even fucking summer man.

JOJO

> You never gave it a chance man.

CARLYLE

> I gave it a chance man, but all I got was the breeze bit... I got stuck in the breeze bit man... I got frozen in time in the breeze man and when I opened my eyes, I was surrounded by frozen bees man. Frozen, non-humming, non-honey making bees man, looking down at me with fucked up bee faces, thinking WHY THE

FUCK DID SOME BASTARD TURN
WINTER ON IN MID-SUMMER IN MID-
AIR IN MID FUCKING HUM, MAN.

The dub changes darkly, heavy.

JOJO
> Do you want to wake the whole fucking
> neighbourhood man? DO YOU WANT FOUR
> MEN WITH MACHETES TO COME
> RUNNING IN HERE AND SLICE YOU TO
> PIECES MAN?!

CARLYLE
> What four men?

JOJO
> Of the apocalypse Carlyle.

CARLYLE
> What apocalypse?

JOJO
> There's only one apocalypse man, and if you
> keep shouting man, four horsemen are going to
> come crashing in here and apocalypse us out of
> existence.

CARLYLE
> No.

JOJO
> Yes Carlyle. So will you quit shouting!

CARLYLE

I can hear them Jojo... I can hear them madcap
horses.

JOJO

I got to get out of HERE MAN.

CARLYLE

I can hear them, I can hear them. Help me
Jojo. Help me.

*The two men race around in a druggy hell as the dub increases in
violence. CARLYLE exits. BENNY enters and noise subsides. Lights
revert to pre-dance state. Silence.*

BENNY

So where the fuck is he Jojo?

JOJO

I don't know man.

BENNY

No Jojo, where the fuck is he?

JOJO

He thought this was a hotel, he was pissed off
when he found out it wasn't.

BENNY

What are you saying?

JOJO

I reckon he's gone to find himself a hotel.

BENNY
> What hotel?

JOJO
> There's only one good hotel in this city Benny.

BENNY
> The Angel.

Lights change. CARLYLE enters and stands at his bed as he did at the end of Act Two, Scene 1. BENNY and JOJO exit. CARLYLE sits at a table staring at a typewriter. He tries to write but fails. Sudden knock at the door.

CARLYLE
> Come in. *(BENNY ENTERS UNSEEN AS YET BY CARLYLE)* Put the bourbon down over there please.

BENNY approaches him. CARLYLE looks up.

CARLYLE
> Benny?

BENNY
> Yes. It's me.

CARLYLE
> What are you doing here?

BENNY
> The Bellboy told me what room you were in. Funny guy huh! What are you doing?

CARLYLE
Writing.

BENNY
Writing?

CARLYLE
Yeh, writing. You got a problem with that?

BENNY
How's it coming?

CARLYLE
It's coming.

BENNY
I thought I told you not to leave the house.
Why the fuck did you leave the house?

CARLYLE
I wanted to go for a walk. Jackson called me a
schmuck...then Jojo was doing my head in.

BENNY
Jackson?

CARLYLE
Jackson said maybe I should go with Amos for a
walk.

BENNY
Amos?

CARLYLE
Amos and me. We were smacked out of our

heads. We went for a walk down the docks. On the waterfront. Me and Amos.

BENNY

No. Carlyle it's...

CARLYLE

Will you just let me finish. It's my story. We passed some kids poking around with a dead animal.... setting fire to it and poking it with sticks. I was about to get out and stop them when Amos turned to me and said - right out of the blue - 'not only have you got a bent and bust up nose Carlyle' he said, 'but you've also got hairs sticking out the end of it.' Those were his very words... I called him a fat Welsh dwarf and that really got him going Benny. He said 'oh yeh?' and I said yeh... and when I find a woman who loves me like Yvonne did, I said, she'll pluck out those hairs for me no trouble... she'll make it a regular occurrence. 'A woman' said Amos, yeh, I said, a woman, cos she'll love me. 'Love and a hairy nose don't mix Carlyle' he said... 'and besides, no woman in this city is going to marry a slag, because that's what you and Yvonne are man, slags.' I got angry Benny... I said I was no slag... but he kept saying 'slag, slag... slag' and I saw the animal burn and the kids' eyes glow... we were drawing their attention... Amos kept saying 'slag, slag, slag'... made me angrier and angrier... He made me so fucking angry Benny, my head just went pop Benny... I grabbed him and hit him... again and again... he went down... the kids were whooping like they'd just gone mad... I must

have picked something up... a stone... a brick...
I was like a mad thing... I was like I'd gone
mad... Then I brought the stone down hard on
his head and I heard his skull crack. *(PAUSE)* I
heard his skull crack... but he still had a smile on
his face... Benny... it was as if he wanted me to
do it... *(PAUSE)* I ran away Benny. I had to
run away. Must have been the kids who saw to
Amos man... nobody else saw it. *(PAUSE)* I
didn't want to do it Benny... it just happened.
(PAUSE) Benny?

BENNY

Amos doesn't exist.

CARLYLE

He's my butty, he came over with Jackson.

BENNY

Jackson doesn't exist.

CARLYLE

Doesn't exist?

BENNY

No Carlyle. It's all in your head.

CARLYLE looks at him, then smiles, backs off.

CARLYLE

(*TRIUMPHANT*) You've got it in one Benny
- what's it matter who Jackson is? It's just a
story.

BENNY
So what are you playing at?

CARLYLE
I'm a writer Benny. I make up stories. I aint a schmuck. I aint ordinary. I'm a writer. Yvonne said I was. *(PAUSE)* I dream of Yvonne Benny. I'd like to have married Yvonne man.... I loved her. I wanted a family... kids... a place you could come and visit Benny... maybe we could sit down and write together Benny. *(PAUSE)* Benny? *(CARLYLE turns around)* Did you ever fuck Yvonne Benny? Did you? DID YOU?

BENNY
I NEVER FUCKED YVONNE.

CARLYLE
Honest?

BENNY
Honest.

Beat.

CARLYLE
But you liked her didn't you?

BENNY
Yeh I liked her... she reminded me of my mother.

CARLYLE
How?

BENNY
She was about the same age as my mother... she

113

reminded me or her... her face... her eyes... her smile...

Fade in music.

We were going on holiday... in 1969... me, my mother and father... in June... in an Austin 1100... we were driving along happy... I was singing to the radio....

We hear the music of his mind.

I was happy man... and then suddenly I saw him. An airman standing on the side of the road. I'd never seen one in the flesh before. It was like the airman from Airwolf. He must have crash landed in a field. My mother was reading Woman's Own in the front when I shouted 'Look at the Airman, look at the Airman'. My father turns around jolted. 'What Airman?' says my father. 'On the side of the road'. 'What Airman?' shouts mam. He was the strangest Airman I'd ever seen. Then SMACK. My father's driving line wanders as he looks for the Airman... wanders over the white line.. When lorry, articulated, doing seventy collides with us... SMACK MAN, SMACK. *(PAUSE).* Family holiday over man. Austin 1100 dies. My mother and father never made it man. Died on the road. *(PAUSE)* I was karted off to hospital with a brain like a balloon. But I survive. Why did I have to survive man? WHY DID I HAVE TO SURVIVE? I grew up in Barnardo's. They said it was the best. But I'm scared... maimed man.... I got an injured head... and a damaged mind man...and I dream of my mother man... I want to hold her tightly and turn back the clock. *(PAUSE)* Sometimes I wanted Yvonne to be my mother... *(BEAT)* I wanted to be in her fingers... with her holding me tight... like I remember my mother doing man... like mothers do... making me feel safe. *(PAUSE)* There's nothing wrong with that is there Carlyle?

CARLYLE

No.

BENNY

I just miss my mother man... you know what I'm saying?

CARLYLE

I know what you're saying Benny... *(beat)* the world is full of dead and missing mothers man. Every time you look at a full moon on a starry night there is a mother who is looking at the same moon and dying. *(PAUSE)* Don't you think that's sad? *(PAUSE)* A mother breathes her last breath. Then she's gone. *(PAUSE)* The moon connects us to all dying mothers. I like to feel connected. I like to feel part of things. Good things. Like a mother's love. Unconditional love. The love of a good mother. A good love. A good connection. Are you capable of good love Benny? Are you? All good things are connected. A network of good things. A city and its people. A dentist to a tooth. *(PAUSE)* Shall I let you into a secret? Inside my head is a city of seven or eight million people. A Welsh city. A metropolis. A city with high life and a low life with stasis in

between. A city of opportunity. A city of death. I can
see the flickering neon. Somewhere on the outskirts
of the city a man and a woman are making their way
to a hotel. The Angel Hotel. On the way to the same
hotel as are three men who bear gifts. They are
travelling by train. Above them is the moon which
connects them to the world. To happiness and pain.
Out at sea a foghorn blows. Can you hear it?
(PAUSE) The woman is heavily pregnant. They
arrive at the hotel to shelter from the wind and snow.
She wants to give birth in the city. She wants it to
happen in the city because she wants to give birth to
a country. Without a city she can't have a country.
She can only imagine the pain of birth. But she wants
to give birth. She wants a country. She imagines the
city. A metropolis. *(PAUSE)* She looks at the moon.
She wants to be a good mother. She wants to feel
connected to that which she's given birth. But she
doesn't know what it will be. She is afraid of what it
might be. How will it all turn out. Will she be
capable of love? A monstrous birth. Can anyone love
a monstrous birth? *(PAUSE)* That's my secret Benny.
I keep it in my head. But I shared it with you. I like
to connect. I dream of a time when all things are
connected. A mother to child, a friend to a man. A
boot to a lip. Me to you. You see my boots Benny?
Those boots have walked the night from dock to
suburb and back again. Searching. For a city. For a
soul... for you. *(PAUSE)* I want to feel connected
Benny. *(PAUSE)* Prove we are connected Benny.
(PAUSE) Put your lip to my boot. *(PAUSE)* You
hear me Benny? *(PAUSE)* Kiss and we will be
connected. *(PAUSE)* Kiss... kiss... kiss.

BENNY moves and kisses CARLYLE's boots. He pulls out a gun.

I love you Benny. I love you. We are connected.
(PAUSE) Kiss... kiss... kiss.

Music builds to a climax as CARLYLE pulls the trigger. BENNY slumps.

CARLYLE
BENNY, BENNY, BENNY.

CARLYLE panics and moves away from BENNY. As he does so, BENNY stands. CARLYLE moves towards him but his hands go right through him. BENNY exits. CARLYLE collapses. NIGHT-PORTER enters.

NIGHT-PORTER
Just because this room's on special offer don't
mean you can go shooting it up... this room is
£49.99 Mr Carlyle.

CARLYLE
Fuck off.

BELLBOY
Don't you tell me to fuck off. WHO THE
FUCK DO YOU THINK YOU ARE! UH?

(PAUSE)

CARLYLE
It wasn't my fault.

NIGHT-PORTER
Excuse me?

CARLYLE
> Can you see him?

NIGHT-PORTER
> See who?

CARLYLE
> I shot him.

NIGHT-PORTER
> Shot who?

CARLYLE
> Benny. I shot him. Here. Now. A minute ago.

NIGHT-PORTER
> There's fuck all there Mr Carlyle.

CARLYLE
> No?

NIGHT-PORTER
> No. I suppose it must have been a dream
> sequence. A major character dream sequence.

CARLYLE
> Don't you fucking talk to me about dream
> sequences.

NIGHT-PORTER
> Don't you talk to me like that or I'll have you
> thrown out. Just cos I'm a minor character
> doesn't mean you can go shouting at me,
> pointing guns at me! Do you think guns and
> shouting is *de rigeur* for this establishment? Do you?

CARLYLE
No.

NIGHT-PORTER
Exactly, so let's have none of your nonsense.

CARLYLE
I'm sorry.

NIGHT-PORTER
So you should be. This was once a respectable establishment, one of the finest hotels in this city, still is in an old-fashioned way, we had the glitterati all here once, we were known for our glitterati... Marilyn Monroe once stayed here man... in 1965, but she signed the visitor's book as Diana Dors... I suppose she didn't want the publicity... *(PAUSE)* This place aint trash man... you got no right to trash it.

The BELLBOY enters.

BELLBOY
Everything alright here Night-Porter?

NIGHT-PORTER
It is now, but look at the mess Bellboy.

BELLBOY
I'll handle this, you go back to the desk.

NIGHT-PORTER
No, no, this is between me and Mr Carlyle. You fuck off back to the desk.

BELLBOY

I don't want to fuck off back to the desk, the
desk is quiet Night-Porter, quiet as fuck... the
whole city is quiet, heavy falls of Welshmen and
a great deal of drifting... a whole tradition
vanished in front of our eyes.

NIGHT-PORTER

What tradition?

BELLBOY

Singing, dancing, winning at rugby... it's enough to
drive a man over the edge.

NIGHT-PORTER

Have you finished?

BELLBOY

No. *(HE WALKS UP TO CARLYLE, POINTS AT
HIS GUN)* Is that real?

CARLYLE

What do you think?

NIGHT-PORTER

Satisfied?

BELLBOY

(NODS) Satisfied.

NIGHT-PORTER

Good. Now fuck off back to the desk.

BELLBOY

Jesus Christ Night-Porter, one of these days.

The BELLBOY exits.

> NIGHT-PORTER
>> Sorry about that Mr Carlyle. Today's defeat
>> getting to his head. *(PAUSE)* International
>> rugby is having a detrimental effect on staff
>> morale.

> CARLYLE
>> Nobody said growing up was easy.

> NIGHT-PORTER
>> How's the writing coming? Any progress?

> CARLYLE
>> Maybe.

> NIGHT-PORTER
>> Oh. I'll leave you to it then Mr Carlyle.
>> *(PAUSE)* If you need anything else, don't
>> hesitate to call. *(PAUSE)* 24 hours a day, 52
>> weeks of the year. *(PAUSE)* Year in, year out,
>> earache, 'ere we are, 'ere we go. *(PAUSE)*
>> There we are then Mr Carlyle. *(PAUSE)* I'm
>> sure something will come. *(PAUSE)*
>> Inspiration. *(PAUSE)* Kippers at 7.30.
>> Goodnight.

NIGHT-PORTER exits.

CARLYLE moves to his desk, presses the cassette.

> CARLYLE
>> 'Binoculars' said my father, 'whatever you do,

don't let him use my binoculars'. She came home early one day, my mother. A pigeon had crapped on her. She didn't want people to stare. She came home to wash it off. *(PAUSE)* He didn't hear her come in. He was standing by the window, binoculars in one hand, Woodbine in the other. *(PAUSE)* He was wearing her clothes, her underwear, wig, make-up, the whole jamboree. He never heard her. *(PAUSE)* 'Walter' she said... 'what you doing?' He dropped the binoculars and they smashed on the floor. She said he made a noise. Like an animal noise. Like a wounded animal. In a trap. She said his face looked as if it was melting. *(PAUSE)* She'd never seen a man look so ashamed. What the fuck did he think she was going to do? 'The binoculars' he said... 'whatever you do, don't let him have the binoculars'. *(PAUSE)* Then she undressed him and took him to bed. *(PAUSE)* She said he was deep. In his head. In his mind. *(PAUSE)* Funny things families. Funny things heads. *(PAUSE)* Why the fuck wasn't I born in a Merc mam?

Sound of wilderness. CARLYLE brings the gun to his head and laughs. He pulls the trigger. He stands there smiling. Fade lights and sound.

END.

Dorien Thomas, Richard Lynch, Russ Gomer
Carlyle, Night Porter, Benny

photograph Brian Tarr

Moving On

Ed Thomas in conversation with David Adams

This book is about the final flowering of a decade of work from one of the leading figures in Welsh drama, Ed Thomas.

1998 saw the release of the film of Thomas's *House of America* (first performed just ten years earlier in 1988), a radically new production of the original stage play (directed by Thomas) and the first production of his last play, *Gas Station Angel*, which opened at the Newcastle Playhouse before moving to the Royal Court in London and then Wales.

1998 saw the creation of the National Assembly for Wales following the narrow referendum vote the year before.

1998 saw the first signs from the Arts Council of Wales that it was radically rethinking the provision of theatre in Wales. This was to be officially proclaimed in January 1999 with the notorious draft drama strategy which proposed investing most of the drama budget in a national company based on Theatr Clwyd and cutting completely Brith Gof, Hijinx and The Magdalena Project, with Bara Caws, Made in Wales and some TIE companies likely to be subsumed by "rationalisation".

We did not realise it at the time but it was not only an end of an era for Ed Thomas but for Welsh theatre.

There is a speech by Ace towards the end of *Gas Station Angel*, that comes the closest to a personal statement by the playwright:

> "I saw most of Wales spread out in front of me…I could see for miles. Into England, Devon, Cornwall and beyond Cornwall, France, then Spain and right at the bottom at the far end of the horizon, I swear I could see the lights of North Africa. All of Europe spread out in front of me, of us… I never thought I'd see this. Maybe I'm imagining it,

my head playing tricks....

"I felt in my bones that the times are a-changing. Maybe I can soon call myself a European. A Welsh European, with my own language and the rudiments of Portuguese, Russian, Czech, even English. Will speaking a new language break the chains of a fucked-up head? Will I be able to be who I want to be then put who I want to be back in the fucked-up bit so it's not fucked-up any more? I hope so, man...."

1998 did not herald the Brave New World people like Ed had hoped for. The arts in Wales, especially theatre, are in crisis, with the Assembly imposing its agenda of populism and accessibility on a weakened Arts Council. Few new writers and no new companies have emerged in the last few years.

But now, several years and nightmares later, Ed Thomas has a renewed vigour.

We talked about past times and the journey that is Welsh Theatre over coffee in his Cardiff home. He looks good, sounds happy...but still has not written a word for the stage since *Gas Station Angel*.

D.A.

1998 was, we both agree, an important year, but in a very different way from, say, 1978-9, with the referendum No Vote and the election of the first Thatcher government that actually led to a decade of crucial development in Welsh theatre, or 1988-9, where we had an exceptionally good year with new work from the then newly-formed Volcano, Brith Gof's *Calamities of War* series, Geoff Moore's radical seasons at St Stephen's and your own Y Cwmni's *House of America*. So was that ten-year period between 1988 and 98 just a blip, an exceptional creative outburst as far as Welsh theatre was concerned? You haven't written anything for the stage since *Gas Station Angel*. What's the reason – were there external forces at work that made this theatre explosion collapse, was it underfunding by the Arts Council, was it the fact everyone went movie crazy and there was a shortage of stage talent or was it that after ten years you lost interest in the theatre? Was the '88-'98 decade just a mini Golden Age of Welsh theatre? With rather less hindsight, what changed in 1998?

ED

Primarily I was knackered. By 1998 I'd written a new play every year since '88, directed them all, toured all over the place, set up a production company, wrote a screenplay, produced and directed three series for TV and did enough interviews to make a budgie sick. I was burnt out.

I think people had gone movie crazy. Including me. Casting *Gas Station Angel* was difficult, a lot of people (or maybe their agents) didn't fancy a long stint touring theatre when new British movies were being cast every week, and that, allied to the Cool Britannia and Cool Cymru thing made theatre even less inviting. I also think that some of the actors I'd worked with in that decade like Rich (Lynch) and Russ (Gomer) were also tired and needed to do new things and that's what happened. It wasn't planned.

But yes, I'm proud of what was achieved between '88 and '98, it was a special time for me and for groups like Volcano and Brith Gof. We did a lot of work between us, toured internationally on a regular basis and pushed ourselves to the limit, with and sometimes without Arts Council support. The theatre created then was created by individuals and companies. That drive and energy is not infinite as I know to my cost. I made a feature film between 1999 and 2000 which undoubtedly is the worst thing I ever got involved with. I got my fingers burnt and my confidence knocked, but you learn, lick your wounds and move on, and a lot of people, especially some of the actors involved, are blameless for what came about.

So now I'm 41 and we return to the much quoted Gwyn

Alf – ten years – rupture, re-invention – true?

D.A.
So is there nothing that can be done by the Arts Council or
National Assembly – it's something cyclical rather than structural?

ED
There should be a structure, like there is in England, where they
have the Royal Court and the National and smaller fringe
companies like the Gate and the Bush to look after new writing. We
just haven't got those institutions.

    The Assembly is in its infancy, but it still has to accept its
cultural responsibility. Its first step is to gain its credibility by
forming a coherent policy for the arts in Wales that's actually got
vision and balls. It may also need to look to the not so distant
future too. Who's to say that in five years time the UK government
won't tell the Assembly that S4C and its funding is its responsibility.
And will the Assembly be able to afford it? It it can't what do we
do? Get political again? What does that mean?

D.A.
Back to the drawing board perhaps ? Was that ten-year period a
time when you had something to say and you don't any more ? Or
are you looking for something to say and don't know what it is ?

ED
For me, yes, I am back to the drawing board, but that's good. I
believe there are seasons of work and cycles of work. You can work
with the same body of actors, then they move on. You can do a
short play, a long play, a short film, a long film, and a performance
piece, but then it moves on.

    I've always had plenty to say, but over the last three or four
years I got tired of saying it. But altered times need altered ways of
working and the work I've been doing over the last six months has
fired my interest again in the possibilities of live performance. Some

of that work I'll do alone, some will be in collaboration with amongst others, Mike Pearson. I'm doing a project with him which might last seven years, who knows ?

D.A.

So this decade between 1988 and '89 could for you be seen as a time of progression, then, with *Gas Station Angel* the climax – especially with the speech about looking to Europe, I get the sense that you knew it was the end of an era, that you were saying, we've had ten years being obsessed with identity, it's time to move on.

ED

Maybe it was the end of an era. The Wales of '88 when I wrote *House of America* was different to Wales now. As I've said before, playwriting then was only a sophisticated form of writing 'Kilroy was here' on the toilet wall to prove we exist; now I think we're far less invisible and that affords new possibilities and as you say it's time to move on. There will always be seasons of work and cycles of work, it would be good to think that those seasons fitted into a coherent and dynamic cultural policy for the arts in Wales that didn't burn people out, or send them away or even worse, get them lost in the blind alleys of volume TV.

D.A.

What was interesting about Welsh performance work was its concern with form but it's really only someone like Eddie Ladd who's taken that on board. It's noticeable how *House of America* is relatively straightforward, old-fashioned almost, but *Gas Station Angel* is much more anti-naturalistic, especially in your production. Might you see your next work as not at all a conventional play?

ED

Probably. But it will start as they always start, with me in the room, chained to my desk, smoking too many fags, setting words to a rhythm to see where that takes me. I also think I'm less self conscious about mixing art forms to find a shape that suits. I'm interested again in ideas, stage, screen, documentary, short film, installation; who knows what it might lead to? Being passionate is a start and being free.

David Adams has written and lectured on Welsh theatre for over twenty years, mainly as the Welsh arts correspondent of *The Guardian* and the theatre critic for *The Western Mail*. He recently edited *One Man, One Voice* for Parthian. He is co-director of the Wales *iti* Cymru, the Welsh centre of the International Theatre Institute.

Sid & Gwenny

HOUSE OF AMERICA

35mm Feature Film Screenplay

Shooting Script, March 1996

"Brilliantly subtle, original and arresting, richly served by an impressive cast. The Welsh for soul is hwyl and *House of America* has it in bucketloads."

The Guardian

HOUSE OF AMERICA *was first screened publicly at BAFTA Piccadilly in October 1996. In January 1997 it screened at the Sundance Festival, Utah, USA, the first Welsh film ever to do so. In October 1997, it opened on general release in the UK and went on to win numerous BAFTA Wales Awards including Best Film and Best Director; it also won the same awards at the International Festival, Gothenberg.*

Credits

The Cast

Mam	:	Siân Phillips
Sid	:	Steven Mackintosh
Boyo	:	Matthew Rhys
Gwenny	:	Lisa Palfrey
Clem	:	Pascal Laurent
Cat	:	Richard Harrington
Roger the Pop	:	Islwyn Morris
Wally	:	Brian Hibbard
The Head	:	Stephen Spiers
Malloy	:	Dave Duffy
Matty	:	Connor McIntyre
Off License Man	:	Andrew Lennon
Receptionist	:	Donna Edwards
Woman With Budgie	:	Stella King
Regular Miners	:	Ron Mills
		Glen Finick
		Terry Arnold
		Alan Jones
		John Weathers

1   <u>**EXT. DAWN. MID-WEST OF AMERICA**</u>   1

A long straight road leads on to the horizon and mountains in the distance. A lonely roadside ranch can be seen nearby.

    SID (V.O.)

> Picture the scene. A mid-western American morning. The dawn sky is beautiful, blueish red with a few stars. He can hear the cicadas mingle with the wind and desert sound. On a nearby ranch of coralled horses and pick-up trucks, a thirsty dog laps at a water bath. The family is asleep man, white cotton clothes dry in the cool morning air. He never thought anything could be this good.

The voice-over gives way to a mid-western radio channel.

2   <u>**INT. RANCH KITCHEN. DAWN**</u>   2

CLEM prepares a lunch-box in a kitchen suggesting idyllic American ranch life. He switches off the radio and exits.

3   <u>**EXT. RANCH. DAWN**</u>   3

CLEM walks out of the door towards the drying clothes on the line. Close up of his unshaven face as he tenderly clasps a young girl's cotton dress.

4   <u>**INT. HOUSE. WALES. MORNING**</u>   4

A pair of lips appear through a letterbox.

    THE LIPS
> Pop?

5   <u>**INT. HOUSE. LOUNGE. MORNING**</u>   5

MAM emerges from behind a newspaper with the headline "Michigan spreads all over Wales."

MAM

    Pop bloody pop bloody pop pop pop.

THE LIPS (O.O.V.)

    Mrs Lewis... it's me... Roger.

6   **EXT. HOUSE. FRONT DOOR. MORNING**   6

ROGER THE POP MAN waits at the front door. MAM suddenly opens it.

MAM

    No Pop... he went to America.

ROGER

    But you owe me six weeks... America?

7   **EXT. RANCH. AMERICA. DAWN**   7

A Zippo lighter fills the screen. A man's finger flicks it on and off a couple of times. It is CLEM, idly surveying the ranch. He lights a cigarette and drives off in a cloud of dust.

MAM (O.O.V.)

    Clem Lewis. Huh. He came in one night and
    said "I'm off" or something like that. "I'm
    going to America," he said "tonight."

8   **INT. LOUNGE. WALES. MORNING.**   8

ROGER THE POP warily reaches for a sugar lump as he sits opposite MAM at a table. She looks at him darkly. He is disconsolate and trapped.

MAM

    I just looked at him dumb. "Brando's dead" I

said. I've just washed him to death, he got
into the washing machine when I wasn't
looking... it was an accident.

ROGER
> Brando?

MAM
> The cat. That was Clem's idea. He thought
> the world of Marlon Brando. "You did it on
> purpose" he said, "you know I liked him, well
> that's that" he said, "now I'm definitely
> going." "I put him over there in the Tesco
> bag" I said, "he's still wet." Clem just turned
> and went. "What about the kids?" I said.
> "Keep them away from the washing
> machine" he said, and he shut the door
> behind him.

9   **EXT. ROAD. AMERICA. DAWN**   9

CLEM drives along in his pick-up. The sun shines in his face.

MAM (V.O. cont.)
> I buried the cat on the mountain behind the
> house, next to the budgie, Billy... well... you
> have to make do, don't you?

*CLEM pulls down the sun visor revealing a photo of three young
children, two boys and a girl. He puts on sunglasses and turns on the
radio - Velvet Underground's "Waiting for the Man". The music fills
the frame as we see him drive off into the distance and plays over:*

10   **INT. HOUSE. WALES. NIGHT**   10

*BOYO, SID and GWENNY dancing ecstatically to the music,
running around, giving each other piggy-backs. Furniture and bric-*

a-brac are pushed around in the mayhem. They tumble on top of each other exhausted.

BOYO, SID & GWENNY
Yeeeessss!

Cut music. Fade to Black. Roll credits: **HOUSE OF AMERICA.**

11   <u>**EXT. MOUNTAIN. OPEN-CAST. WALES. DAY**</u> 11
A hooter sounds. A huge silver sign declares "Michigan International Mining". The site is busy with men and machinery. A red flag is raised and a detonator is fired. On the mountain-side, beyond the mine - two small fading wooden crosses with the names 'Brando' and 'Billy' etched into them.

12   <u>**INT. BEDROOM. HOUSE. MORNING**</u>   12
*(The room is divided into two parts. **SID's** side is black and littered with American memorabilia - The Doors, Easy Rider and a photo of his father, **CLEM** on a Harley Davidson in 1973. **BOYO's** side of the room is white with rugby posters, cups and junk. An x-ray of a dislocated shoulder sits proudly on the wall.) **SID** stands half-dressed in a mirror gelling back his hair. Lou Reed's 'Smalltown' plays on the radio. **BOYO** groans and rolls over. **SID** puts on his black leather jeans and jacket and admires himself. He exits after a kung-fu flourish.*

13   <u>**EXT. BACKYARD. HOUSE. DAY**</u>   13
*A Harley Davidson sits in a puddle of mud and oil amongst a ramshackle assortment of broken furniture, cars, lawn mowers etc. It begins to rain. **SID** emerges from the kitchen in yellow waterproofs, the opposite of the cool man we saw in the room. He sits astride the Harley, kicks it but nothing happens. He kicks it a couple of more times before it fires into life.*

14   <u>**EXT. ROAD. MORNING**</u>   **14**

SID screams through the deserted village streets on his Harley.

         GWENNY (V.O.)
               What would happen if all the planets round
               the sun...

15   <u>**INT. KITCHEN. DAY**</u>   **15**

BOYO, half dressed, waits in the kitchen for the kettle to boil.

> **GWENNY**
>> ...slow down then Boyo?

> **BOYO (O.O.V)**
>> What sort of question's that?

16   <u>**INT. GWENNY'S BEDROOM. DAY**</u>   **16**

GWENNY stands at the window looking up at the sky through a telescope then EXITS to meet BOYO coming up the stairs, carrying MAM's breakfast on a tray.

> **GWENNY**
>> Heard it on the radio I did, the earth is travelling at eighteen miles a second round the sun.

> **BOYO**
>> So?

17   <u>**INT. LANDING. DAY**</u>   **17**

> **GWENNY**
>> If all the planets, like earth right, decide to slow down, then we'd just fall into the sun and burn.

> **BOYO**
>> Better keep my fingers crossed then or pray to Jesus or something.

> **MAM (O.O.V.)**
>> Jesus is a busy man.

BOYO

Uh?

18   INT. MAM'S BEDROOM. DAY   18

MAM sits at her dressing table carefully putting on make-up as
BOYO and GWENNY enter.

MAM

I said Jesus is a busy man, you can't always
get through to him when you call, but he
knows me. I say Jesus, it's Mrs Lewis from
Wales, and if I'm lucky, on a good night he'll
answer. Was it you who wanted him Boyo?

BOYO

No, me and Gwenny was just talking.

MAM

Like I got through to him the other night,
asking forgiveness, but I wasn't at my best,
but you know what he said, he said there was
so much going on down there it's hard to
keep track, and if it carried on like this he'd
just have to go and put his head in the sand,
Jesus himself.

BOYO

Well, if he feels like that, what have we got to
worry about, innit?

MAM

All I'm saying is that he'll have to watch out,
we can't have him drunk in charge of the
world can we?

BOYO

> What did you want him to forgive you for?

MAM

> That's between him, me, and the
> deep blue sea.

19   <u>EXT. STREET. DAY</u>   19

SID pulls up outside a doctor's surgery in a deserted street stuffed between a boarded up chapel and a butcher shop.

20   <u>INT. DOCTOR'S SURGERY. DAY</u>   20

*SID appears at the **Receptionist's** window. She slides back the glass.*

SID

> Repeat prescription please *(hands prescription over counter)*

RECEPTIONIST

> Name?

SID

> Mrs Eileen Lewis

RECEPTIONIST

> And you are?

SID

> Sid Lewis.

RECEPTIONIST

> Take a seat Mr Lewis, we won't
> be long.

SID looks around at the full surgery of people. It is a grim place to be *ill in. **SID** sits opposite an old woman with a dead budgie in a cage.*

OLD WOMAN
He's dead, but I didn't like to
leave him see.

21   EXT. HOUSE. DAY   21

***CAT** pulls up to the house in a battered Reliant Robin. Tom Jones'
'Detroit City' plays on his cassette . **GWENNY** races out of the house,
followed by **BOYO**, still getting dressed. They get into the car. What
follows is a well-rehearsed routine.*

GWENNY
Ready?

*enter **BOYO** and **CAT** nod, then put on dark sunglasses.*

GWENNY
She sat in the back, as her brother Boyo
turned to his best friend Cat and said...

BOYO
Drive.

*All three point towards the windscreen as the car pulls away towards
the road.*

22   EXT. MOUNTAIN. DAY   22
***SID** sits astride his Harley in front of the huge Michigan Mining sign.
He pulls out some pills from his pocket and takes them, then rides away.*

23   INT. PANTYDDRAENEN PUB. DAY   23
*The pub is almost empty. **GWENNY** feeds a juke-box. **CAT** joins
BOYO and **SID** in mid-conversation at the bar.*

SID

> Lou Reed's better than John Cale
> anyway.

BOYO

> Never, John Cale's Welsh mun.

SID

> He's not, he's American, New York band.

BOYO

> I'm telling you, he comes from Ponty or
> somewhere, innit Cat?

SID

> Huh, what do you know?

CAT

> My brother once tuned the piano for
> Lindisfarne, that's what I know mate, last
> time they were in the Rank in town.

SID

> Lindisfarne... who the fuck are they?

BOYO

> That's not the point Sid.

SID

> No, the point is, it don't matter if Cale came
> from fucking Banwen, he's living in New
> York now, and I bet you that's where he'll
> stay. Huh, can you imagine Lou Reed
> walking around Banwen? Alright Lou? How's
> it going was, like on the wild side? Not cool

enough for him, no way, probably never even heard of Wales.

BOYO

He don't know nothing that's why.

*Suddenly the door opens and six silver hatted Michigan Mining workers enter and make for the pool table. One of them, with 'THE HEAD' written on his helmet approaches the bar; he is an enormous man. **WALLY** the Barman serves him.*

THE HEAD

Five lagers, two whiskies and five scampi fries.

WALLY

Coming up.

THE HEAD

Alright?

BOYO

Alright.

CAT

Alright.

GWENNY

Alright.

(PAUSE)

THE HEAD

They call me The Head.

GWENNY, CAT and BOYO nod.

BOYO
> Boyo.

CAT
> Cat.

GWENNY
> Gwenny.

SID
> Sid.

WALLY returns. THE HEAD pays.

THE HEAD
> Ta.

THE HEAD rejoins his friends.

CAT
> Big bastard.

BOYO
> Crap pool players.

GWENNY
> What they wearing their hats in here for?

24   <u>**INT. LOUNGE. HOUSE. DAY**</u>   24
A Tom Jones ballad plays on the record player in an empty lounge.
Sound of growling motorbike arriving outside.

25   <u>**INT. HOUSE. STAIRS. DAY**</u>   25
*The music can be heard in the background as **MAM** walks warily up*
the stairs towards the landing. She approaches her bedroom door and

pushes it open. Suddenly there is the sound of a door slamming from downstairs and she spins round, listens, then runs to the landing.

MAM

Clem? Clem?

*There is no reply, so she runs downstairs and into the lounge where **SID** puts the newly prescribed pills on the table.*

SID

Bit early for Tom Mam.

MAM

Women were his weakness, didn't smoke, didn't drink much and everybody thought he was handsome, just had a soft spot for women, that was his trouble.

SID

Yeh?

MAM

Yes. I've told Mr Snow all about him.

SID

Mr Snow? Who's he?

MAM

She was a floozy see, I was too busy looking after you three, said I had no time for him and then she got her hands on him behind my back, he was a dreamer and he fell for the glitter.

SID

Frontier man, see Mam. Took his horse and

his woman, headed West and built a ranch
for himself.

MAM

You think that's funny do you?

BOYO and GWENNY enter from the kitchen.

SID

It's not great no, but it's a joke, and a joke's a
joke, you know what I mean?

GWENNY

What's up?

SID

Mam's just having a little rant that's all.

MAM

Is that what you call it is it?

BOYO

Hey come on now Mam, what's wrong?
(Pause) Mam?

MAM

My room's been painted blue.

SID

See what I mean?

SID exits.

MAM

It's the wrong colour.

GWENNY

It's been blue as long as I can remember Mam.

MAM

Nobody's painted it behind my back then?

BOYO

No mun, Mam I...

MAM

Don't make fun, I wouldn't have asked if I didn't think it. (*Beat*)

MAM exits.

26   <u>**EXT. BACKYARD. HOUSE. DAY**</u>   26

*An axe comes down hard on a log. **BOYO** is chopping wood as **SID** piles them up. A can of lager sits nearby from where **BOYO** takes occasional swigs.*

BOYO

What she want to bring him up for now innit?

SID

Maybe she's heard from him, written her a letter or something.

BOYO

I haven't seen no letters.

SID

Fuck, a trip to America, be alright I reckon.

BOYO

Bollocks.

SID

>It's a big country mun. Plenty of work there too Boyo, plenty of space, sun, sand. Fancy riding across it on a Harley Davidson, chasing the sun, money in your pocket, tiger in your tank, Hendrix on the Walkman, no helmet, just free and moving West.

BOYO

>You can do that in Pembroke, Sid.

SID

>Pembroke? Don't give me Pembroke. What happens when you reach the sea? It's the end of the line.

BOYO

>I don't know. You lie down on the beach and look at the sky.

SID

>Yeh, watching the rain come down, no way mate, what you do is wait for a low tide and ride hell for leather across the Atlantic. Watch out there's a wave.

BOYO

>Can I ask you a question Sid?

SID

>Sure, anything... say.

BOYO

>Can you swim?

*SID's face drops, **BOYO** smiles.*

SID

> Don't give me any of that shit now
> will you.

SID marches away towards the Harley.

BOYO

> Hey mun, Sid.

SID

> Fuck off.

BOYO

> Don't be like that, I was only having
> the crack.

SID

> Is that what you call it?

BOYO

> I'm sorry.

SID

> I'm your brother for fuck sake, not a
> piece of shit.

BOYO

> I said I was sorry.

SID looks at him, concedes, they put their heads together.

BOYO

> Things are bound to get better mun, just got

to give it time.

SID

Time? I'm pushing thirty for fuck sake. And I
haven't had a shag for eighteen months.

BOYO

It's longer than that, it's two years.

SID fails to start the Harley.

SID

So fucking what if it was? Eighteen months?
Two years? What's the difference? It's all
Mickey Mouse anyway, small time, fourth
division, second class toys.

SID fires up the Harley.

SID

I just got to get out of here Boyo before...

BOYO

Your balls explode.

SID

Typical, that is bastard typical!

SID looks at him in disgust and rides away. From a bedroom window,
GWENNY watches him go.

MAM (V.O.)

It's the wrong colour, shows up the dirt too
much... red's my colour.

27   **INT. MAM'S BEDROOM. DAY**   **27**

*MAM sits in a chair, staring at a blue wall as GWENNY turns
away from the window and approaches her.*

> **GWENNY**
> I'll paint it red in the summer, alright?

MAM nods.

> **MAM**
> What's wrong with me Gwenny?

> **GWENNY**
> You just get confused sometimes that's all.

GWENNY puts her arms around her.

> **MAM**
> You still love me don't you?

28   **EXT. FARMHOUSE. DAY**   **28**

*SID arrives at a remote farmhouse ruin. He cuts the engine. He looks
at the distant open-cast.*

29   **INT. LOUNGE. DUSK**   **29**

*The TV is on. BOYO eats a TV dinner, trying to ignore the nearby
conversation between GWENNY and MAM who are looking at a
photograph album.*

> **GWENNY**
> And that one?

> **MAM**
> That's on our honeymoon in Trafalgar Square.
> He went to stand by a fountain and a pigeon did a

mess in his hair. *(GWENNY laughs with MAM)* I thought it was funny too, he was angry, went to the gents to clean it off.

We see a close-up of the photograph album. There are no photographs, just the outline of where they've been.

MAM

We were happy then.

GWENNY

What year was it?

MAM

1957.

GWENNY

There's a coincidence now.

MAM

Is it?

GWENNY

That's the year Jack Kerouac and Joyce Jonson met, January 1957.

MAM

What's that got to do with my wedding then?

GWENNY

Nothing. Just a coincidence.

30   **INT. FARMHOUSE. NIGHT**   30

Broken rafters and abandoned furniture litter the floor. A fire crackles amidst the ruins in front of a small pyramid of stones. **SID** *sits* *nearby sipping bourbon and popping pills. He lights a cigarette with a Zippo. He smiles and puts out his hand as if rehearsing for a future meeting.*

> **SID**
>> I missed you dad.

Happy with his performance, he pours a little paraffin on the fire, making it glow. He opens Jack Kerouac's "On the Road" and reads. Sound of welding and sparks.

31   **<u>INT. FACTORY. AMERICAN MID-WEST. DAY</u>**   31
*A man hidden behind goggles is welding, sending a stream of orange sparks into the air. We notice his 1970s wrist watch. After a moment, he takes off his helmet and reveals himself as **CLEM**.*

32   **<u>EXT. OPEN CAST. DAY</u>**   32
As the light comes up there is already great activity in the mine. Labourers warm themselves by lighted braziers as the diggers load coal into the backs of trucks.

> **GWENNY (O.O.V.)**
>> It's massive dad. Like a big round basin, and the cranes, you should see the cranes, they're like electric dinosaurs and you can see the tops of them from our house. Sid heard they'd be wanting labourers up there so we're waiting every day for news.

33   **<u>EXT. HOUSE. EARLY MORNING</u>**   33
*Trucks pass along the ridge above the house, their headlights on. A light shines from **GWENNY**'s attic bedroom.*

34 <u>INT. GWENNY'S BEDROOM. EARLY MORNING</u> 34

GWENNY rummages in her dressing table. She pulls out a small heart-shaped pot containing some pills. She takes a few. In the drawer we see a doll and some neatly laid out doll's clothes, a girl's writing case and a copy of Joyce Jonson's 'My Life with Jack Kerouac'. She lies on the bed and starts to write.

> ### GWENNY (V.O.)
> I have got one piece of news though. I didn't get the check-out job in the supermarket. Donna Leadbetter beat me to it, but what they saw in her I don't know. I was gutted but Sid told her I didn't need a job because we were moving to America to live with you. Cheeky huh?

35   <u>INT. LOUNGE. DAY</u> 35

BOYO is building a fragile house of cards on the lounge table. MAM watches a T.V. set covered in snow. GWENNY passes through the room, unnoticed almost, and exits.

> ### GWENNY (V.O.)
> You don't think I'm pestering you do you? I love you dad and I know in my bones you still love us. It's been too long dad, I'm not a baby anymore.

36   <u>EXT. VILLAGE STREET. DAY</u> 36

GWENNY posts a letter.

> ### GWENNY (V.O.)
> Please write back soon dad,
> we all love you.
> Gwenny

She does a kung-fu flourish and looks around at the forgotten street. As she walks away, a Michigan Mining Land-Rover passes her and a man waves.

37   INT. LOUNGE. HOUSE. DAY   37

*A scene from 'On the Waterfront' with Marlon Brando and Rod Steiger in the back of a taxi plays on the T.V. and **GWENNY** sits enthralled in front of it. **MAM** watches impassively. **BOYO** is unimpressed.*

> **BOYO**
>
> On the bloody Waterfront, seen it twelve times. You're worse than Sid mun.

> **GWENNY**
>
> Shut up mun, Boyo and watch the film.

*BOYO pulls faces as we watch **GWENNY** respond to Brando's "I could have been somebody..." speech.*

> **BOYO**
>
> I could have been somebody... huh... actor.

> **MAM**
>
> Not my kind of film.

> **BOYO**
>
> Who does he think he is? Uh mam?

> **MAM**
>
> Musical I wanted.

BOYO

> It's me that could have been
> somebody, not him.

GWENNY

> Sssh will you Boyo...

BOYO

> I mean, I could have played rugby for
> Banwen, for Cardiff, the World, the fucking
> lot, not sit in and watch bastard films, lies,
> fucking cloud cuckoo buckoo!

GWENNY turns off the film in a temper.

GWENNY

> What the hell is wrong with you Boyo?

MAM

> Not my cup of tea either.

GWENNY

> Him and his bloody rugby, you're not the
> only bloke to get injured you know, so
> there's no point feeling sorry for yourself.

BOYO

> I'm not feeling sorry for myself.

GWENNY

> He always has to spoil everything
> mam.

Suddenly SID enters breathlessly. BOYO looks at him puzzled.

BOYO
>What's wrong?

GWENNY
>Sid?

SID tries to catch his breath, looking serious and worried.

SID
>Upstairs.

BOYO
>Uh?

SID
>Now... the two of you.

SID exits upstairs, followed by BOYO and GWENNY.

38   <u>INT. SID & BOYO'S BEDROOM. HOUSE. DAY</u> 38
SID walks breathlessly into the bedroom, and stands with his back to the room looking out of the window. SID turns around slowly, looking very solemn.

SID
>Bingo.

GWENNY & BOYO *(Together)*
>Bingo?

SID
>On Monday morning... *(PAUSE)*... me and you Boyo, will be getting up very early, getting on the back of the Harley, and with the rest of the rabble in the village will be

going up to the open cast... *(PAUSE)* TO
SIGN UP FOR JOBS AS LABOURERS.

BOYO
What!

39   <u>EXT. JOB CENTRE. DAY</u>   39

A sign in the window says:
Michigan Mining International.
Labourers Wanted
Immediate Start
Apply to Site Manager
M. Molloy
Wages Negotiable

BOYO, SID and GWENNY stand outside.

BOYO, SID & GWENNY
YEEEESSS...

SID
You got to promise me something brother.

BOYO
What?

SID
Fix the bike and turn it round by Monday.

*All laugh as they enter the job centre. Fade in Dionne Warwick's "Do
you know the way to San Jose" over.*

40   <u>EXT. CAT'S HOUSE. DAY</u>   40

CAT asleep in his Reliant is rudely awoken by banging on the roof.

CAT

What the fuck?

SID

Jobs, that's what what's the fuck.

CAT

Fuuuck...

SID

And?

BOYO

Lager, pint of...

CAT

Bitter, half of...

GWENNY

Campari, lots of...

SID

Campari?

*From a distance we see **BOYO** and **GWENNY** jump into the Reliant and drive away in pursuit of **SID** on the Harley.*

41 INT. PANYTDDRAENEN PUB 41

*News of the jobs has travelled fast and the pub is a warm, lively, beery atmosphere of celebration. **BOYO** and **SID** are at the bar.*

BOYO

We didn't go to Sunday School in velcro-fronted waistcoats for nothing.

SID

No, or elasticated yellow ties.

BOYO

And shorts.

SID

Exactly, a man doesn't know who he is
without his shorts.

*They laugh and put their heads together. Near the pool table, **THE
HEAD** is in mid-conversation with **GWENNY** and **CAT**.*

HEAD

You're standing on coal innit. That machine
over there is and that lorry is. The machine
fills the lorry with coal and the labourers' job
is to throw the bits of coal that tip over, back
on the lorry. But the trick is, how can you tell
which bits fall off the lorry? Cos it all looks
the same don't it? So you either shovel it all
back on or you don't bother.

GWENNY

And you don't bother?

HEAD

No, my head's gone.

CAT

Jesus.

41   <u>**INT. GARDEN SHED. NIGHT**</u>   41

*Moonlight spills through the window. **MAM** is staring at the moon, a* *screwdriver dripping red paint in her hand. Paint is also spattered across clothes. She's a ghostly, fearful figure.*

MAM

We'll make a dream baby Ei, a sweet pea dream baby that runs in the Florida sun in winter, sleeps all night and smiles all day, a baby to be proud of. We'll roll him round and write poems on his belly. I love you Ei... how many bees in baby?

42   **INT. PANT PUB. NIGHT**   42

Music plays on the jukebox. **GWENNY** *dances exuberantly with* **CAT**. **SID** *watches at a distance.*

CAT

You're a good looking girl Gwenny.

GWENNY

You're a good looking Cat, Cat.

BOYO *joins* **SID**.

BOYO

Put a pint behind the bar for me.

SID

Where you going?

BOYO

Things to do, people to see.

SID

Mammy.

BOYO

> Lend us the bike.

SID

> Fuck off.

SID reluctantly hands BOYO the keys. CAT joins them.

CAT

> Fix it while you can Boyo baby, because I bet
> you a tenner my Reliant will be on that site
> before you.

BOYO

> Bollocks.

BOYO exits.

CAT

> You want a bet Sid?

SID

> Boyo's giving the Harley a service, it'll go like
> a bird mun.

CAT

> Tenner I'll be there first.

SID

> Deal.

43   <u>**EXT. BACKYARD. HOUSE. DAY**</u>   43

*BOYO walks round to the backyard and sees the kitchen window
splattered with red paint. His face falls.*

BOYO

    Fuckin hell...

His eyes follow a trail of red to the Garden Shed.

BOYO

    Mam?

BOYO runs inside.

44   <u>INT. GARDEN SHED. DAY</u>   44

MAM sits in the corner of the garden shed surrounded by junk. She is covered in red paint. The doors suddenly open and BOYO stands there.

MAM

    I ran out of paint. Is it too late to get
    some tonight?

45   <u>INT. MAM'S BEDROOM. NIGHT</u>   45

The room is a mess - red paint splatters on the wall and some furniture. BOYO is not looking too happy. MAM sits quietly nearby. Silence.

MAM

    I'm sorry. I didn't mean to upset anyone...
    but no-one understands.

BOYO

    Obviously not.

MAM

    I don't want to go back to the hospital.

BOYO looks at her.

MAM

Don't send me back will you?

BOYO

If it will make you better Mam, I...

MAM

No it will make me worse, I just panic that's all... worry.

BOYO

About what?

MAM

Everything... I want you to be together... and I'm afraid. It's the open-cast's fault... I don't want you and your brother to work up there.

BOYO

Oh come on now Mam, it's work mun, Jesus, I thought you'd be happy.

MAM

I would be but...

BOYO

It won't come near the house, they're only digging the mountain, is that what you're afraid of?

MAM

This house is all we've got.

BOYO

Coal they want, not houses.

MAM

This house is full of lies.

BOYO

What lies?

MAM

Kept us together, that's the main thing, but Gwenny and Sid want to go to America after him, but there's nothing there for him, and Gwenny's been writing him letters.

BOYO

How do you know?

MAM

I've got eyes, I can see, but you're on my side, I heard you call your father a bastard. Do you think I haven't got ears?

BOYO

Yeah, on the side of your head by the looks of it.

MAM

(Grabs him) Don't laugh at your mother.

BOYO

I'm not laughing, leave me go.

MAM lets him go.

BOYO

What's my father got to do with

anything anyhow?

MAM

Everything. He's not in America, he's never been to America, all he ever did was dream about America.

BOYO

Everybody knows he went to America mun, Mam.

MAM

Lies, all lies.

BOYO

Then where the hell is he? (*Silence*) Mam? Answer me?

MAM kisses him then laughs.

46   <u>**EXT. BACKYARD. HOUSE. NIGHT**</u>   46

BOYO with the aid of a lamp is fixing SID's bike. He is covered in oil. Both he and SID are drinking cans in the half-light.

SID

She's talking though her hat mun. She don't like it cos he chased his dream without her.

BOYO

Women he was after Sid, not dreams.

SID

He saw his chance and woosh, he

took it.

BOYO

> He was a bastard Sid, he had
> responsibilities.

SID

> Yeh, only half the size of his dreams mate,
> that's the way I see it. I mean, nobody called
> Tom Jones a bastard and he went there.

BOYO

> Yeh, but Tom went cos of the tax, anyway
> he's back in the Vale now.

SID

> Like Tom do you brother?

BOYO

> He's good yeh, but Elvis is the king.

SID

> Exactly, and where are our kings? One answer
> mate, we haven't got any. I mean, let's face it,
> Harry Secombe isn't a bloke you'd stand out
> in the rain for is he?

BOYO

> No, but Harry Secombe never said
> he was a hero.

SID

> No, and he's fucking well right and all.

47 **EXT. OPEN CAST. NIGHT** 47

MAM looks down at the open cast from the top of the mountain. A digging machine digs away at the topsoil. She weeps.

> **SID (V.O.)**
>> The only ones for me are the mad ones, mad to live, mad to talk, the ones who never yawn or say a commonplace thing, but burn, burn, burn like fabulous yellow roman candles.

48 **INT. GWENNY'S BEDROOM. NIGHT** 48

The lights from a passing truck spill into the house. GWENNY stands at her window lit by the moon. SID holds her hand.

> **GWENNY**
>> Exploding like spiders across the stars.

They smile. SID offers her a tablet. GWENNY takes one. They stand arm in arm at the window.

> **GWENNY**
>> We will get out of here won't we Sid?

> **SID**
>> No worries.

49 **EXT. AMERICAN RANCH. NIGHT** 49

A full desert moon. From inside the ranch we hear the sound of a family happily dining, a comedy plays on TV. Outside the sound of cicadas mingles with a desert wind. CLEM walks towards the pick-up in the backyard and gets in. From the glove compartment he pulls out a letter with 'Gwenny Lewis, The Ranch, The Ynys, Banwen' written on it. His face is a picture of turmoil. Suddenly he flicks open his lighter and burns the letter. The family photo in the sun visor lights to the flickering flames.

FADE TO BLACK.

50   **EXT. ROAD. DAWN**   50
A long, straight road leads nowhere. The only sound is bleating sheep and a light wind.

51   **INT. BOYO & SID'S BEDROOM. DAWN**   51
It is 6.25 a.m. as the alarm goes off. BOYO and SID's eyes flick open and they hurl themselves out of bed.

52   **INT. BOYO & SID'S BEDROOM. DAWN**   52
SID and BOYO race to put on shoes, socks, trousers etc as the ticking clock seems to increase in volume. On SID's bedside table lie neatly ordered goggles, helmet and gloves. He grabs them and exits.

53   **EXT. BACKYARD. HOUSE. DAWN**   53
SID and BOYO emerge from the house and walk towards the Harley. Their faces drop.

>   **SID**
>   What the fuck?

>   **BOYO**
>   Shit.

The front tyre of the Harley is flat.

54   **EXT. ROAD. DAWN**   54
The road we saw earlier is much busier with half a dozen or so cars moving along. At the back of this convoy is CAT in his Reliant driving like a man possessed. CAT overtakes, the Reliant struggles, the other drivers none too impressed by his manoeuvres.

55   <u>EXT. BACKYARD. HOUSE. DAWN</u>   55

SID is frantically blowing up the Harley's front wheel with a foot pump. An argument is in full flow.

> **SID**
>> You should have checked it.

> **BOYO**
>> Don't blame me it's your bike.

> **SID**
>> But you're the mechanic!

> **BOYO**
>> It was alright last time I looked.

> **SID**
>> Fuckin' hell.

> **BOYO**
>> Keep pumpin' and stop shoutin'.

56   <u>EXT. OPEN-CAST SITE. DAWN</u>   56

CAT screams into the open-cast site at the front of the convoy and pulls up triumphantly. He gets out as more cars arrive.

57   <u>EXT. OPEN-CAST CANTEEN. DAY</u>   57

THE HEAD stands outside the canteen doors guiding the prospective labourers inside. CAT approaches beaming broadly.

> **CAT**
>> A tenner's a tenner in any language.

CAT nods towards the site entrance where we see SID and BOYO come screaming in on the Harley.

58   <u>**EXT. OPEN-CAST SITE. DAY**</u>   58

*CAT greets a hassled **SID** and **BOYO**, still arguing.*

> **SID**
>> What's the form?

> **CAT**
>> Go to the office and sign in.

> **BOYO**
>> Thank fuck for that.

> **SID**
>> He nearly cocked it up.

> **BOYO**
>> It wasn't my bastard fault.

SID and BOYO run to the office.

59   <u>**INT. OPEN-CAST CANTEEN. DAY**</u>   59

*Cigarette smoke and the rumbling chatter of forty or so men fills the room, among them is **SID**, **BOYO** and **CAT**. The Foreman, **MOLLOY**, enters with a site manager and draws the men's attention.*

> **MOLLOY**
> *(without any decorum, American accent)*
>> Welcome to Michigan Mining, my name is
>> Molloy and I'm the foreman on the site. I'm
>> here because I'm hard, fair and don't take any
>> bullshit. I like my men to show up on time,
>> work hard and uphold the standards of the
>> company. We only hire the best. *(PAUSE)*
>> As there are only ten jobs available and most
>> of you have similar qualifications we've

decided to pick the first ten men out of the hat. Any questions?

Murmuring from the men. The tension on **SID** *and* **BOYO's** *faces increases.*

> **MOLLOY**
>> Good, so the following men report to the site office:
>> Ron Jaws
>> Russ Gomer
>> David James
>> Cat Stevens....

CAT's face is a picture of relief and joy. **SID** *and* **BOYO's** *faces remain tense. As the remaining names are called out, the tension builds to a peak:*
>> Micky Butts
>> Danny Loughor
>> Danny Beynon
>> Kevin Bartlett
>> Terry Gabala
>> and Idris Amrott

MOLLOY *puts down the list, surveys the men.* **SID** *and* **BOYO's** *faces are frozen in disbelief.*

> **MOLLOY**
>> All those men whose names I called out go with Sparky here to get kitted out and then to the admin office where we'll do all the paperwork. All you other men, we'll keep your names on file, till next time. Remember Michigan Mining is an expanding company; it needs good workers. Thank you, now go

home and fuck your wives.

The canteen erupts in a mixture of happiness and disappointment.
MOLLOY *leaves.*

> **CAT**
> Sorry boys.

*CAT exits leaving **SID** and **BOYO**.*

> **BOYO**
> Fuckin' hell. Fuckin' fuckin' hell!

*SID turns and exits sharply, pursued by **BOYO**.*

> **BOYO**
> Sid?

60   **INT. SITE OFFICE. DAY**   60

*A man scribbles at a desk. **BOYO** watches him blankly, **SID** is angry and aggresive.*

> **SID**
> Look at me when you're talking to me you
> bastard.

> **MAN**
> What did you say your name was?

> **SID**
> Sid... Sid Lewis.

> **MAN**
> Address?

SID

The Ranch, The Ynys, Banwen

The man writes it down.

SID

Well?

MAN

Well what?

SID

Can you get me and my brother a job?

MAN

No, I was just writing down your details.

The man smiles.

SID

You think it's funny do you?

MAN

Look mate, there's nothing I can do, I'll put you on file for any vacancies.

SID

You're taking the piss out of me.

MAN

I am not taking the piss.

SID

You are.

BOYO

Come on Sid, lets go.

SID

No, this bastard's goin' to give me a job.

MAN

Get out.

SID

No.

MAN

GET OUT.

*The office worker springs out of his seat and tries to chuck **SID** out. **SID** retaliates and a scuffle breaks out, **BOYO** tries to break it up, when suddenly, **MOLLOY** and two heavies appear.*

MOLLOY

Problems Mattie?

MAN

Just this trash.

SID

Trash huh?

*SID butts the office worker and a brawl starts, spilling out of the office and on to the site, drawing the other men's attention who cheer but don't join in. Amongst them is **CAT**, who, on seeing that **BOYO** and **SID** are outnumbered, tries to intervene but is held back by **THE HEAD**. CAT watches horrified as **BOYO** and **SID** take a brutal hammering. The watching men become silent because of its one-sidedness. SID and **BOYO** are punched and kicked into the mud,* *bloodied and defeated.*

MOLLOY
Don't ever fuck with me again.

MOLLOY walks away.

61   **EXT. RIVERBANK. DAY**   61
*The rain has stopped. The Harley is parked near a river flowing under a bridge. **BOYO** is splashing water on his bloodied face. He joins **SID** sitting against a wall looking a mess and crying. **BOYO** puts his arms around him.*

BOYO
Stop crying Sid.

SID
I'm not fucking crying alright. (***Silence***) How the hell am I going to tell Gwenny?

BOYO
She'll understand mun... it's not your fault.

SID
Bastards.

They draw closer together, both of them fighting back tears.

62   **INT. LOUNGE. DAY**   62
GWENNY puts on lipstick in a mirror. MAM methodically plays patience with the cards on the table. Suddenly we hear the sound of an approaching motorbike. GWENNY runs out excitedly.

63   **EXT. BACKYARD. HOUSE. DAY**   63
*She runs into the backyard to see **BOYO** get off the Harley. Her face*

drops and she freezes at the sight of the two boys.

> **GWENNY**
> No...

She weeps. **BOYO** *comforts her.*

> **GWENNY**
> No... NO!

The scene is all to much for **SID** *and he rides off recklessly.*

> **GWENNY**
> SID!

> **BOYO**
> Leave him go.

GWENNY *cries in* **BOYO's** *arms for a moment before breaking and running into the house and upstairs in tears.*

64 <u>INT. LOUNGE. DAY.</u>   64

MAM watches him from the lounge as she plays patience at the table. BOYO walks inside and sweeps away the cards.

> **MAM**
> I'm sorry.

> **BOYO**
> Why us Mam... why is it always us who loses?
> Why Mam? WHY?

He holds his head in his hands, **MAM**, *stares at him blankly.*

65   <u>**EXT. ROAD. DAY**</u>   **65**

SID rides hell for leather along the road. He turns too quickly into a narrow track still wet with rain. He skids, regains control at a lower speed but has to abandon the bike which careers into a hedge. SID ends up on the floor. He gets up and looks at the bike before laying into it with his boots and a piece of wood, trying to work out his rage. He collapses exhausted.

66   <u>**INT. BAR. PANT. NIGHT**</u>   **66**

CAT and the successful new labourers are celebrating boisterously and drunkenly with their new workmates, amongst them is THE HEAD. All are wearing new silver hard hats. WALLY is kept busy at the bar. Sitting on his own and staring into his beer is BOYO, his beaten face and morose mood a total contrast to the celebration.

> **BOYO**
>> Oh, Wal.........

> **WALLY**
>> What?

> **BOYO**
>> *(Holding out a tenner)* Give this to Cat when he's ready.

> **WALLY**
>> I'll give him a shout for you now.

> **BOYO**
>> No, not now, just give it to him that's all. A bet's a bet.

BOYO exits, WALLY watches him go.

67   <u>**INT. LOUNGE. HOUSE. NIGHT**</u>   **67**
*The only light comes from the T.V. set on snow and the orange glow of the electric fire. **BOYO** enters and looks around. He sees a picture of himself as a youth winning a rugby award. He switches off the T.V.*

68   <u>**INT. GWENNY'S BEDROOM. NIGHT**</u>   **68**
***GWENNY'S** face, close. Running mascara. She is drunk and wild. Huddled in a corner. Close on the rotating fan of the electric coal fire, and in front of it a melting plastic doll. The room glows red.*

69   <u>**INT. LOUNGE/STAIRS. NIGHT**</u>   **69**
***BOYO** goes up the stairs towards **GWENNY'S** bedroom.*

70   <u>**INT. GWENNY'S BEDROOM. NIGHT**</u>   **70**
***BOYO** enters the room to find GWENNY's childhood memorabilia scattered all over the place. **GWENNY**, frightened and abandoned looks at him.*

> **GWENNY**
>> You left me on my own.

> **BOYO**
>> Gwenny?

> **GWENNY**
>> Sid?

***BOYO** switches on the light and we see **GWENNY** huddled in a corner with a bottle of bourbon. She is glassy-eyed and child-like.*

> **GWENNY**
>> Oh...

> **BOYO**
>> You haven't drunk all that have you Gwenny?

GWENNY nods.

> **GWENNY**
>> I'm afraid Boyo...

BOYO hugs her.

71 **EXT. OPEN CAST. NIGHT** 71

MAM looks down from the mountain at the flood-lit open cast. She wears sun-glasses. We see CAT, THE HEAD and some others react as she sings a Tom Jones number in front of them.

> **MAM**
>> The old home town looks the same... as I stepped down off the train...

72 **INT. FARMHOUSE. NIGHT** 72

SID's battered face can be seen through the flames of a newly built fire. He drinks. His shirt is spreadeagled over the heap of stones in the corner. He pours bourbon onto the flames.

> **SID**
>> Burn... burn... burn...

73 **EXT. ROAD. AMERICA. DAWN** 73

CLEM's pick-up pulls out of the ranch onto the long, straight road. Cicadas can be heard and a light wind. A radio is turned on and a country music station introduces Tom Jones' 'I'm Coming Home'. We see the pick-up screech to a halt in a cloud of dust. The desert silence is filled with the sound of Tom and the radio. Inside, tears run down CLEM's cheeks. He pulls down the sun visor to look at the family photo, but there is nothing there, just an outline of where the photo used to be. CLEM's face collapses, we mix in the sound of the fire, he looks around panicking as bits of scrub and grass start to combust into a blaze. He screams.

74   <u>**INT. RUINED FARMHOUSE. DAY**</u>   **74**

SID opens his eyes to the droning of the open-cast. His face is a mess. It is raining heavily.

> **ROGER THE POP (O.O.V.)**
>> You alright?

SID looks at ROGER who stands at the door in a soaking anorak.

> **SID**
>> Yeh.

> **ROGER**
>> I saw your bike... came off did you?

> **SID**
>> Can you give me a lift?

> **ROGER**
>> I suppose, one of the Lewises aren't you?

> **SID**
>> Yeh. Sid Lewis.

75   <u>**INT. POP VAN. DAY**</u>   **75**

SID smokes a Marlboro as ROGER drives in the rain.

> **ROGER**
>> What happened to your face then?

> **SID**
>> Bitten by a dog.

> **ROGER**

Must have been a big dog.

*SID looks at him with disdain, **ROGER** shrugs. (PAUSE)*

ROGER
Mother better?

SID
No.

ROGER
Oh... *(PAUSE)* Not worth me calling round then... for the money... eight weeks... is there any...

SID
No.

ROGER
... Just wondering... that's all...

*The van drives along. In the back amongst the pop bottles is **SID's** bike.*

76   **EXT. STREET. DAY**   76
*It is raining heavily as **GWENNY** posts another letter to America. The street is deserted, apart from a silver Michigan Mining wagon which beeps her as it passes. MINERS in the back wolf-whistle at her and **CAT** blows her a kiss.*

77   **INT. SUPERMARKET. DAY**   77
GWENNY looks like a drowned rat as she walks down the aisle of a 'build them high, sell them cheap' Kwik Save store. A SPOTTY YOUTH stacks shelves as she steals some black stockings and hair dye. He sees her but she disarms him with a smile and walks out past the check-out counter where the two check-out girls are too vacant and

bored to notice.

78   <u>**EXT. BACKYARD. HOUSE. DAY**</u>   78

*ROGER the Pop's lorry drives away, leaving the Harley in a mess on the floor and **SID** standing looking at it. **BOYO** appears behind him wearing only a t-shirt despite the rain.*

> **SID**
>> I took the corner too sharp, it ran from under me. *(Pause)* Then I smashed it up.

> **BOYO**
>> I can fix it.

> **SID**
>> What's the point?

> **BOYO**
>> Seen the state in you?

> **SID**
>> Seen the state in you?

> **BOYO**
>> Fuckheads.
> **SID**
>> Shits.

> **BOYO**
>> Fuckin' Yorkie eaters. Who the hell do they think they are?

79   <u>**INT. SID & BOYO'S BEDROOM. DAY**</u>   79

*SID stands smoking at the window dressed peculiarly in **MAM's** dressing gown. **BOYO** lies on the bed.*

SID

I wasn't born to live in this, see.

BOYO

In what?

SID

In rain... it's not natural mun...

BOYO

Where do you reckon you should be
born then?

SID

If I had to answer a straight question, I wish
I'd been born somewhere else, someone else.

BOYO

Like who?

80   <u>**INT. BATHROOM. HOUSE. DUSK**</u>   80

*Steam fills the bathroom as **SID** wipes the mirror and looks right into
it.*

SID

Jack Kerouac.

*He turns off the bath-water. **GWENNY** enters. **SID** takes off his
dressing gown as **GWENNY** gently cleans **SID's** wounds. Steam
engulfs them in a word-less, almost erotic encounter which only **MAM**
witnesses, unseen from her bedroom door.*

FADE TO BLACK.

81   EXT. OPEN CAST. DAY   81

*From black we hear **MAM's** voice counting.*

> **MAM (O.O.V.)**
>> One hundred and seventy one...etc.

*We see that **MAM** is walking up the mountain towards the house. Suddenly she stops dead in her tracks next to the graves marked Billy and Brando. A hooter sounds and after silence we see an explosion rip open a fresh seam of coal behind **MAM**.*

82   INT. BOYO & SID'S BEDROOM. DAY   82

BOYO *is woken by the explosion and gets out of bed. All traces of the beating have disappeared, yet he still manages to look bleary-eyed and unshaven. Cans litter the foot of his bed.*

83   INT. LOUNGE. HOUSE. DAY   83

*The lounge is in a similarly scruffy state with cans and take-aways littering the floor. **SID**, dressed in Kerouac gear looks identical to his father as he sits in front of a perfectly constructed house of cards. His face, like **BOYO's**, has completely healed since the fight. **BOYO** enters and looks stunned at **SID's** card creation.*

> **BOYO**
>> Jesus Christ.
>
> **SID**
>> It's a masterpiece mate.

> **BOYO**
>> How did you get that far then?

> **SID**
>> Solid foundation Boyo... everything Sid Lewis builds is solid. Skill too, two of them together, fatal combination mate.

BOYO

> No flies on you see, are there
> brother?

SID

> No, and the odd ones I do find flying round
> my head either went to Oxford or
> Cambridge.

BOYO

> On a day trip.

SID

> No, Boyo, only because of their brains see,
> only because of their brains.

GWENNY enters, breathless, her hair is dyed black and she is looking more like a woman than a girl.

GWENNY

> Never guess what I've just seen. I was walking
> down the street right, and it's raining, the
> clouds were low, and in front of me is
> someone walking a dog, it's a chihuahua.
> *(SILENCE)* And I can hear an open cast
> lorry coming down the road behind me, and
> it passes me, whoosh, like that, and it's just
> about to pass the dog, who's on the lead,
> when the dog strays into the road, and gets
> squashed flat, and the owner's still holding
> onto the lead, just staring at the squashed
> dog. And all of a sudden, I feel like laughing,
> not just giggle, but a hysterical one.

SID

> Yeh, what it is right, is that somewhere deep
> down inside, you just hate chihuahuas.

GWENNY

> Why? Then I go and see if I can help. The
> man's just staring down, I feel sorry for him
> now. When he turns round and says "I've
> only just given him a whole tin of 'Chum',
> and now the poor bugger's gone and got
> squashed." Then I ask him what the dog's
> name was, and he turns round and says Jack.

SID

> Kerouac?

GWENNY

> That's what I said, and he says who's that,
> and I say, he's an American who wrote books.
> So the two of us stand there looking at this
> American novelist who's squashed on the
> road, and you know what?

SID

> What?

GWENNY

> I haven't thought of an ending
> to it yet.

BOYO

> Oh Christ mun, Gwenny.

SID

> Hey c'mon baby, there's got to be an ending, got to be an ending.

GWENNY

> And the girl turned to her friends and I said I made it all up. I've never seen a chihuahua and what's more, I haven't been out of the house either. I've been in my room reading, and trying on clothes.

GWENNY laughs, SID laughs, BOYO frowns, slumps down at the table where the house of cards sit. He accidentally bangs the table, notices the cards don't move. BOYO smiles broadly.

BOYO

> You conniving little, oi... Gwenny look at this, that's why his cards stay up, he's glued them all together!!

BOYO shows them triumphantly, SID is annoyed, GWENNY laughs.

GWENNY

> That's cheating Sid baby.

BOYO

> Too right it is.

SID

> Yeh well, it just goes to show see Boyo, don't believe everything you see.

BOYO

> I'll remember that.

84 **EXT. DOLE OFFICE. DAY** 84

*A Transglam bus pulls away as **BOYO**, **SID** and **GWENNY** rush out of the DOLE OFFICE in nearby town. **BOYO** looks forlornly after the bus. **GWENNY** puts shades on him, then puts hers on. **SID** already wearing his, walks away with his thumb out hitching a lift. **GWENNY** follows as does a disgruntled **BOYO**.*

85 **EXT. ROAD. DAY** 85

*A long straight road, no sign of traffic. **BOYO** brings up the rear as **SID** and **GWENNY** head out of town with their thumbs out.*

86 **EXT. PANTYDDRAENEN PUB. DAY** 86

*As they enter the village, **BOYO** turns into the Pant Pub **SID** and **GWENNY** continue walking.*

> **BOYO**
>> Where you going?

> **GWENNY**
>> Home.

> **BOYO**
>> But this is the Pant.

> **SID**
>> Yeh.

> **BOYO**
>> It's Thursday.

> **SID**
>> And?

> **BOYO**
>> We drink.

SID

Not in here we don't.

SID and GWENNY continue walking.

BOYO

(*Shouting*) How else we going to get pissed?

Suddenly we hear the sound of an elaborate car horn and we see CAT pull up in a jazzy orange Ford Capri. He gets out of the car looking as pleased as punch. SID and GWENNY look less than impressed.

BOYO

Fucking hell.

CAT

Like it?

BOYO

Flash as fuck mun, what you reckon Sid?

SID

It's alright.

CAT

Fancy a spin?

SID

You got to be kidding.

SID walks away.

CAT

Gwenny...?

GWENNY

No thanks.

She follows **SID.**

CAT

What the hell's wrong with them?

BOYO

You know how Sid is mun, still a bit
touchy.

CAT

Gwenny's dyed her hair and all, I preferred it
as it was.

BOYO

(To **CAT***)* Orange by Jesus.

CAT

Yeh... engine by Ford.

87   **EXT. ROAD.DAY**   87

CAT's orange Capri comes screaming down the road with **BOYO**
inside.

88   **INT. CAPRI. DAY**   88

CAT and **BOYO** *are inside in mid-conversation.*

BOYO

When did you meet her then?

CAT

Couple of weeks ago.

BOYO

Nice is she?

CAT

Fucking gorgeous, she's a typist.

BOYO

Do I know her?

CAT

Nah. Sharon her name is, comes from Stoke, mirror glass figure.

BOYO

Hour glass.

CAT

She's got nice jugs that's all I know, and her friend has. I'll get you an introduction if you want, you'll have to come to town though.

BOYO looks away.

CAT

I'll lend you the money.

BOYO

Goes like a bullet fair play.

CAT

Two litre engine, overhead cam shaft, twin choke webers, re-conditioned, the works.

BOYO

Great mun.

CAT

You wait till Sharon sees me in
this mate.

BOYO

Jammy bastard

CAT

Capris and women, jelly and
blancmange.

They laugh.

BOYO

What have you done with the
Robin then?

CAT

Scrapping it, what else?

BOYO

Straight up?

CAT

Straight up...why?

89 **EXT. MOUNTAIN. DAY**   89

*SID and GWENNY are leaning on the MICHIGAN MINING
sign, looking down into the mine below.*

SID

Clem Lewis from Dodge City, we stayed with him
when we were on the road, came looking for the
dream with us, tried to talk about his baby all the
time. He said I know a girl on the other side of

>Heaven man, you've got to meet her Jack, she'll take you to dreamworld.

GWENNY
>Was he a good man Sid?

SID
>The best Gwenny, the best.

GWENNY
>Then why don't he write to us then?

SID
>Well I don't know do I? Christ Gwenny mun, I'm only telling the story.

SID is indignant. (Pause)

GWENNY
>It's no good without the Bourbon is it?

SID looks at GWENNY then walks away.

90   <u>**EXT. BACKYARD. HOUSE. DAY**</u>   90
BOYO walks around the newly acquired three wheeler Robin Reliant. It is in less than mint condition. SID and GWENNY enter the yard as MAM looks on.

MAM
>It's nice Boyo.

SID

It's crap.

BOYO

It's a car. 50 quid in instalments
after I get myself a job.

SID

He ripped you off.

BOYO

I've just got to look after it
that's all.

GWENNY

I wouldn't be seen dead in it.
(Laughing)

BOYO

Nobody's asking you to be seen
dead in it.

MAM

I like it Boyo.

SID

But it's only got three wheels
Mam.

MAM

Three wheels is enough.

SID

It's only three quarters of a car, typical of
him, not all there.

BOYO

> Bollocks.

MAM

> I'll come for a spin with you
> Boyo.

SID

> Yeh, go on Boyo, take Mam for
> a spin.

GWENNY

> Yeh.

MAM

> It will be nice to go out. I haven't been out in
> ages.

SID

> And we all know why.

MAM

> What did you say?

SID

> I said you'll enjoy it Mam.

BOYO

> Come on then Mam, get in.

MAM smiles and gets in the car. BOYO sighs.

SID

> Enjoy the trip brother.

*BOYO starts up the Reliant. **SID** and **GWENNY** watch it pull
away.*

SID

Fancy going on the road in that, wouldn't get
you as far as Swansea.

GWENNY

Who needs to go to Swansea?

*GWENNY pulls out some pills, **SID** laughs.*

91   EXT. MOUNTAIN ROAD, DAY   91

*The Reliant climbs a winding road, overlooking some beautiful
rugged Welsh landscape. **BOYO** and **MAM** are in conversation.*

MAM (O.O.V.)

Why does he have to wear your father's
clothes anyway?

BOYO

They're not my father's clothes mam.

MAM

Reminds me of her she does.

BOYO

Who does?

MAM

Gwenny. You were in school, it was a
Monday. I came home from work early,
dental appointment. I saw his motorbike. He
should have been in work, he skived off. He

always skived off, I tried to tell him, but he
wouldn't listen...

92   <u>EXT. STREET. DAY.</u>   92

*GWENNY cuts a striking figure as she walks down the street followed
by SID. She enters an off-licence as SID walks nonchalantly by.*

> **MAM (V.O.)**
>> ... I walked into the house, I saw her clothes,
>> the floozy...a skirt, stockings, pair of shoes,
>> her handbag. They'd been drinking; there
>> were bottles everywhere. There was music on
>> the record player, Tom Jones it was, he knew
>> I liked Tom Jones.

93   <u>INT. OFF-LICENCE. DAY</u>   93

*GWENNY puts two bottles of Jack Daniels bourbon on the counter.
The off-licence worker obviously fancies her.*

> **OFF LICENCE MAN**
>> Wasn't I at school with you?

> **GWENNY**
>> Maybe.

> **OFF-LICENCE MAN**
>> Lewis innit?

> **GWENNY**
>> Maybe.

(Pause)

> **OFF LICENCE-MAN**
>> You got a boyfriend?

> **GWENNY**
> Are you asking?

Putting her leg on a chair and letting her skirt ride-up. **OFF-LICENCE MAN** *looks admiringly.*

> **GWENNY**
> You got a washroom I could use?

> **OFF-LICENCE MAN**
> Yeh.

> **GWENNY**
> Can you show me?

> **OFF-LICENCE MAN**
> Yeh.

GWENNY walks provocatively around the counter past the OFF-LICENCE MAN who follows her out the back and thinks it's his lucky day. As soon as they've gone, SID enters the off-licence and rifles through the shelves putting bottles in a bag, smiling and exiting.

94   <u>INT. OFF-LICENCE. WASHROOM. DAY</u>   94

GWENNY looks at herself in the mirror and smiles, puts on lipstick and opens the door where the OFF-LICENCE MAN is waiting.

> **GWENNY**
> Thanks.

She walks away towards the shop.

> **OFF-LICENCE MAN**
> Hang on a minute, I thought we...

GWENNY
> What?

OFF-LICENCE MAN
> We... I... I could shut the shop.

GWENNY
> Are you real?

*GWENNY exits. **OFF-LICENCE MAN** is defeated.*

95   **<u>EXT. STREET. DAY</u>**   95
*In a little alleyway, **GWENNY** re-joins **SID**. They laugh exuberantly and race away in victory.*

96   **<u>EXT. MOUNTAIN CAR PARK. DAY</u>**   96
*The Reliant is parked up overlooking the view. **BOYO** eats an ice-cream. **MAM** ponders.*

MAM
> Do you love me Boyo?

BOYO
> Uh?

MAM
> You heard.

BOYO
> What you asking me that for?

MAM
> I want to know.

BOYO
> Yeh.

MAM

I want to hear you say it.

BOYO

Oh come on Mam, give me a break.

MAM

I want to hear you say it.

(Pause)

BOYO

I love you alright. You're my mother
aren't you?

MAM

Would you still love me if you knew I'd done
something wrong, something bad?

BOYO

Yeh, course I would.

MAM

No matter what it was?

BOYO

I'd know you had your reasons.

MAM

Good boy.

(Pause)

BOYO

Why do you ask?

MAM

> I wanted to be sure you wouldn't
> shout at me.

BOYO

> What have you done then?

MAM

> I let the air out of the tyre the day you went
> for those jobs.

BOYO

> Oh Jesus Christ Mam. *(Angry)*

MAM stuffs her cornet into his cheek.

MAM

> I knew you'd shout at me, I knew it, let's go home.

BOYO

> Bloody hell Mam.

97   <u>**INT. BATHROOM. HOUSE. NIGHT**</u>   97

*SID is in a bathful of water wearing only his jeans. He holds a bottle
of Jack Daniels. GWENNY sits on the toilet, drunk.*

(SINGING)
> **SID**

> > Home in Missoula, home in
> > Truckee...

> **GWENNY**

> > Home in Opelousas ain't no
> > home for me.

SID

Home in old Medora...

GWENNY

Home in Wounded Knee...

SID

Home in... what is it?

GWENNY

Ogallalla...

BOTH

Home I'll never be...

Whistles and cheers as they end the song. **BOYO** *enters uncomfortably.*

BOYO

What's the crack?

SID

The crack is...

GWENNY

I'm peeing, but he won't get out of the bath.

SID

Is that a problem to you brother?

BOYO

No, but Mam wants you to keep the noise
down.

SID

And what Mammy wants, Mammy gets.
Look at you all dead, dead, dead. Have you
got a penny for me to go to the fair?

GWENNY and SID laugh.

BOYO

You two ought to have a good look at
yourselves, laughing at Mam.

BOYO exits.

SID

Why do you always take her side. What are
you, some kind of Mammy's boy?

GWENNY and SID laugh.

98   **INT. LOUNGE. HOUSE. NIGHT**   98

*BOYO opens a can of lager and watches some rugby on the T.V.
MAM sits with her arms folded, listening to the continuing shouts
from SID and GWENNY upstairs.*

MAM

They're laughing at me, can't you hear them?

BOYO stares at the T.V. MAM gets up and switches off the T.V.

BOYO

Put the rugby back on mun Mam.

MAM

No.

BOYO

Mam, please mun. I want to watch the rugby.

MAM switches on the T.V. set but it is off channel.

BOYO

    Mam mun!

MAM

    Mr Snow's the only friend I got in here. We get on like a house on fire. I get up in the morning and say hello Mr Snow, and then before he's got time to answer, I turn him off.

She switches off the T.V.

BOYO

    Jesus Christ.

BOYO gets up and puts on his coat.

MAM

    Where you going?

BOYO

    For a bloody spin...

MAM

    That's it, you leave me on my own...

BOYO exits. We hear the Reliant start up and drive away.

MAM

    With Jack and Joyce.

99   <u>INT. WASHROOM. AMERICA. NIGHT</u>   99
CLEM washes his face then dries it. He looks at himself in the mirror then exits.

100   <u>EXT. GAS STATION. AMERICA. DAY</u>   100
In a gas-station in the middle of nowhere, an elderly gas attendant

fills **CLEM**'*s pick-up.* **CLEM** *gets out and gets him to fill a gasoline can as well.* **CLEM** *then sits in the front and lights a Marlboro.*

> ### SID (V.O.)
> Clem Lewis from Dodge City, we stayed with him when we were on the road, came looking for the dream with us...

101   INT. SID'S BEDROOM. HOUSE. NIGHT   101

SID lights a cigarette with a Zippo as he stands in the mirror. **GWENNY** *lies on the bed drinking...*

> ### SID
> He said I know a girl on the other side of Heaven man, she'll take you to dreamworld...

Suddenly **MAM** *bursts in angrily and starts to spank* **SID**.

> ### SID
> What the fuck...

GWENNY *laughs.*

> ### MAM
> STOP LAUGHING AT ME!

> ### SID
> Don't ever do that to me again.

> ### MAM
> You were laughing.

> ### SID
> Never!

*The threat in **SID's** voice is obvious. **MAM** crumples and starts to weep.*

> **MAM**
> Not safe for me in this house no more.

She exits. Silence.

102   <u>**INT. PANT PUB. NIGHT**</u>   **102**

***BOYO** is at the bar, drowning his sorrows. A Tom Jones ballad starts to play on the jukebox. **MOLLOY** and his heavies suddenly enter.*

> **HEAVY 1**
> Well look who it is.

***MOLLOY** looks at **BOYO** and smiles malevolently. **BOYO** avoids eye-contact not wanting any trouble. **WALLY**, sensing trouble, pours him another pint. **MOLLOY** comes up to the bar close to **BOYO**, and stares at him. **BOYO** doesn't want a confrontation.*

> **BOYO**
> How much do I owe you Wal?

WALLY
> Pay me next time... here you go.
> *(handing him a beer)*

MOLLOY *(sings)*
> "I'm coming home, to your loving arms
> etc..."

BOYO is humiliated by MOLLOY's malevolent singing and is forced to exit the pub to the cheers of the heavies.

103   INT. MAM'S BEDROOM. NIGHT   103

MAM stands at her window staring out at the backyard. Her face shows consternation and from her POV, we see a fire burning in the yard.

SID: (Voice in Mam's head)
> What you burning mam?

104   INT. RELIANT. NIGHT   104

Close-up on BOYO's defeated face as he drives along. He turns the corner into the backyard of the house. His face falls.

BOYO
> What the fuck?

105   EXT. BACKYARD. HOUSE. NIGHT   105

SID's Harley Davidson, covered in clothes is ablaze. BOYO screeches to a halt in his Reliant. He opens the car door, but as he does so, the Harley explodes. The windows in the kitchen smash to pieces. MAM stands nearby calmly staring at the blaze which reflects on her dishevelled and dirty face. SID and GWENNY race out from the house, still only semi-clothed from their previous adventure. They stare in horror. BOYO is first to recover, turning on a hosepipe, helped by SID. The flames are eventually extinguished against the night sky.

106   <u>INT. LOUNGE. NIGHT.</u>   106

The kitchen windows are smashed. **BOYO** *and* **GWENNY** *stand together, angry and disappointed.* **SID** *stares at the electric fire.* **MAM** *giggles at the kitchen table.*

> **SID**
>
> Shut up Mam.

> **MAM**
>
> How can I? I killed him. *(Silence)* The cat's out of the bag. *(**MAM** laughs watched closely by the others)* The cat is out of... the bag. *(laughing)*

> **SID**
>
> Shut up Mam. *(She continues to laugh)* SHUT UP I SAID!

The steel in **SID**'s *voice changes* **MAM**'s *mood and she controls herself.*

> **MAM**
>
> What did I say?

> **BOYO**
>
> You said you felt like sleeping.

> **MAM**
>
> Did I? I do too, bed is best.

BOYO *moves as if to take her upstairs,* **MAM** *rejects it.*

> **MAM**
>
> No, no, I can manage on my own... but I'll go to your room Gwenny, my room gives me nightmares.

MAM moves towards the stairs, stops, surveys the scene.

MAM

> I'm still your mother.
> Goodnight.

She exits upstairs, shutting the lounge door behind her, we hear her footsteps going upstairs.

BOYO

> Fucking hell.

*Holding his heads in his hands as he sits on the chair, **GWENNY** starts to cry in the background. **SID** gets up and goes to comfort **GWENNY**.*

SID

> Putting it on she is Gwen.

GWENNY

> Is that what you think?

SID

> Course it is, you don't believe
> her do you? Boyo?

BOYO

> I don't know what to believe
> Sid.

SID

> Everybody knows he's in America, you ask
> anybody. *(Pause)* She never killed him, she
> probably wished she did and now with her
> nerves and everything. She's got it all mixed
> up and thinks she's done it, that's all.

GWENNY

That's all?

SID

Yeh... believe me.

BOYO

I don't know Sid, she's too much for me she is. *(Breaking down)*

SID moves over to BOYO to comfort him.

SID

Don't let it get to you brother, it's all in her mind, all in her head.

BOYO

How come we haven't heard a word from him since he went then?

SID

Because he probably thought it was for the best, didn't want to upset us... I bet you he's laying plans for us to go over for a visit, what do you say Gwen?

GWENNY nods.

GWENNY

Perhaps...

BOYO

How can you be that sure Sid?

SID

I don't know, just got a feeling

about it. *(pause)*

All three think about the ramifications.

> **SID**
>> No point getting worked up about it, the best thing to do is to forget about it and get mam into the hospital.

BOYO nods.

> **BOYO**
>> Yeh... suppose it's for the best.

> **SID**
>> Hey c'mon, let's cheer up and forget it, it's not the end of the world.

> **BOYO**
>> Fucking feels like it.

> **SID**
>> Hey c'mon, the two of you.

SID draws GWENNY and BOYO into a huddle.

> **SID**
>> This is family... it'll be alright.

They cling tightly together.

107   **EXT. MOUNTAIN. NIGHT**   **107**

The crane digging the topsoil eats a way at the earth. Not far away and right in its path are the two crosses in the undergrowth with " Brando" and "Billy" on them.

108   **EXT. RANCH. AMERICA. NIGHT**   108
*Tumbleweed blows across the yard. No clothes hang on the washing
line, no horses stand in the corral and the woodwork all around needs
a coat of paint.*

109   **INT. RANCH, AMERICA. NIGHT**   109
*In the kitchen, the sink is full of dirty dishes, cans, bourbon bottles and
cigarettes litter the table. No family photos can be seen. It looks as if the
family no longer lives in it.*

110   **EXT. RANCH. AMERICA. NIGHT**   110
CLEM *gets out of his pick-up with a can of gasoline. He looks at the
ranch for a moment before lighting a cigarette. He starts to laugh
loudly.*

111   **INT. BATHROOM. WALES. NIGHT**   111
SID *stands in the bathroom mirror in moonlight, staring at his
reflection.*

>   SID
>   R.I.P.

FADE TO BLACK.

112   **EXT. HOSPITAL. DAY**   112
BOYO *drives his Reliant through the gates of the hospital. A couple of
patients can be seen taking afternoon walks.* **BOYO** *pulls up at the
main entrance.*

113   **INT. HOSPITAL LOUNGE. DAY**   113
BOYO *looks around the lounge. The T.V. is on.* **MAM** *is in the corner
staring blankly at it. The only other person is a young woman playing
with a Barbie doll.* **BOYO** *approaches* **MAM** *who doesn't notice him.*

>   BOYO
>   Hello Mam.

MAM

Hello Jesus, it's me... Eileen Lewis.

BOYO

No Mam, it's me, Boyo.

(Pause) MAM's face shows disappointment as she re-adjusts.

MAM

Oh... I thought you were Jesus.

BOYO's face says it all, MAM gets up and walks past him. BOYO follows.

114   INT. MAM'S ROOM. HOSPITAL. DAY   114

MAM opens the door to her room and walks in, followed by BOYO. It is very sparse and clinical with a bed, a chair, desk, wardrobe, window and curtain.

BOYO

I brought you some Jaffa Cakes and fruit.

MAM nods, BOYO puts them on the desk.

BOYO

Not a bad room, Mam.

MAM doesn't answer.

BOYO

How you feeling?

MAM

I thought you'd forgotten about me.

BOYO

Don't be so soft Mam, I...

MAM

How's the house?

BOYO

Alright. *(Pause)* Gwenny keeps writing him letters to America.

MAM

You'll have to tell her to stop.

BOYO

I've been reading them. I don't want to upset her, but they're calling her Miss America.

MAM

Who is?

BOYO

The Post Office. The woman told me she comes in every week to see if there's a letter.

MAM

What fruit did you bring?

BOYO

Apples, do you want one?

MAM takes an apple.

BOYO

Did you give her an address Mam?

MAM

I can't remember.

BOYO

Sid told me you gave it to her.

MAM

She was pestering me.

BOYO

So you did then?

MAM

Yes.

BOYO

So he is in America?

MAM

An address doesn't mean anything.

BOYO

What's the address then? *(Silence)* Mam?

MAM

You better ask her that, she's the one sending
the letters. Me and Gwenny were sitting there
one day and there was a Western on, and I
turned round to her and said that's where
he'll be. But you know what the worst of it is,
you don't have to go to the Wild West to find
America, they've built a Wild West up the
valley. The bloke who told me is a cowboy,
he thinks he's a cowboy. Montgomery Clift
he calls himself. You ever heard of him?

She laughs. **BOYO** *shakes his head.*

> **MAM**
>
> I think I'm lucky to be in here, nobody'll hurt me in here. I hear you can see the open-cast from the window now. (*PAUSE*) They're coming nearer, won't be long now.

> **BOYO**
>
> I love Gwenny mam, and I don't want to lie to her.

> **MAM**
>
> Then tell her the truth.

> **BOYO**
>
> I don't know what it is.

> **MAM**
>
> Ask Sid then, if you don't believe me.

MAM exits. **BOYO** *looks defeated.*

115   **EXT. RANCH. MID WEST AMERICA. DAY**   **115**

*A light wind blows the smouldering ruin of the ranch. It has been burnt to the ground and looks completely desolate. Tumbleweed blows in the ruins, vultures call and circle in the sky. Nearby **CLEM** stands looking a dishevelled mess at the edge of the road looking at the devastation. He has a gun in his hand.*

> **SID (V.O.)**
>
> Picture the scene. A typical Mid-Western American morning. The sky was bluish red with a few stars.

116   <u>**INT. SID & BOYO'S BEDROOM. WALES. DAY**</u>116
*Cans and take-aways litter the bedroom. The house has not been cleaned in weeks. **SID** stands at a mirror, looking at his reflection.*

> **SID**
>> The sound of cicadas mingle with the early dawn sound of the desert. *(Pause)* Does it fuck.

117   <u>**INT. BATHROOM. HOUSE. DAY**</u>   117
GWENNY is violently sick in the toilet. She washes her face and looks at herself in the mirror.

> **SID (V.O.)**
>> You could look as pretty as Joyce, see Gwen.

118   <u>**INT. LOUNGE. HOUSE. DAY**</u>   118
GWENNY turns from a mirror.

> **GWENNY**
>> Even without the copper earrings?

> **SID**
>> They don't have to be copper, just big and round.

BOYO sits alone with a beer in the mess-strewn lounge.

> **GWENNY**
>> And Boyo, you can be Allan Ginsberg or somebody.

> **BOYO**
>> It's alright, I'll stick to being Boyo.

GWENNY pulls a face at him behind his back.

SID

It was him who introduced Jack to Joyce.

BOYO

Oh, great mun.

GWENNY

It's a love story see Boyo.

BOYO

How long am I going to have to listen to this crap?

GWENNY

Don't be like that.

BOYO

Well Christ mun, it's the same old crack every day, Jack this, Joyce that, why don't you give it a rest?

SID

Read the book, then you can join in.

BOYO

I don't want to read the book, I'm not interested, you're like a pair of kids mun, playing.

GWENNY

There's nothing wrong with that is there?

BOYO

I'm not saying, but it's all this yankage, give it a rest for Christ sake.

GWENNY

Oh, poor Boyo, he feels left out
Jack.

She puts a baseball hat on his head. **BOYO** *grabs the hat, spits on it and then throws it across the room.*

GWENNY

There was no need to do that.

SID

If he doesn't want to play, baby, we can't
help him.

BOYO

(Exploding) No, I don't want to fucking play
alright, I just want you to stop, look at
yourselves and face the truth.

GWENNY

Oooooohhhhhh...

BOYO

He's not in America Gwenny.

BOYO *holds up a letter with* **GWENNY**'s *handwriting.*

GWENNY

Where did you get that from?

BOYO

Your room.

GWENNY

Snoop.

BOYO

It's a Mickey Mouse address Gwenny... mam made it up.

GWENNY

How do you know?

BOYO

Well it's bastard obvious mun - Clem Lewis, Main Street, Dodge City, The West. She got it out of a Western!

GWENNY

I don't care... he'll get it somehow.

BOYO

Don't be so soft mun, Gwenny. There's a million Lewis's in America.

GWENNY

I don't care alright, I don't care what you say, you're not going to stop me.

GWENNY exits angrily, slamming the door.

BOYO

Sid mun, talk to her.

SID

What is there to say?

BOYO

You can tell her it's bollocks and help me do something about it.

SID

Nothing we can do.

BOYO

> There's got to be something. *(Pause)* Sid
> mun, it's me Boyo, talk to me.

SID

> The only ones for me are the ones who burn
> Boyo, you got me?

119   <u>**INT. PANTYDDRAENEN PUB**</u>   119

BOYO is the only customer, he and WALLY are in mid-conversation.

BOYO

> Do they make cars in Dodge City
> Wally?

WALLY

> What sort of question's that?

BOYO

> Do you know the answer?

WALLY

> Detroit is the car capital of America innit?

BOYO

> Not Dodge?

WALLY

> Don't think so. Dodge is in the Wild West
> somewhere, by Kansas or Colorado.

BOYO

> How far's that from Detroit?

WALLY

> Must be couple of thousand miles mun, but

I'm not sure... I can ask Pat for you, she
knows tons about America.

BOYO

No, don't bother.

WALLY

You sure?

BOYO

Yeh. *(Pause)* Did my old man know anything
about cars?

WALLY

The only thing your old man knew about cars
was he never had the money to buy one.

120   <u>EXT. FARMHOUSE. NIGHT</u>   120

*A fire blazes near the pile of rocks. GWENNY circles the fire with a
bottle and popping pills. SID stands in the doorway looking up at the
moon.*

GWENNY

We can go out in the moonlight when the
dinosaurs are sleeping, they've eaten the
dragon, tin men, clankety clank, boom buddy
boom buddy hiccup clanks the wind will
make them feel better.

She stumbles and falls over near the rocks.

SID

Get away from there Gwenny.

GWENNY

The girl from the prairie got a ladder in her

stocking Jack...

SID

I said get away from there.

*We close in on **SID**. He turns away and sits by the fire, staring at it, the fire sound increases.*

121   <u>EXT. BACKYARD. HOUSE. NIGHT</u>   **121**

MAM turns her head in front of a roaring fire in response to:

SID (O.O.V.)

What you burning Mam?

Her face is blackened, her eyes wild.

122   <u>INT. RUINED FARMHOUSE. NIGHT</u>   **122**

SID suddenly extinguishes the fire. He looks at the burning embers. GWENNY stands next to him, staring down.

GWENNY

What's wrong Jack? Now's the chance to run when the world's asleep but my legs have got pins and needles Jack. Look at them.

GWENNY lifts up her skirt provocatively. SID looks at her legs. He then turns away. GWENNY approaches him.

GWENNY

Music we need. It's all quiet in forgotten town, Jack.

SID

Lets go home.

He exits. GWENNY follows.

GWENNY

> Is it raining or what? Jack wait for me!

123   **INT. LOUNGE. NIGHT**   123

*The T.V. set plays with the volume off. **BOYO** is attempting the impossible at the lounge table - building a house of cards while drunk. **SID** enters, supporting a paralytic and drugged **GWENNY**. His cards fall.*

BOYO

> Fuckin' hell, lovers just about on their feet
> then are they?

SID

> Shut up and give us a hand will you?

BOYO

> Where you been?

GWENNY

> Whaddy say?

SID

> I said sit down before you fall down,
> shit for brains.

BOYO

> You can talk.

GWENNY

> Whoisit Jack?

BOYO

> It's Bill and Ben the Flower Pot
> Men.

BOYO laughs, stumbles.

SID

> On second thoughts I'll manage on
> my own.

SID heads upstairs.

BOYO

> *(Shouting after him)* You could have told me
> where you were going... I eat popcorn and
> drink coke too... Hey mun!.. I'm talking to
> you! *(Laughs)* Prefer chips though. Have a
> chip, have a kip... you listening to me Jack
> Kerouac?

SID (O.O.V.)

> Fuck off Boyo.

BOYO

> Don't be like that mun, come down and have
> a drink with your brother... 'bout time we
> had a talk... you listening? *(Pause)* Oi?
> Detroit is where the cars are, not Dodge.

A door slams.

BOYO

> I got cans and everything... Sid?

Silence.

BOYO

> I want to talk... oi...

He gives up and slumps in the chair.

BOYO

(Shouts) Fucking shambles the lot of
you.

He chucks the cards in the air.

124   **EXT. OPEN CAST. DAY**   **124**

*Heavy rain. The diggers are working away at the topsoil, getting
nearer the graves of 'Billy' and 'Brando'.*

125   **EXT. BACKYARD. HOUSE. DAY**   **125**

*Rain falls in the yard. The charred remains of **SID**'s Harley
Davidson can be seen amongst the rubble and charred earth. The
kitchen windows are boarded up.*

GWENNY (V.O.)

Jack, you remember when we were small?

SID

Small?

GWENNY

Like little.

SID

Yeh.

GWENNY

I had a dolly.

126   **INT. MAM'S BEDROOM. DAY**   **126**

***MAM**'s room is a mess of bottles, pictures, some of **GWENNY**'s clothes.*

GWENNY (V.O.)

I played with it in front of the fire Jack. Our
mammy and pappy were arguing. You
listening Jack?

*We see **SID** sitting on the bed, half wasted.*

SID

I'm listening.

GWENNY

I heard mammy scream. I saw her cry. She
told me to go upstairs. I left my dolly by the
fire. I stayed upstairs a long time.

*We reveal **GWENNY** rolling black stockings on her legs, in black
underwear, then mini-skirt and jumper - the perfect image of Joyce
Jonson. **SID** watches her.*

GWENNY

Then I came downstairs, there was nobody
there. I picked up my dolly, but my fingers
went straight through her. Melted by the fire.
All the way from Hong Kong to melt on the
carpet in my house. Then mammy came in
and said that pappy had gone to America.
(Pause) She's not lying is she Jack? Jack?

SID

You're a good looking woman Gwenny.

GWENNY

Joycey.

SID

You're a good looking woman Joycey.

GWENNY

Thank you Jack.

***SID** looks at her and smiles.*

SID

Time we hit the road baby.

127   <u>**EXT. STREET. DAY**</u>   127

*An American Convertible Car sits in a dead end street. **SID** and **GWENNY** suddenly appear, moving towards it. **SID** smashes the side window and jumps inside as does **GWENNY**. He hot-wires the wagon to life, they roar away, whooping and cheering as a **MOLLOY** from a house angrily, pulling up his trousers.*

MOLLOY

Oi!

128   <u>**EXT. ROAD. DAY**</u>   128

***SID** and **GWENNY** pop pills and drink bourbon wildly. **SID** is driving erratically and at high speed, drawing the attention of other drivers as they roar past.*

GWENNY

Its the wolf, its the wolf, its the
WOOOOLLLUUFF.

***SID** steps on the gas.*

129   <u>**EXT. OPEN-CAST SITE. DAY**</u>   129

*The entrance of the site is marked by a huge 'Michigan Mining' sign, its silver glinting in the light. **SID** and **GWENNY** speed into the site, screaming manically inside.*

GWENNY

Burn them, burn them, burn them
Jack.

130   <u>**EXT. OPEN-CAST. DAY**</u>   130

The Convertible weaves a perilous path through the mud and machinery of the site. Huge lorries and road making machines swerve to avoid the lunatic car from hell.

131   <u>EXT. OPEN-CAST. DAY</u>   131

A coal lorry, unaware of the convertible's presence on the site comes hurtling round a blind corner, the wagon is heading straight for it.

132   <u>INT. WAGON. DAY</u>   132

SID and GWENNY panic.

>   **GWENNY**
>   Watch out.

>   **SID**
>   I got it, I got it.

133   <u>EXT. OPEN-CAST. DAY</u>   133

There is no room for the lorry to swerve, there is a huge 100ft drop to one side and a wall of mud and stone on the other. The lorry driver is powerless - he screams on the brakes as SID at the last minute swerves the convertible into the mud heap which operates like a ramp and he flies through the air, miraculously avoiding the lorry.

134   <u>INT. CONVERTIBLE. DAY</u>   134

SID and GWENNY scream like banshees, completely exhilarated and speeding.

>   **SID (O.O.V.)**
>   He went to the gas station and got himself
>   some gas, a whole pick-up full of it, drove
>   back to the ranch, doused the whole place
>   with gasoline, torched it and watched the
>   whole shithouse go up in flames!

135   <u>EXT. ROAD. DAY</u>   135

The wagon screams out of the site and drives down the road as dusk falls.

GWENNY (O.O.V.)
> Burn... burn... burn.

136　**EXT. RANCH. MID-WEST AMERICA. NIGHT** **136**
*The ranch is engulfed in flames. **CLEM** stands in the middle of the road watching it. The pick up in the front of the house explodes in a fireball which cascades into the air. After a moment **SID's** voice is heard.*

SID (V.O.)
> He stood on the road, a lonely figure
> watching his whole dream fall apart. He
> didn't feel sad. He always knew that one day
> it would happen, and he was sick too, sick of
> hiding out in his farmhouse with his secret.

137　**EXT. FOREST. WALES. DUSK**　**137**
*A light wind rustles in the trees. Burnt out shells of various cars sit in a forest clearing in the fading light. It is strangely eerie sight, with the forest reclaiming some of the cars, growing through the floor and engines of the wrecks. **SID** and **GWENNY** sit reclined in the battered convertible staring up at the sky.*

GWENNY
> What was his secret Jack?

SID
> He knew they'd come looking for him, so he
> went on the run. For five whole days he lived
> in the desert, living on berries, even smoked a
> pipe with a Navaho Indian. He wasn't afraid,
> he just didn't want to die a nobody.

GWENNY

He died Jack?

SID

He died young... all his life he knew he could have been something, but something happened when he was young that stopped the real man from ever showing himself.

GWENNY

What happened Jack?

SID

He saw his pappy die, Joycey.

GWENNY

He died?

SID

> And nobody knew. Nobody on the whole
> earth knew, not even his brothers and sisters,
> it was a secret. A secret between him and his
> ma.

GWENNY

> His ma?

138   INT. MOTEL ROOM. NIGHT   138

*A typical Mid-West roadside motel. A TV plays in the corner in black
and white - a comedy show with canned laughter. Bottles of bourbon
and cigarettes litter the place. We hear a sudden gunshot.*

SID (V.O.)

> He took his life in a motel bathroom. He
> drew himself a bath, lay down in his clothes,
> brought a Colt 45 up to his temple.

*In the bathroom we see **CLEM** with a single bullet in his head lying
dead in the bath. We hear the sound of a ticking watch and see his
distinctive seventies wristwatch.*

139   EXT. FOREST. WALES. DUSK   139

SID and GWENNY lie reclined in the convertible.

SID

> He knew in his bones he wasn't long for this
> world. Some men know from ever since they
> were little that they've got doom written on
> the inside of their hands.

GWENNY

> You're not doomed are you Jack? *(pause)*
> Jack?

SID

> He left a note on the side of the bath saying
> he was sorry. With it was a letter home and a
> photo of his three kids.

GWENNY

> That's sad Jack.

SID

> I know.

GWENNY

> I'm afraid Jack... *(Pause)*... hold me.

SID holds GWENNY, fade in music which plays over and is the dominant sound of the following scene.

140   <u>**INT. PANTYDDRAENEN PUB. NIGHT**</u>   **140**
BOYO sits at the bar with a pint and a double whisky in front of him. He is pissed out of his mind. In the background, THE HEAD and his cronies are dressed as schoolgirls except for their silver hats. The local Banwen rugby team are dressed identically except they are wearing bowler hats. They sit on opposite tables, taunting each other in a beery hell.

BANWEN BOYS

> *(Singing)* Who the twats in the steel hats...
> Michigan... Michigan.

MICHIGAN WORKERS

> Who the twats in the bowler hats, Banwen
> RFC.

BOYO exits wobbily.

141 <u>INT. PANTYDDRAENEN PUB TOILET. NIGHT</u>   141

BOYO leans against the urinal wall lit only by moonlight, he starts to bang his head slowly and lightly against the wall.

142   <u>EXT. FOREST. NIGHT</u>   142

SID and GWENNY dance closely together in the moonlight and the ghostly shadows of the cars. It is a beautifully romantic picture. The music comes to an end. SID and GWENNY stand in silence.

> **GWENNY**
>> Do you love me?

> **SID**
>> I love you Joycey.

> **GWENNY**
>> Kiss me Jack.

They look at each other for a moment before slowly beginning to kiss, tenderly, then passionately. They undress and make love, erotically on the forest floor in moonlight. The mood is interrupted by BOYO screaming.

143 <u>INT. PANTYDDRAENEN PUB. TOILET. NIGHT</u> 143

BOYO dismantles the toilet and fittings in a drunken frenzy. A window smashes and BOYO rips out the water pipe from the urinal sending water cascading all over the place. Some of the site workers and rugby players rush in to see the mayhem but do nothing about it, they just watch in silence. WALLY jostles through the crowd and shouts:

> **WALLY**
>> What the fuck to you think you're doing? BOYO?

BOYO who is soaking, drunk and filthy stops and collapses in a heap crying.

> **WALLY**
>> Get out.

BOYO doesn't move.

> **WALLY**
>> I said get out...

*BOYO still doesn't move, so **WALLY** takes things into his own hands and grabs **BOYO**, dragging him out. **BOYO**, doesn't resist. Cheers from the workers.*

144   <u>EXT. PANTYDDRAENEN PUB. NIGHT</u>   **144**
*BOYO is thrown roughly into the street by **WALLY**.*

> **WALLY**
>> And stay out... you're banned.

> **BOYO**
>> Wally... I'm sorry. WALLY MUN!

*The pub door slams. **BOYO** leans his head against the door. In the pop wagon nearby sits **ROGER**, drinking Dandelion and Burdock through a straw and listening to Patsy Cline's "Crazy" on the radio. He winds down the window.*

> **ROGER**
>> Lift?

145   <u>INT. LOUNGE. NIGHT</u>   **145**
*The TV set is on snow. **BOYO** opens his eyes on the lounge floor, surrounded by cans. He is disorientated but gets his bearings. He looks terrible. He gets up and goes upstairs.*

146   <u>INT. MAM'S BEDROOM. NIGHT</u>   **146**

SID and GWENNY are sprawled out on the bed semi-clothed. The room is a mess. BOYO looks in from the door; it is not a sight which makes him happy. He closes the door. SID opens his eyes.

147   INT. BOYO'S ROOM. NIGHT   147
BOYO lies down on his bed. He weeps silently and painfully.

148   INT. MAM'S ROOM. NIGHT   148
SID lies awake. He too is upset. We hear the sound of fire.

149   EXT. BACKYARD. NIGHT   149
The fire blazes. MAM turns her head, her face is blackened as before.

> SID (O.O.V. - his voice is a child's)
> What you burning Mam?

We reveal SID as the speaker. He looks vulnerable and afraid.

150   INT. MAM'S BEDROOM. NIGHT   150
Tears stream down SID's face as he weeps openly. GWENNY rouses and puts her arms around him.

> GWENNY
> Don't cry Jack. I don't like it when you cry. Nobody cries in Dodge City.

> SID
> It's not Dodge City and it never was.

> GWENNY
> Don't say that Jack... we're happy here. We're safe. Nobody can hurt us. We're the heart of America baby and we're free... we can live on wild flowers and sunshine, we'll be happy together Jack, you love me and I love you.

SID

No Gwenny.

GWENNY

We'll make a love baby Jack, one that can
sing and dance and fly in the air. *(pause)* Jack?
Say we will?

SID

The game's over Gwenny.

He hugs **GWENNY** *and weeps bitterly in the early dawn light.*

151 <u>**INT. BOYO'S ROOM. MORNING**</u>   **151**

BOYO opens his eyes. He gets up and walks into the landing. The toilet flushes and GWENNY appears in the door frame, half-dressed. Her hair is messy and her eye make-up has run down her cheek.

>BOYO
>>Gwenny?

GWENNY looks at him blankly.

>GWENNY
>>Don't call me that.

>BOYO
>>It's me.

>GWENNY
>>I don't know you.

She goes into MAM's bedroom and sits hugging her knees. BOYO enters, GWENNY looks at him suspiciously.

>GWENNY
>>Go away.

152 <u>**INT. LOUNGE. HOUSE. MORNING**</u>   **152**

SID sits at the lounge table smoking. He looks pale and wasted. Lou Reed's "Coney Island Baby" plays softly on the record player. BOYO enters and looks at him. There is a long silence. BOYO sits opposite SID at the table.

>BOYO
>>Tell me.

>SID
>>What is there to tell?

BOYO

Don't fuck with me Sid.

SID

She said she killed him.

BOYO

So where is he?

SID

That's what she said.

BOYO

*(Grabbing **SID**)* WHERE THE FUCK IS HE?

Pause

SID

Take your hands off me man. I'm your brother. *(**BOYO** releases him)* Was a time when I thought he'd meet us in the airport, me and Gwenny. Waiting for us. I'd see him walk towards us. Funny that, don't you think? *(Pause)* I love you man, you're my brother.

BOYO *looks at him, pained, confused and hurt. He exits to the backyard, we hear the Reliant start up and scream away. **GWENNY** enters, smiles at **SID** who can only look away.*

GWENNY

I've got morning sickness Jack. *(Pause)* Happens when you're pregnant.

SID

You're not pregnant Gwenny.

GWENNY

> Please don't call me Gwenny, Jack, you know
> I don't like it. *(Pause)* Give me a hug Jack,
> you're supposed to kiss me and tell me I'm
> the best woman in the world. Tell me you're
> happy, please tell me you're happy. *(Pause)*
> Do you want a drink? *(Pause)* Do you want
> to go to bed and play then? *(Pause)* Why
> don't you look at me?

SID

> Because you're my sister Gwenny.

GWENNY

> Stop it, I don't like this game, just say you
> love me Jack.

SID

> I'm not Jack Gwenny, I never was
> Jack either.

GWENNY

> But I'm going to have your baby, a love
> baby, what's happened to you Jack?

SID

> It's over Gwenny.

GWENNY

> No. No... Why don't you love me anymore?

SID holds her in his arms.

153   INT. HOSPITAL LOUNGE. DAY   **153**

MAM is sitting in a Welsh costume, complete with hat and daffodil, *clapping and singing along to an electric organ led rendition of "Myfanwy" by an over-enthusiastic staff nurse. Sitting around are five or six other patients all similarly dressed in Welsh costumes. Some of them are very ill and schizophrenic. **BOYO** enters the circle and walks straight up to **MAM**. The music stops suddenly.*

NURSE
Can I help you? *(sternly)*

BOYO *ignores this and looks straight at **MAM**.*

MAM
What you looking at me like that for? It's St.David's Day... *(she looks around)*... got to show willing here. Do you like my daffodil? It's plastic, they didn't have any real ones, but the plastic ones stay yellow forever.

BOYO *doesn't respond.*

BOYO
Where is he Mam?

154   INT. MAM'S ROOM. HOSPITAL. DAY   154
*Organ music re-starts in the background. **MAM** stands by a window. **BOYO** approaches her. **MAM** plays with her daffodil, in silence.*

BOYO
Mam?

MAM
I did it to keep us together under one roof. He didn't want to belong anymore. She had black hair see, over her shoulders. Awful. She was wearing tights. She left without them.

Made her run I did. Never moved so fast in all her life. Your father said he was sorry. I nearly believed him, but I knew she wasn't the first. She was the only one I caught that's all. *(Pause)* I remember lying in bed one night long after wondering whether I was going to forgive him or not. After all, he was a good looking man. I turned to him and smiled. He kissed me. He said everything was going to be alright, he said he'd never do it again. I knew in my bones he'd never do it again. *(Pause)* Clem told me to undress. I told him I wasn't in the mood. I pretended to sleep. I waited till I could hear him snoring. I looked at him. Never seen him looking so peaceful. *(Pause)* I hit him with the coal hammer. Twice. I'd got it waiting and ready by the side of the bed. I finished him off with a pillow. Must have kept it over him for ten minutes. He didn't feel a thing. And nobody knew, the whole world was asleep. *(Pause)* "What you burning Mam" said Sid.

MAM (cont.)

He saw the blood on the clothes and the fire. I told him there and then. Keeps a good secret your brother.

BOYO

Where is he Mam?

155 **EXT. MOUNTAIN. DAY** 155

The digger digs away at the mountain topsoil, only yards from the two wooden crosses etched with "Brando" and "Billy".

156   <u>EXT. HOSPITAL MAIN ENTRANCE. DAY</u>   156

BOYO runs out of the door and sprints across the car-park towards the Reliant. He gets in and screams away as fast as the Reliant can take him.

157   <u>EXT. OPEN CAST. DAY</u>   157

The digging machinery smashes into the topsoil at the top of the mountain. It is only a few feet away from the two wooden crosses with "Brando" and "Billy" on them. The sound is brutal and deafening as the trees of the wood get uprooted. The wrenching of the roots should feel like an earth screaming.

158   <u>EXT. STREET. DAY</u>   158

BOYO screams around a corner and past the Pant pub and eventually pulls up near the lane leading to the house at the foot of the mountain. He starts to run up the mountain, and as we do so, we intercut between BOYO's feet, knees, legs, pumping face showing his exertion and the cruelly digging digger getting nearer to the crosses. Eventually we see the digger rise in the air and come crashing down to earth on the crosses. BOYO shouts:

> **BOYO**
>> NO!!!

But to no avail, the digger digs up soil leaving a crater behind it. We follow the digger in its arc where it tips its load on the open cast site in the back of one of the enormous euclid lorries. We look for remains of a body. But there is nothing.

159   <u>EXT. MOUNTAIN. DAY</u>   159

BOYO is scrabbling on his hands and knees in the crater looking for his father's remains. He suddenly comes across a bone but it is only the small carcass of a budgie. He looks at it in despair. There is no father's body. The crane driver blows his horn in frustration, motioning for BOYO to get out of the way. BOYO does so and from the POV of the crane driver, we watch BOYO move away as the digger crashes into the earth and scoops up the topsoil and swings around.

160   EXT. BACKYARD. HOUSE. DAY   160

BOYO sits with his head on the wheel of the Reliant as the drone of the open cast can be heard nearby. He gets out of the car. He is filthy, covered in soil adding to the lost dishevelled look of previous scenes. He is at the end of his tether.

161   INT. LANDING. HOUSE. DAY   161

BOYO comes up the stairs and stands at the top of the landing. He approaches MAM's room and slowly pushes open the door. GWENNY sits alone crying. She is unaware of BOYO being there.

> **GWENNY**
>> He's left me on my own.

> **BOYO**
>> Gwenny?

> **GWENNY**
>> *(Pause)* Jack was a fraud.

GWENNY looks up to see BOYO standing there.

> **BOYO**
>> Where is he, Gwenny?

> **GWENNY**
>> He doesn't love me anymore.

> **BOYO**
>> WHERE IS HE GWENNY?

> **GWENNY**
>> He wants to kill the baby, but I'm not going
>> to let him.

BOYO
> The what?

GWENNY
> A love baby. *(Pause)* Can you tell why I can't
> move my arms mister?

BOYO
> You stay there, I won't be long, I'm going to
> find him okay?

BOYO exits.

GWENNY
> The truth of it was, he said he was a poet. *(Pause)*

162   <u>**EXT. STREET. DAY**</u>   162
*BOYO runs down the deserted street approaching the Pantyddraenen
Pub, he enters hurriedly.*

163   <u>**INT. PANT PUB. DAY**</u>   163
*A western plays on the T.V. in the empty pub. **WALLY** looks round to
see **BOYO** enter breathlessly.*

BOYO
> Where's Sid.

WALLY
> You're banned... get out.

BOYO
> Wally... you've got to help me
> I...

WALLY
> Help you? Have you seen the mess you've

made of my bog? Get out. I never want to see you or any of your bastard family in here ever again. Go on... get.

BOYO stares at him, then turns and exits.

164   INT. RUINED FARMHOUSE. DAY   164
SID dismantles the pyramid of rocks. He works methodically as though in a trance.

165   EXT. PANT PUB. DAY   165
BOYO sits at the entrance to the pub with his head in his hands. Slowly we hear the sound of a trundling van, and very soon we hear the unmistakable rattling bottle sound of ROGER the POP's van. He pulls up at the Pant and looks at BOYO. BOYO raises his head.

166   INT. RUINED FARMHOUSE. DAY   166
Rocks scatter all over the floor as SID stops digging and stares down at a pit with plastic sheeting. He weeps openly. He pulls out a plastic bag. From inside he pulls out a watch - the watch on CLEM's arm when we saw him dead in the bath. He wipes the face of the watch and puts it on.

167   INT. POP LORRY. ROAD. DAY   167
BOYO sits in silence in the passenger seat of the lorry. ROGER drives occasionally looking at him.

> **ROGER**
> Dog bitten you too is it? *(BOYO doesn't respond)* Mother in hospital then? *(BOYO doesn't respond)* They tell me she's in for keeps. *(BOYO doesn't respond)* Suppose we'd better call it quits then. *(BOYO looks at him, puzzled)* The pop. *(BOYO nods)*

ROGER pulls up near a dirt track leading to the mountain.

>   **ROGER**
>   This is it.

BOYO looks towards the track.

>   **ROGER**
>   Always wondered what he was doing up
>   there, thinking of buying it is he?

BOYO gets out.

>   **ROGER**
>   About quarter of a mile up the
>   track, can't miss it.

BOYO looks at him then starts to walk. ROGER drives away. BOYO starts to run.

168   **INT. RUINED FARMHOUSE. DAY**   168
SID drags a chair into the middle of the building and places it under a beam. He stares once more at the covered pit and then takes a petrol can and frantically starts dousing the pit and the furniture in paraffin.

169   **EXT. TRACK. DAY**   169
We stay right on BOYO's face as he runs.

170   **INT. FARMHOUSE. DAY**   170
SID takes a cigarette and lights it with the Zippo. The tobacco crackles as SID inhales. He looks around him at the scattered rocks and furniture.

| 171 | <u>EXT. FARMHOUSE. DAY</u> | 171 |

BOYO approaches from a distance, running as fast as he can.

> **BOYO**
> SID... SID...

| 172 | <u>INT. FARMHOUSE. DAY</u> | 172 |

SID hears BOYO's shouts but is impassive. He flicks the cigarette into the plastic sheeting in the pit and it explodes back into his face. The fire spreads quickly along the floor and furniture as SID steps onto the chair beneath the beam.

| 173 | <u>EXT. FARMHOUSE. DAY</u> | 173 |

BOYO sees the smoke and flames as he approaches. He reaches the door to find SID hanging by a rope from the beam as the whole farmhouse burns.

> **BOYO**
> No, no...

BOYO makes his way through the burning building towards his brother's body.

BOYO

NO! NO! NO...!

174   EXT. FARMHOUSE RUIN. DAY   174

BOYO carries SID out of the fire. He embraces his dead brother and howls as the farmhouse is engulfed in flames.

*We slowly **FADE TO BLACK**.*

175   EXT. ROAD. WALES. DUSK   175

BOYO drives his Reliant down a long, straight road.

GWENNY (V.O.)

Picture the scene. Jack sat on his Harley watching the sun rise. He looked at the inside of his hand. He saw doom there as he knew one day he always would. He was a hero. He knew he was a hero at last. Sid Lewis... March 2nd.

*Inside the car, **BOYO**'s face is impassive. On the dashboard is the charred remains of **CLEM**'s watch. He drives into the distance.*

EPILOGUE

176   EXT. HOUSE. DAY   176

The house is only fifty yards away from the approaching open-cast. It is boarded up and deserted. The backyard remains a mess.

BOYO (V.O.)

Dear Gwenny,
Hope you are well... weather is good here, and am enjoying the job.

177   INT. HOUSE. DAY   177

The downstairs house seems decayed, deserted and desolate. Coal dust blows through the open door, covering the ramshackle furniture in a fine black sheen.

BOYO (V.O. cont.)
> They say they'll make a mechanic out of me yet. Will send money as soon as I can. Have found lodgings outside Poole. Love, Boyo.

178   **INT. MAM'S BEDROOM. HOUSE DAY**   178

GWENNY lies in MAM's bed reading BOYO's postcard. She puts in in the empty album. MAM is rummaging for clothes in a wardrobe.

MAM
> Mechanic. Huh... try this.

MAM holds out a dress. GWENNY gets out of bed, wearing maternity clothes.

GWENNY
> I always knew he'd land on his feet.

MAM
> He's a good boy.

GWENNY
> Too small.

MAM continues to rummage. GWENNY stands by the window.

GWENNY
> We're thinking of calling the baby Dodge, Mam.

MAM
> That's nice.

GWENNY
> It was Sid's idea.

MAM
> Silly bugger... when's he going to come and
> see me then?

GWENNY
> He'll come when he's ready, but it's a bit
> difficult at the moment.

MAM
> How's that?

GWENNY
> Well... he's in America isn't he.

*GWENNY looks honesty at **MAM**. **MAM** moves towards her and
touches her face. They hug.*

179   EXT. ROAD. AMERICAN MID-WEST. DAWN   179
*Two roads converge into one which leads on to the horizon and
mountains in the distance. The beautiful dawn sky is bluish red with a
few stars. Cicadas mingle with the wind and desert sound. This is
broken by the sound of an appoaching motorbike and then a station
wagon.*

180   EXT. ROAD. AMERICAN MID-WEST. DAWN   180
*SID dressed in black leathers and no helmet is riding down the road
smiling.*

181   EXT. ROAD. AMERICAN MID-WEST. DAWN   181
CLEM, wearing sunglasses drives his station wagon down a road,

nearing the crossroads he waves as he sees **SID** *arriving on the other road.*

182   <u>EXT. ROAD. AMERICAN MID-WEST. DAWN</u>   182

From high up we see the meeting of father and son at the crossroads. Their engines die. The only sound is light wind.

Roll Credits.
FADE TO BLACK.
THE END

The Filmmakers

Director	:	*Marc Evans*
Screenplay	:	*Edward Thomas*
Producer	:	*Sheryl Crown*
Director of Photography	:	*Pierre Aim*
Co-Producer	:	*David Green*
Casting Director	:	*Joan McCann*
Costume Designer	:	*Amy Temime*
Editor	:	*Michiel Reichwein*
Original Music	:	*John Cale*
Production Designer	:	*Mark Tildesley*
Production Manager	:	*Gina Carter*
1st Assistant Director	:	*Dafydd Arwyn Jones*
Production Accountant	:	*Peta Inglesent*
Art Directors	:	*David Bryan*
		Edward Thomas
Locations	:	*Bryan Moses*
		Andrew Pavord
Sound Recordist	:	*Simon Fraser*
Camera Operator	:	*Georges Diane*
Make Up	:	*Pamela Haddock*
Chief Hairdresser	:	*Amanda Warburton*
Wardrobe Supervisor	:	*Linda Alderson*

Production Co-Ordinator:		*Sophie Fante*
Script Supervisor	:	*Bev Tatham*
2nd Assistant Director	:	*Jon Williams*
3rd Assistant Director	:	*Graham Anderton*
Focus Puller	:	*Muriel Coulin*
Clapper Loader	:	*Andrew Banwell*
Grip	:	*David Hopkins*
Boom Operator	:	*Ed Brooks*
Wardrobe Assistant	:	*Miles Johnson*
Post Production Supervisor:		*Alistair Hopkins*
Producer's Assistant	:	*Clare Alan*
Construction & Set Painters:		*Matthew Hywel Davies*
		Tristan Peatfield
		John Pinkerton
Standby Construction	:	*Rod Wilson*
Properties Buyer	:	*Fran Cooper*
Property Master	:	*Mike Malik*
Dressing Prop	:	*Nick Thomas*
Standby Prop	:	*Arwel Evans*
Special Effects Supervisor	:	*David Harris*
Senior Technicians	:	*Paul Knowles*
		Steve Lloyd
		Paul Whybrow
Technicians	:	*Judith Harris*
		Nick Smith
Rain Effects	:	*Mark Turner (MTFX)*
Stunt Co-Ordinator	:	*Tom Lucy*
Stunt Performers	:	*Helen Caldwell*
		Abbi Collins
		Ray-De-Haan
		Ian Jaye
Lighting Gaffer	:	*Mark Taylor*
Best Boys	:	*Ray Brown*
		Mark Hutchings
		Andrew Taylor
Electricians	:	*Chris Davies*

Stuart Hurst
Alyn Lewis
Danny Pryday
Steve Slocombe

Assistant Editor	:	*Mark Atkins*
Dubbing Mixer/Editor	:	*Adrian Rhodes*
Dialogue Editor	:	*Colin Ritchie*
Foley Editor	:	*Jacques Leriode*

Floor Runner	:	*Ashley Way*
Production Runner	:	*Jerry Lockett*
Stills Photographer	:	*Mark Tillie*
Specials Photographer	:	*Martyn James Brooks*
Unit Publicist	:	*Lysette Cohen*

Production Lawyers	:	*Jonathan Berger*
at Theodore Goddard		*Jonathan Blair*
Completion Guarantor	:	*Film Finances Inc.*

World Receipts Collected and Distributed by
National Film Trustee Company Ltd

For September Films

Post Production Co-Ordinators:		*Elaine Day*
		Fiona Alderson
Assistant Production Accountant:		*Peter Sarandon*

Production Trainees	:	*Zoe Spyropoulos*
		Annabel Marner
Camera Trainee	:	*Rachel Pillar*
Sound Trainee	:	*Llion Gerallt*
Special Effects Trainee	:	*Neil Todd*
Location Vehicles	:	*Andy Dixon Facilities*
Driver	:	*Chris Malone*

Motorbike Technician	:	Mike Peters
Unit Driver	:	Dave Hawkins
Caterers	:	Champion Catering

Canadian Crew

Production Manager	:	Linda Chapman
Art Director	:	Ken Rempel
Production Co-Ordinator:		Tracy Long
Location Manager	:	Richard Richter
1st Assistant Director	:	Andy Price
Production Assistants	:	Pamela Wintringham
		Brooke McGill
Focus Puller	:	Dean Frissc
Clapper Loader	:	Damon Moreau
2nd Camera Focus Puller:		Reagan Enderl
Script Supervisor	:	Amanda Alexander
Set Decorator	:	Robin Swiderski
Set Dresser	:	Tom Edwards
Construction Co-Ordinator:		Warren Simmons
Head Painter	:	Rick Jansen
Key Grip	:	John Adshead
Dolly/Company Grip	:	Tim Milligan
Gaffer	:	Tracey (TC) Chapman
Genny/Lamp Operator	:	Robin Loewen
Lamp Operator	:	Jim Manduca
Make Up/Hair	:	Bryon Callaghan
Wrangler Co-Ordinator	:	John Scott
SPFX Co-Ordinator	:	Lee Routly
Transportation Co-Ordinator:		Arnold Holmes
Drivers	:	Karen Holmes
		Danny Klepper
Catering	:	Sandstone Catering
Craft Service	:	Averline Adshead

Shot on Location in South Wales and Canada.

Costumes Supplied By	*Angels & Bermans*
Titles/Opticals	*G.S.E.Dolby*
Moviecam Camera & Lens From	*Media Film Services*
Lighting From	*AFM*
Shot On	*Kodak*
Processed by	*Rank FilmLaboratories*
Post Production Facilities	
& Re-Recording By	*De Lane Lea*

Based upon the original stage play "House of America" by Edward Thomas.

The Producers would like to thank:
Stephen Cleary, Simon Perry, Menna Richards, Euryn Ogwen Williams, Ryclef Rienstra, Welsh Development Agency, Jeroen Arnolds, Graham Easton, Llionos Wyn Jones, Ruth Kenley-Letts, Stavros Stavrides.

With special thanks to:
Celtic Energy (Philip Jarman, Anthony Evans, Kevin Dow, Roger Evans, Tom Addey, Iona Jenkins), Walters Mining (Huw Richards, Glyn Hughes), Derlwyn Open Cast Mine.

Supported by the National Lottery through the Arts Council of Wales.

Looking Forward, Looking Back
Some notes on a film

Marc Evans

I
Looking Forward

January 1989

Chapter Arts Centre, Cardiff.

Manage to get tickets for *House of America's* last performance at Chapter. Word of mouth has brought a whole bunch of us there. There's a real sense of occasion. At half-time we come out stunned – I am overwhelmed. Not only is the play terrific, but it seems to be talking to **me**. Ed Thomas has entered my world. At full-time I decide to enter his. I am completely enthusiastic and full of admiration, probably embarassing. Ed says something about Welsh mythology. I haven't a clue what he's talking about. An argument starts – well, almost – about what I can't remember. It proves to be our last and the beginning of a friendship.

January 1989

The New Ely, Cardiff.

I track down Ed who's living in an attic in Partridge Road. He's forgotten about the almost argument and agrees to meet for a lunchtime drink. He'll bring me some scripts of *House of America*. My immediate plan is not to try and make the play into a film but to take the scripts around some production companies in London (Red Rooster, Working Title) to try and get some interest in a new Ed Thomas screenplay. He's never done one

259

before but seems quite keen.

The dark beer flows, and so does the conversation. Every subject is covered, although I can't remember details. I exit drunk – with scripts – into a righted world.

- - - - - - - - - - - - - -

9 March 1995

I have become the weak link in the chain. Ed is already proven – the script is written and speaks for itself. Sheryl, though a first-time producer, has the backing of a reputable production company September Films and British Screen. But what about the director?

I get organised. First I make up a show reel and then I sit down to write my "Director's Notes" – which are to be sent out with the script to prospective backers. Stephen Cleary of British Screen says that these are very important in giving the reader an impression of what kind of film it is that I'm going to make. They should suggest its visual possibilities – its colour perhaps, or its flavour – an appetiser for the feast ahead. My mind goes blank.

I ask Stephen for an example and he quotes the director's notes to *The Cement Garden* in which Andrew Berkin proposed that the main character's bikini should become progressively more lurid during the film. A visual tease. It's a very good example, but my mind is still blank.

The most common misunderstanding of *House* as a script is that it is seen as a dreary piece of social realism ("God it must be so depressing living in Wales...") but I don't want to spend too much time telling people what the film is **not** going to be like. But nothing as tantalising as a chameleon bikini has come to mind, so I try very hard to imagine the finished film and settle down to watch it in the cinema of my head. I am swept away by its vitality and mood and I am impressed by its use of music and the poetry of the story-telling.

The problem with trying to describe the film of your imagination is that whatever you write will sound like pretentious bullshit. It can only be the work of a genius because, inevitably, you are describing the perfect film!

Pretentious bullshit or not, this is what I wrote:

HOUSE OF AMERICA - Director's Notes

The screenplay to House of America *is dripping with Welsh rain but should be read through rose-tinted sunglasses, for the film is a perverse celebration. Rather than issuing a very British warning against dreaming too much, it invites us into a world in which dreams can take flight. Its characters dream impossibly of America and the film impudently attaches itself to that great tradition of American cinema (films like* On the Waterfront, Hud *and* Badlands*) in which the losers become heroes. Heading for the open road with the roof down and the radio blaring,* House of America *is desperate to escape the tyranny of its post-industrial landscape. It ignores the rain and is hell-bent on heroism.*

Sometimes the film is forced to face the hang-over greyness of its surroundings but, like Sid, it is forever finding ways to shirk this responsibility, to bunk off and get high, to celebrate and be damned. For what other choice is there when reality lets you down? As Mam herself might say, "You have to make do, don't you?"

With Sid in the driving seat there is no room for doubters. The radio is at full volume and the landscape rushes past in such a blur that this might as well be America. Welcome to the "Sid Lewis Experience" where anything seems possible. Believe in the dream and it becomes bigger than the dreamer, more resilient than reality.

And when finally it seems beaten by the fact, it re-invents itself again, providing the film with its last image, a kind of America beyond the grave!

At the beginning of the film there is a clear and obvious clash of images, with Clem's idyllic ranch life contrasting starkly with the family's troglodyte existence in the shadow of the open-cast mine. But this distinction soon falls away and as the film progresses the lines get blurred. Instead of the poetic juxtaposition of Wales and America, there is a strange merging of these two worlds.

Clem's story is obviously idealised and told uncompromisingly in American clichés. Wide vistas of the long, straight road, loving close-ups of the well-thumbed Zippo and the crumpled pack of Marlboros. But when Clem dies, self-destructing in a bad short story, the film is left in a no-man's land, stuck somewhere between Wales and America. It is no longer the dream that distracts from real life but real life that distracts from the dream, and threatens to destroy it.

Sometimes we enjoy a cliché for its own sake, and this is especially true in the earlier scenes. Sid astride his Harley Davidson popping pills beneath the Michigan Mining sign is self-consciously iconic. Sid lives out his fantasy and the camera aids and abets him. There is humour in this self-conscious role-playing and the camera plays games with labels. The Head's silver helmet reads "Head", the tail-gate to Clem's pick-up reads "Dodge" and his lunch-box reads "Clem" (nestling convincingly between those marked "Hank" and "Bud" at the fictitious car factory). The sunstrip across the windscreen of Cat's new orange Capri boasts two names - "Cat" and "Sharon". Labels, constantly reinforcing the idea that our fate is decided, our luck pre-determined. Thus Sid's re-invention (and finally Gwenny's) takes on great poignancy. A beautiful but hopeless fight against circumstance. A bid to be different. As Sid says to Boyo, "If I had to answer a straight question, I wish I'd been born someone else, somewhere else", and he almost pulls it off!

As the seriousness of Sid's intentions finally dawns on us, the imagery becomes less playful, less intrusive, allowing the incipient tragedy to unfold. In the later scenes when Sid and Gwenny are Jack and Joyce stealing cars and booze around the town, they are no longer kids dressing up, no longer play-acting. The roads across the valley tops are long and straight, crossing a kind of symbolic hinterland. Small design details suggest the infiltration of the dream into reality. A white diagonal criss-cross at the level crossing, road-signs to nowhere, brown paper bags from the "drug store", tumbleweed up the high street. Sounds suggest an unseen mythical landscape, beyond the dark woods where Jack and Joyce make love. The howl of a lone coyote, the distant whistle of the Memphis train. The effect is sadly ironic, bathetic almost, with each incongruity suggesting Sid's ultimate failure, for the transformation can never be complete.

And the music keeps on playing, giving House of America *a great energy and mirroring its cultural confusion. Elvis, for example, evokes a mythical, unattainable America whereas the Velvet Underground (having a genuine Welsh member in John Cale) offers up some realisable hope. If only Sid could play guitar, if only Boyo hadn't broken his shoulder, they too could be contenders, if only... As in life, the "soundtrack" is everywhere, giving our characters hope and inspiration, helping them to define themselves and conjuring up their imaginary America. Tom Jones singing "Detroit City" says it all. The landscape is American but the passion is most definitely Welsh.*

"It's not Dodge City, and it never was," says Sid, and he speaks from bitter experience. Ultimately even he admits that you cannot escape from the facts (you can ignore the rain but you'll still get wet!). This is not America but Banwen, a two-bit by-pass town in the Valleys. South Wales will always show through in the end, wet and weary, to dampen the dream. The joke is not lost on us as Welsh film-makers. We are getting tired of setting up our cameras in the

rain and seeing, well… just rain. House of America *is desperate to take us somewhere good, to show the world that we have some heroes of our own. It is more about hope than despair, funny and sad at the same time, claiming that an impossible dream is still better than "if only…"*

28 August 1995
Dutch Film Committee, Amsterdam.
We have come to appeal directly to a committee of Dutchmen to put money into our film. It's all starting to feel a bit absurd. If nobody in Wales wants to make *House of America*, then why should anybody in Holland ? The Dutch have already tried to shake us off but there are political pressures in our favour. British Screen, our main (i.e. only) backer helped them to make Marleen Gorris' film *Antonia's Line* last year and now it's payback time. Simon Perry at British Screen has recommended *House* for reciprocal funding in the strongest possible terms and Hans de Weers - the reciprocal Producer - supports him. But there are hostile elements within the Dutch Film Board. They feel manoeuvred and would, given the choice, rather get involved with something a bit more potentially lucrative. We are caught in a battle of wills. We meet Hans at the headquarters of Bergen films - a beautifully converted church in the middle of Amsterdam which serves as a theatre and office space. He drives us to our meeting at the Dutch Film Committee offices. Sheryl, the producer, reminds me once more not to speak too quickly and Hans tells me to sell myself – we are on a mission to enthuse. There are canals everywhere….

After a short wait we are greeted rather coolly by Reikliff – who Hans has identified as our enemy – and ushered into a narrow room where the committee are seated on either side of a long table. Piles of scripts are laid neatly along the centre and a large monitor sits at the far end as though the whole meeting is to be chaired, via satellite, by a Mekon. We huddle together at the opposite end – miles away. I tell myself to speak loudly. Reikliff is flicking through my Director's notes and I can see that certain lines have been highlighted in fluorescent yellow. Oh my God! I suddenly feel vulnerable. Reikliff speaks. "How can you possibly call this film celebratory ?" His English is perfect, he has even mastered the superior tone. I wish we had the Mekon. I answer slowly, and loudly, giving the overall impression of an idiot. A bearded man is smiling and nodding at me. I can't work out whether this denotes pity or encouragement. I decide that he is friendly and direct my answer at him. Things get better, although I am completely at a loss to guess the overall reaction. Sheryl is also questioned which gives me my first chance to look around properly. I am reminded of Frans Hals' portrait of the *Regents of Haarlem*. What are they thinking? Then it's my turn for questions again. Then it's over. Hans says we did O.K. but I have my doubts.

Back on the plane, we speculate like mad. I make a bet with Sheryl. I think we'll get the money, she thinks we won't, but really – I suspect – it's the other way round.

Wednesday 29th November 1995

Hans de Weers, our Dutch co-producer, is insisting that we use a Dutch cameraman. At first I am enthusiastic – Robbie Muller is Dutch. But Hans thinks that Robbie is too big for our film and suggests another (Marc Ferperlaan). I watch his tapes and I am disappointed. I feel cheated – there seems to be a choice of only one.

I know that Sheryl is at a conference. I send her a long and pedantic fax which states my case. I am feeling defensive, so most of the fax reads like a manifesto.

Photography is what distinguishes a film, providing it with its key or colour but it's not an easy thing to talk about. It is strangely invisible and most people's attitude towards it, even within the industry, falls into the "I don't know much about art but I know what I like" category. Directors who are too interested in photography give out the wrong signals. In television any enthusiasm in this area is regarded as a pretentious failing, and every features producer's dread is to find their pup director held in thrall by some 'slow' (and usually foreign) cinematographer!

It's not that I intend the film to be "heavily photographed" (is this English?) like an expensive commerical, but it shouldn't be "domestic British miserabilist" either... House *deals with a heightened reality and the photography should represent this. It must have <u>mood</u> - i.e. guts, inventiveness and a sense of humour.*

So how can photography have guts, inventiveness and a sense of humour? Well, in the operating and the framing for a start. Two recent (but very different) films prove this – La Haine *(Mathieu Kassovitz) and* Chungking Express *(Wong Kar Wai). The camera-work in both films oozes "personality". The inward camera movement of* La Haine, *for example, takes us towards the characters rather than skirting around them. The film has a penetrating eye, choosing to show us specific aspects of the action (following the gun in Vinz's pocket through one scene, for example) and surprising us with moments of grace in a bleak world (Hubert's boxing with the punch-bag becoming slow-motion as we watch). The overall effect is seamless – clean – and yet on analysis it is highly stylised. Some of the camera set-ups are very ambitious and must have been technically difficult to achieve. (Examples - contra-zoom on the balcony or Vinz at the mirror ducking out and back into the track.) Exactly the kind of shots that get dismissed as "wanky" on the day!*

I know that you're not supposed to be too admiring of other people's films. They become ghosts in your house. But La Haine *shows perfectly how a film can be photographically inventive while not losing sight of the story, and can be both personal and distinctive as a result.* House *is a strong emotional drama but it needs a photographic style that can accommodate moments of transcendental grace as well as dark unreality. Photography can achieve this at no expense to the vitality and poignancy of the human drama. There doesn't have to be a battle between style and content.*

(How light can influence a scene – a random example... Scene 21 in the pub. When the kids first see the Michigan miners in their silver hats. This could be a very "ordinary" scene. Or it might be suffused with bright sunlight after the rain, creating one of those perfect pub mornings, before the dole money is spent with the alcohol just starting to take hold. There's a great song on the jukebox – Gwenny's choice. The miners enter, in slow-motion perhaps, their silver hats blindingly bright in the winter sun, epitomising for a moment their first impression on the kids. Sid lights a fag and the moment is gone. But the image remains in the head, incandescent, like an indelible memory....Then the dialogue kicks in, taking the piss as usual.)

House of America *is full of poetic possibilites. I would love a cameraperson to do more than simply fulfil a brief by bringing a "personality" or cultural perspective to the project. It is for this reason that the idea of Robbie Muller seemed so appealing. A European (Dutch!) cameraman who had helped define the "American Independent" film. I suppose what I'm saying is that if we are going for a Dutch d.o.p., then let's go for the best there is, or the most interesting for the film. Let's not settle for the one who happens to be available. Otherwise, what's the point? There are plenty of young, up-and-coming camerapeople in this country who would bring energy and commitment to the job, not to mention some of the older, more experienced ones... or what about the bloke who shot* La Haine*?*

December 1995

The last stages of Development Hell are probably the worst. You're waiting for that elusive "end money" and you feel abandoned in a new kind of limbo. You've been assuring everyone for months that the film will be made ("We only need

£250,000!" you say, smiling) but your enthusiasm is wearing thin. What seems like a small amount of money to you seems like a fortune to anyone normal. Yet you can't understand why your Producer doesn't just hurry up and FIND THE MONEY. Your friends look at you with a combination of incredulity and pity – "Oh you're still trying to get *that* made are you?" – like you're the nutty next-door-neighbour who spends every weekend trying to build a space rocket out of dustbins. You feel foolish. You've cancelled all appointments and turned down work, which means that you're completely skint. And to make matters worse, you're Welsh.

The National Lottery administered by the Arts Council of Wales is our last chance of salvation, before reverting to "Plan B"*. The Lottery Committee hold the key that can release us from our black hole of despair. THEY POSSESS END MONEY. We have applied to them for our final funding way back in September and we are waiting for news.

It seems like a very hopeful scenario. Welsh film = Welsh funding. Well, er, no... actually. Wales has so far been less than enthusiastic about *House of America*. HTV Wales have chipped in recently, but most of the money has come from elsewhere. England mostly and even Holland! There was a stage when Ed and I got a perverse pleasure out of this situation (well, at least nobody can accuse us of nepotism... and we've become truly international artists into the bargain, rejected in our own land but welcomed in the bistros of London and the cafés of Amsterdam!). Now we want to kiss and make up. But in matters of the heart, Wales can be unpredictable.
(*There is no Plan B)

8th December 1995
Sheryl takes my fax to heart and decides to search out "the bloke that shot *La Haine*". It turns out to be two blokes, and yes they are interested in working in Britain and yes they are theoretically

free. Sheryl sends them a script and asks me to follow this up with an introductory fax. I tell them why I like *La Haine* (the thesis is already written!) and try to introduce myself – which is more difficult. I feel like a lonely heart. This is what I write.

Well, I'm thirty-six years old and House of America *will be my first feature film. My work up until now has mostly been (drama, on film) for television. As you probably know we have great t.v. in this country but no film industry so it's tough getting started. It's already been five years since Ed Thomas (the writer) and I started talking about* House of America, *which seems like a long time, although everyone tells me that this is normal! I met Sheryl Crown while directing for the BBC and I suppose the project really started to happen when Sheryl took it with her to September Films and we got the backing of British Screen. Anyway this is all history.*

What I want to tell you is that this is a very personal film for me. Ed and I come from South Wales which has been almost invisible in terms of the cinema in recent years and we both feel passionate about putting "ourselves" on the screen. We both speak (and work) in Welsh and although House of America *is written in English, the language is very particular to our part of the world, as is the life and attitudes depicted. I can't help feeling that there is a new movement, a new kind of film-making starting to happen around Britain, allowing areas like Scotland and Ireland and the "forgotten regions" of England to express themselves in a new way. Although Wales is not considered by film-financiers or distributors to be a very easy place to sell (not sexy!) I want* House of America *to change all that. Needless to say we haven't got a big budget but the prospect of making the film is very exciting.*

I don't know how well you know Britain, but perhaps I should give you an idea of the landscape of the film. "The Valleys" are like the fingers of a hand, running North from the sea. Narrow and rich in coal they were highly industrialised in the Nineteenth Century and became very crowded. The Valleys towns flourished, becoming famous for their "community spirit" and spawning a million clichés about terraced streets and black-faced miners singing on their way home from the pit (maybe you have seen John Ford's How Green Was My Valley *of 1941?) The real landscape of scarred earth and coal tips was ugly but strangely photogenic, wet and black in my memory. The coal tips dominated until the Sixties when the Aberfan disaster and the gradual decline of the mines led to a lot of strange green landscaping taking over.*

Over the last ten years the mining industry has all but disappeared leaving a close community with nothing to do. There are some small private pits around, looking like klondikes from the Old West, and some large open-cast mines at the valley tops, but there is not much work for the locals. The Valleys are a strange place now, greener but somehow bleaker. But not totally depressing. Some of the towns have the atmosphere of a Western, sleepy but pregnant with possibilities! People make their own fun (television, drink, drugs) and there is a lot of black humour. On the right day, in the right pub, anything could happen!

This is what House of America *is trying to capture. A way of life in which the kids are forced to make up their own rules and left to indulge their private fantasies. Some people see it as a depressing script, but Ed and I feel that it is a celebration. There is a lot of poetry in the landscape - a kind of Welsh hinterland - and a lot of life in those mad forgotten towns.*

Wednesday 13th December

Meet Fizzy Oppé at Cyngor Ffilm Cymru to talk about another project. You can't walk into any institution down here without seeing at least three people that you know. Dave Berry is one of them – a true believer – asking me when *House* is getting started. I give him that "true believer" smile and just say "soon". He wishes me luck and an image of an exploding rocket, made entirely of dustbins, crashes into my mind. I go home and find out that riots have broken out in Brixton. Meanwhile in Cardiff everything is cold and quiet... and tomorrow is Lottery day.

Thursday 14th December

I go up to Trefforest in the morning to speak to the students about "Script to Screen". Optimistically the staff assure me that there will be a "lively discussion" afterwards. It is the end of term and below zero conditions so I don't feel too bad about the fact that only half of the class turns up. But the small group that does attend seem to be visibly hung-over and one of them keeps nodding off. Perhaps I should crack some jokes? This teaching lark is more difficult than it looks. If there's a silence you feel you have to fill it which only makes things worse. You know that you've failed when the teachers start asking you questions. They're only being kind, trying to hide the fact that you've succeeded in completely stupefying a normally vibrant and enquiring group of young adults. There must be a knack to it....

I wait for the train back to Cardiff, with Ponty looking cold and unloved in the distance. ("The old town looks the same as I step down off the train....") I like the train journey from the Valleys to Cardiff – it reminds me of school. Then I make my way to London. I don't know what to expect at Brixton and feel apprehensive as I walk up into the High Street. The "Seven-Eleven" has been burnt out and there are lots of policemen walking around in pairs. At the end of our road, the windows to the Frank Johnson sports shop have all been smashed and all the trainers extracted – someone's Christmas shopping. Does the atmosphere seem edgy? It's probably all in my mind.

At about 5.30 I find out that we've got the Lottery money. A magic moment, but nobody to tell as there's nobody in at home. I crack open a bottle at September Films where we are meeting some actors – a very good bunch of Welsh boys. Richard Harrington and Michael Sheen especially. I suppose this means that the film will be made. We won't have to lie anymore.

Sunday 17th December

We arrange for the "Men from *La Haine*" to come and meet us in London. There is an almost comical air of expectation as Sheryl and I wait for them in the empty September Films offices. We have no idea what they will look like. We haven't even seen photographs! They (Pierre – lighting cameraman – tall / Georges – operator – short) turn out to be of French Algerian extraction – but not very dark – French Algerian Jewish.... "We are all bastards" Pierre says, which I think is an excellent starting position for any relationship. We watch a tape of *L'Assasins*, a Matthieu Kassovitz short which they've shot. They describe Matthieu's humour as very Jewish, very dark. They like the humour in *House* too, although some of the lines need clarification. Who is Harry Secombe for example? And what is "shagging"?

Georges is the more talkative, mainly because he has the better English but they both come across as extremely likeable. They are reassuringly older than I expected. I had imagined them to be thrusting and trendy, French groove-bags with pony tails and attitude. They had imagined me to have long hair and a beard.... We go for lunch at "L'Odéon" in Air Street which is very new and swanky. Unfortunately it turns out to be a complete Terence Conran copy of a French brasserie. I search for something British - or even Welsh - on the menu and pathetically suggest the Hereford Duck.

I've already shown Pierre and Georges some photos of the "Beloved Country", and they've read my "introductory fax" so it isn't too difficult to swap ideas. Georges even tried to find Banwen in the atlas, and failed. We all end up speaking a kind of Franglais.

I suppose that I am interviewing them, but they interview me too. There is a much bigger divide between t.v. and features in France. Budding French directors are weaned on "courts mettrages" (shorts), whereas we get to do telly. This creates a certain difference of outlook and experience and perhaps some French prejudice against "television drama". They haven't seen my work so I am guilty until proven innocent. They ask how many set-ups I intend to shoot each day and, of course - the camera department's eternal obsession - do I like to move the camera?

I love the camera department, but to a certain extent their agenda is always the same. They want a challenge – to execute the interesting, well-made shot and they crave difficulty almost as much as actors. But the desire to move the camera is also, subconsciously, about controlling a scene. The cut is ultimately the director's means of control, his intervention. Actors and cameraman love doing scenes "in one" because there is no intervention. They feel more in control. The trouble is, if a scene becomes too complicated it becomes more about organisation than anything else, with the director acting like some kind of referee between the interested parties. Sometimes a cut is exactly what's needed!

I think it's been a good meeting. Pierre and Georges seem enthusiastic about the project and I feel comfortable with them. We exchange tapes coyly. They ask questions about shape, colour, feel and I try to use specific examples from the script. Pierre talks about metaphor and Georges likens the film to Ken Loach meeting Tennessee Williams in Wales – which I think is pretty terrific. As they leave for Paris I feel, if nothing else, that we have made a connection.

Monday 18th December

I go with Sheryl to meet the distributors (First Independent). A courtesy meeting but the conversation is pretty lively with lots of jokes about sheep. It's very interesting for me to find out which actors are considered to be "box office" by them. Julie Christie for example is not considered a draw for the public, whereas Brenda Fricker is. I can't get my head around this. How do they know? The distributors of course would like us to have a "star" in the film which seems impossible and unnecessary to me on our budget, but we have to show willing. They seem to agree that the music of the film could be a help in attracting a younger audience (as well as the not so young) and I'm glad about this, because it is an essential part of the script.

I ask them why cinema posters are generally so horribly designed and trailers so predictable. I have always assumed that there must be a reason. Some tyrannical guidelines laid down by the studios or some marketing "received wisdom" that stops them from being more imaginative, but apparently not. I know why they need to show breasts and guns wherever possible – but it's the graphic design that really gets me down. It always seems so dull and old-fashioned compared to say album covers – which can be true objects of desire. If the boys from *Trainspotting* have proved anything it's that originality gets you noticed. I loved their specially shot trailer and their poster campaign. Even if you can't afford this kind of exposure there's no reason why the design can't be as good.

Thursday 27th December
Still very cold outside. My diary confirms that 1995 has not been a good year for me (about four months paid work in total). Too much time spent waiting for things to happen. I find one quote which I copied down in June from Howard Brenton's *Hot Irons* (re. "Romans in Britain"): "... cooks and runaways are our ancestors. We have the genes of survivors not heroes in us – the heroes got killed. The cowards were our fore-fathers and fore-mothers". My 1996 diary looks blank but hopeful.

Saturday 29th December
Strange apocalyptical weather hits Cardiff – freezing rain. Water in the atmosphere but frozen on the ground. Ice falling like sheets of glass from the car window, roads silver and icicles hanging from everything. It reminds me of a scene from "The

Singing Ringing Tree" – an East German kids' programme that terrorised a generation. I venture out in my hired Honda to Ed's house. 5 mph all the way. A blazing fire, coffee and cigarettes await me. We have a good time – plotting a film that we now know will be made.

We settle down to some work on Act One. Ed thinks it's too busy and frenetic, with no room for the camera. It has a different rhythm to the rest of the film. There are a lot of choices to be made... It feels good to be talking like this. Up until now most conversations have been about the narrative only. It's healthy after all the "script editing" to consider some reckless solutions, poetic possibilities.

I suppose deciding where to put the camera is partly instinctive, like deciding which character should speak first in a scene. Your first choice could almost be arbitrary, forcing its own resolution. Not every shot is functional. There is not necessarily a correct shot waiting to be found. The whole process is one of diminishing choices - which is what makes it interesting.

Saturday 30th December

"All the way from Hong Kong to melt on the carpet in my house." I love the detail in Gwenny's dialogue as she pieces together the fragments of her memory. "... and then I came downstairs... but there was nobody there, I picked up my dolly but my fingers went straight through her..." I have a picture in my head, a piece of my own memory - a battered "Magicoal" fire, with the false coal broken, exposing the mechanics of the "magic" within - a little fan rotating above a glowing red filament. I see Gwenny's doll from a small child's point of view. A fantasy plastic teenager (wearing hotpants or similar) sitting by the red electric bar, legs splayed and smiling - helplessly melting. The camera examines her with morbid interest, in close-up, and the sound is unbearably loud. A squeaking fan and the crackle of her nylon hair.

David Levinthal's *Dark Light* photographs remind me of Gwenny's doll. I love them. They bring so many things to mind simultaneously. The child (us) as malign narrator, for example. Who can honestly say that they haven't hung, burnt, or tortured their Action Man at some point, or decapitated or tortured their sister's Cindy or Tressy doll? (Remember the t.v. commercial : "Tressy's got a secret – her hair grows". Well, not any more it doesn't...) But most of all it's the quality of light that really makes these photographs exciting – golden but fetid, like sunlight through closed curtains.

Monday 1st January
London enveloped in hangover – a real pea-souper. The bottle-bank at Tesco's surrounded by its own thick cloud of guilt and regret. New leaves turning over with every smash of green glass. Bad head day.

Tuesday 2nd January
The central heating packs in so I put on lots of clothes and make lists. I write the back-story to the Lewis family. It's funny how you identify with the kids, when in fact you're old enough to be their father! By my reckoning Gwenny wasn't even born until 1979 – which is the year I went to university.

I pick up *War And An Irish Town* by Eamonn McCann, given to me by Red Saunders back in 1990. Of course it is describing a specific situation and has a specific agenda, but it is interesting in a general way about the mythologies of nations – how historical truths become "encrusted in myth".

"When a man lives in a world of bookies' slips, varnished counters and Guinness spits he will readily accept an account of the past which tends to invest his living with dignity."

Friday 5th January

From Andy Gimberg, *States of America*
"Why is there such an urge to encompass America when it is made up of so many parts? Because America is really a mirror, and in the process of describing it we cannot help but describe ourselves."

Saturday 6th January

Early train to Paris. Another adventure! Pierre and Georges are waiting for me at the barrier, full of enthusiasm. I am not sure whether to kiss and shake hands – so we do a little dance which accomplishes both. Georges drives us to his flat in the Vingtième. We sit around a small table with our scripts etc. and start consuming lots of coffee and cigarettes. We discuss the film until lunchtime and walk to a local café – Lebanese. Lots of kissing and joking – Georges seems to know everyone – and the food is great. Kebabs, potato cakes and Lebanese beer. Then more coffee, cigarettes and talking back at Georges' place.

By the end of the afternoon we are very tired, especially Pierre and me. Georges seems indefatigable. All this thinking and talking – in French and English – has worn us out. Also there's an element of fear. We discuss many sequences for which I am not even close to finding a solution. The task of making the film suddenly seems enormous to me. But I remind myself that these are early days. Conversations like this are the process by which the problems are identified and then solved. We agree to continue with our meeting tomorrow.

As Georges bids farewell to Pierre and I on the landing to his flat (kissing and waving) his next-door-neighbour comes up the stairs dressed in cycling gear. He looks vaguely familiar. There is a lot more embracing and kissing before I am introduced. This is Mathieu Kassovitz – director of *La Haine*! A strange moment. I feel like the mistress meeting the wife. We shake hands but don't kiss. Mathieu asks us in for a drink, although he has none. A typical director's flat – small but immaculately tidy. Well organised space. A bowl of jelly-beans on the kitchen table. He opens the window as soon as Georges lights up.

He is very very gracious, and curious about British films. How can we produce the anarchy of Monty Python and Benny Hill and yet have such a *sober* film culture – the only recent exports to France being Mike Leigh and Ken Loach? Our meeting ends warmly. He wishes me luck.

I go back to my hotel in the Bastille. I lie on the bed and look at the ceiling. I told Georges and Pierre that I might call a friend – but I have no intention of doing so. I just wanted to save them the trouble of entertaining me for the night. I watch some sport on t.v. (Cardiff Arms Park! Tomorrow is the final of the European Cup between Cardiff and Toulouse), then fall asleep. I wake up looking at the ceiling. I'm hungry. It's raining outside.

I look for a restaurant which isn't too full (so I feel conspicuous) nor too empty (so I get depressed). The Bastille is very lively. Men talk to women who lean on their elbows and cradle glasses of warm red wine in their hands. Occasionally they pick wax from the candle, or reach lazily for a strong cigarette as they listen, rapt, to their artist boyfriends – oblivious to the Welshman at the window. They all look so beautiful and so French. I'm getting very wet so I settle for an Indonesian with an aquarium. Plenty of fish to watch. The English menu translations are hilarious. I wonder what "Flicker in Stuff" could be.

Sunday 7th January
After breakfast at Georges', we discuss the opening sequence in some detail. We drink some Jamaican punch and toast the film and I leave about lunchtime – feeling that the morning has been worthwhile. We embrace and kiss with ease. I promise to write.

On the train I make notes about everything that we have discussed so that I don't forget. It seems that the most important decision we made was to use BLEACH BY-PASS.

BLEACH BY-PASS

Pierre is keen to use a process called senblanchiment for the Welsh sequences - what we call bleach by-pass or silver enhancement. Its effect is to harden the contrast of the film. More of the silver is retained at the printing stage, darkening the blacks and brightening up the whites. It can give a strong, almost monochrome "monumentality" to the film which might be just right for House of America.

(Film references - Mike Radford's 1984 *or, more recently, Jeuno et Caro's* City of Lost Children, Seven, Silverado. *Other examples are* Naked *or* An Awfully Big Adventure, *although I felt that these were not such a good use of the technique.)*

The only possible cost implications of bleach by-pass are in the processing of the final print, which is basically put through a different machine. Sometimes an inter-neg is required, although my contact at Ranks Laboratories did not think this was necessary and did not feel that there would be any significant difference in price. The effect has certain design implications however (strength of colour, darkness of tone) so the decision to use it would need to be made in advance of shooting.

The strong clean "dark" look of the bleach by-pass process seems like a good option for "House of America". The colours of South Wales would respond very well to this effect – even the bright green grass has, in reality, coal beneath it which provides a kind of underlying blackness.

FORMAT

Before discussing which format we should choose, we tried to define the kinds of shot we would be using. (For example, how many characters are likely to be in the frame at any one point – it is not a big cast of characters). If the scenes were to be very cutty, Georges would favour the 1.66:1 aspect ratio. I thought that we would quite often use a moving camera to reflect the internal politics of the family or to stress one character within a scene (e.g. showing Sid as "architect" of the fantasy). We all thought that America immediately suggested Westerns and wide vistas so we tended towards the wider format (1.85:1), although this decision is not urgent.

WORKING PRACTICES
We had a brief chat about working practices. The exact job descriptions vary (they always have a second grip instead of a stand-by chippie) but there do not seem to be any great discrepancies. They like to start the day with an Italian! This is what the French call blocking for some reason (!) i.e. to play out the action with the actors on the set before any work begins so that everybody has an idea of what is going to happen.

January 1996
Getting the money for your film is one thing, but GETTING THE MONEY for your film is something else. The cash doesn't turn up in a suitcase when you sign on the dotted line, and with a total of six partners involved there are six dotted lines to sign. I am impatient. Not only am I seriously skint but I am anxious to get started. I want to use this time constructively. Sheryl's problem, of course, is cash-flow. David Green – our Executive Producer at September Films – has already supported the project through Development Hell and is understandably reticent about throwing more cash at it.

Somehow Sheryl manages to access enough money to get us underway while all the paperwork is being sorted out. September Films agree to *lend* me some money to live on.

It's all a question of priorities. Since Joan McCann has already been working (for nothing) on casting at the London end, we agree that there are two priorities as far as Wales is concerned:
1. Local casting

2. Locations

Llinos Wyn Jones – an old friend – agrees to help out on the casting and we employ a young gun called Euros to start looking for open-cast mines. Since I have sold my car, I am allowed to keep the hired Honda and I hit the road immediately in search of the Welsh badlands.

Monday 8th January

Torrential rain in Cardiff as I get to our borrowed offices at the HTV building. God, it's a depressing place – the "Taff Mahal" – a horrible example of Eighties corporate architecture, with the worst carpets in Europe. Llinos negotiating in a sparse basement room. She has the smile of a stoic and the patience of a saint. Her task – to scour the job centres, schools and colleges for unknown talent – a possible Gwenny or a Boyo – and to set up workshop-style auditions. A romantic idea, but who knows?

Tuesday 9th January

After talking through the script and location ideas, my brief to Euros is very simple – find every open-cast mine in South Wales and photograph it! I suggest that he starts from the West and that I start from the East. He should photograph anything that he finds interesting along the way and we should meet every day to look at photographs and take stock. The nature of the valleys makes them difficult to recce, it takes time to explore them all. We are dealing with a big little country.

Wednesday 10th January

I am determined to conquer Gwent. Start in Garn Diffaith in glorious sunshine and end up at Bargoed in the rain. A massive land clearance like a scar through the town. I get totally drenched. Later on – fantastic view from the hills above Blaenavon as the sky clears to reveal the sea in the far distance.

Friday 12th January

After a few days travelling, Euros remarks that we are not only looking for a mythical America but also a mythical Wales. He is right. The picture in our heads does not really exist. I was in Gwent again today and found some remarkable places around Blaenavon (like Llanelly Hill by Brynmawr and the Bedwellty Pits beneath Tredegar) but the place we are looking for is really an invention, a composite. The closest to it is Banwen and Onllwyn - the area about which *House of America* was written in the first place. The roads here are long and straight and the grass is yellow like in an Andrew Wyeth painting, but there is not much else. The open-cast has long gone, there are no shops and the pub is boarded up.

Landscape is a difficult thing to photograph - because what you're really trying to capture on screen is not a vista but the atmosphere or the experience of a place. What you need is time – time to look and time to shoot.

Saturday 13th January

I travel beyond the badlands of Banwen and Coelbren and venture into the villages of Gwaun Cae Gurwen, Brynaman and Garnant – the edges of our own Wild West. I notice that dotted along the roads in all these villages are sheds of various kinds, constructed from odd bits of corrugated iron and painted timber. On closer inspection, some reveal themselves to be customised kit-form chapels built by God-fearing frontiersmen, but others are less obvious in shape or function, someone's mad afternoon or midnight impulse. Whereas some have been built sensibly on the roadside, others have been placed darkly in the middle of bogs or on the slopes of grassy coal tips. What for? Cries for help? Rites of passage? Or do they hold some higher symbolic significance for their demented authors?

Equally inexplicable to the uninitiated is the obvious commitment throughout the West to playing rugby in the rain. In almost every village I pass through there are games taking place. Small groups of spectators huddle under umbrellas, while their kids play murder in the car park, patiently watching the steam rising from a knot of drenched forwards who are locked in combat, desperately searching for a ball in the cold oily mud. I can almost feel the velcro burn of the stubble through the vaseline, the searing pain of the dislocated thumb and the sting of embrocation in the disgorged eye. And the backs just wait in ragged lines, like doomed sheep dogs, stamping their feet and holding their damp sleeves in sullen expectation, hoping that the strange lumbering monster before them will give birth to their only source of joy – that wet brown leather egg! To hold it is their only aim, to carry it for some yards before being felled and winded and buried in the mud their greatest triumph! While far away in the outfield, a young winger is momentarily distracted by the sight of a figure in the distance. A stranger in an anorak, dragging a piece of corrugated iron towards the soggy dunes beyond the clubhouse. A man on the edge of society. A lonely shed-builder in the rain.

Tuesday 16th January
Mist over Wales. I leave early for the open-cast at Nant Helen with Euros. Visibility nil. We turn back and talk mostly about films as we drive theoretically home. Why does everybody love Tarantino *so* much? We pass the McDonald's in Glyn-Neath – shining like a beacon through the dampness.

In the evening I go with my father and a friend to see Wales playing Italy at the Arms Park. There's a continental atmosphere in town, and the floodlights make the stadium look very impressive in the mist. I sit next to a man in a Ganex mac who is desperate for this game to have some significance – just so he can say that "he was there"... Arwel Camber Thomas seems his best bet – a first cap for the twenty-two year-old outside-half from Cwmtawe. He gets his first conversion attempt within five minutes, with the ball coming off the cross-bar. "That's it!" says the man conclusively, "We've got an outside-half!" and of course I agree. "Exactly the same happened to Johnathan [Davies] with his first conversion," he continues, as though I needed proof, "although on that occasion the ball came off the upright, rather than the horizontal." Well, you can't argue with such a technical reading of the omens, can you? His silent wife gets out the celebration butterscotch.

Sunday 21st January

I phone John Cale at a recording studio in New York. At exactly six o'clock, our time, as instructed by his agent. They put me on hold and I listen to the local radio traffic report. I imagine glistening station wagons heading out of town along the freeway. Then a Welsh voice comes on – John Cale. A superficial chat, but he seems interested in doing the music for *House of America*. I straighten and I'm off to the Welsh BAFTA Awards with my old friend Geraint (Producer of *Arthur*). A ridiculous, drunken bun-fight attended by over 700 people. I don't feel that comfortable at the TAFTAs, which is why I always end up drinking too much. There's something about the event that doesn't quite ring true. Yet it somehow seems like a perverse gesture *not* to turn up....

Sunday 27th January

The papers are full of Richey James – the Manic Street Preacher who disappeared a year ago. He left his car at the Severn Bridge Service Station, a well-known suicide spot, and hasn't been seen since. No body has been recovered. A real-life Sid Lewis.

Friday 2nd February

Gothenburg Film Festival.

Wednesday 7th February

Catch my favourite train – the 06:45 to Cardiff. The end of the line, so you can fall asleep. But we talk - Mark Tildsley (the designer) and I, who turns up despite a strange lung complaint. We look at magazines and books – the stills from *Kids* by Larry Clark, photographs of Hollywood low-life by Philip Lorca DiCorcia. Blue snow turning to white snow as we enter Wales, fucking cold outside. Cardiff as dismal as hell on arrival. Greasy spoon in Canton does the job – marvellous poached eggs and industrial strength sausages. We visit an old bakery in Taff's Well which smells of Chinese takeaways and armpits but looks like it could be a perfect "studio" for us. The Estate Agent thinks we're weird.

Thursday 8th February
Wake up early to work on the script. Mark Tildsley snoring like thunder from the next room which I put down to his emerging pleurisy. We do some work on sets. We invent Sid's hideaway. Scattered rocks on the floor boards, a single home-made chair beneath a dangling noose. *Shane*, Van Gogh, Heavy Metal, Navajo Indians, Robert Frank, corrugated iron, Jasper Johns and the Resurrection. All you need is a pen and paper.

Saturday 10th February
Back in London. Joan and I go to meet Siân Phillips at the National Theatre canteen. She is charming. Can she play Mam? She has a great face, and great poise. Currently performing in *A Little Night Music* for Sean Mathias and working on a one-woman show for him about Marlene Dietrich. She could be a very interesting Mam, a bit older than written. A Valleys Blanche du Bois. And if she finds the girl from Alltwen beneath that hard-won sophistication, who knows?

The afternoon is taped readings with Steve Mackintosh and Richard Harrington, Richard Lynch and Michael Sheen at the Soho Laundry. Very impressive. Lynch comes in looking brown (he's been to Australia) but a little defeated. It's hard working with actors that you know really well – you have to show some kind of even-handedness. Steve Mackintosh's Welsh accent is terrific, Harrington is nervous, Sheen is great too but a different version of Sid (a bit Dennis Hopper!)

Sunday 11th February

Meet Meichiel, our Dutch Editor. Seems shy but confident. Buy some more Manic Street Preachers albums.

Thursday 14th March

A fourteen hour day, during which the Art Department buy a Harley Davidson Sportster for the film. They reckon it's a bargain at £2000. Everyone at "Rhondda Studios", an empty WDA factory, is very excited. Now all we have to find is a Capri, a Robin Reliant, and an American Classic.

Sunday 17th March

London readthrough.

Monday 18th March

Crisis management. Visit East Pit.

Tuesday 19th March

Rehearsals in Chapter.

Friday 22nd March

I get a fax from Chris Monger (all the way from L.A.). It reads as follows:

"To make films is to prolong the games of childhood." François Truffaut. Marc! Whatever you do, don't forget that we do it to have fun. Congratulations / Best wishes / Bon voyage / Pob Hwyl – Chris."

Sunday 24th March

Shoot starts in Banwen.

II
Looking Back

I first saw *House of America*, the play, in Chapter in Cardiff in 1989. It was a Saturday night and I almost didn't go. I had no idea what to expect. What I saw was the last performance by the original cast, fast and furious, of a play that took my breath away. I remember going out at half-time and saying "Oh my God! It's her isn't it. It's Mam! She did it!". Then at full-time meeting Ed. We spoke Welsh to each other (and have done ever since) although I didn't understand exactly what he was going on about. I was full of praise, he was full of theories.

We talked a lot about *House of America* that night and it seems that we have been talking about it ever since. About turning the script into a screenplay, about raising the money for the film, about casting and shooting, about lines of dialogue, camera angles, costumes, cars, minutiae. On top of Welsh hills, wet with rain we talked about it some more and then again with our eyes half-closed in Soho cutting rooms late at night. We talked to journalists about it, to students, to family, to friends, to each other, to ourselves and to the walls. Until eventually we bored even the walls, not to mention ourselves, and we stopped talking about it anymore.

What remains is 98 minutes of celluloid, a film, our film, stuck somewhere in time. I haven't seen it for a while nor thought about it that much. Until now, for this book. So here I go, talking about it again, on these pages.

I'll start with a quote.

Someone once said (Shaker Kapur I think) that you always make three films: one that you write, one that you shoot and one that you cut. He is undoubtedly right although there is actually a fourth film that you also make, over which you have no control. It is the film that you can only see once you have walked away from it and put some distance between you. It is the film that after a time, jumps out and surprises you once more by becoming an artefact of the past. Made by another you at another time.

For better or for worse this is never the film that you thought you were making and this is certainly true of *House of America*. Reading back over notes that I made at the time, thinking over ideas and their execution it seems obvious now that a lot of what happened was accidental. We had a plan alright, it was mostly there in the screenplay and I, as director, thought I was in control (a necessary illusion for getting out of bed in the morning) but of course I was not. I remember phoning Ed in the middle of the shoot and saying "I don't know what it is" and he just said "go with it". The flurry of activity and constant chaos that constitutes a shoot almost inevitably leads to this kind of confusion and leaves you finally with the fragments of celluloid that seem mysterious to everyone involved. It is a film that you have imagined for a long time (six years for *House*) and now it's lying there in bits, just waiting to be found. And the truth is it is no longer yours. For the die has long been cast, your job now is simply to try and make sense of its multiple strands. What you end up with is some unrecognizable flawed thing, a diabolic baby, that you will love anyway, warts and all because you were responsible for its birth.

Ed and I have been loving parents to *House* although it takes time to see your offspring as they really are. We did our best to bring something beautiful into the world, we really did. Take a look at the screenplay, it's all there in black and white! And from the directing side of things too there was a scheme, an image system which sort of guided our actions. This came from wanting to establish a visual language for the film before the chaos took over. We had decided to use a French camera team (Pierre Aïm and Georges Diane) who had been responsible for the previous year's

La Haine a film I had much admired. Beautifully photographed in black and white it seemed to approach its grim subject matter with the sense of poetry I was looking for with *House*. The fact that "the eyes" of the film were French was I suppose one of those happy accidents which brought into the mix an outsider's view of a familiar landscape and in a more practical sense forced us to spend a lot of time carefully trying to explain ourselves, especially to Pierre whose English was not great. This lack of a common language helped us define things better and look at things differently. By the time we came to shoot we felt we knew what film we were making.

Thinking about it now, memories come flooding back... I could go into far too much detail here about how things developed visually.... On the first recce to Banwen for example (the main location) Pierre commented that "the grass is black". It was indeed so, having been planted like so much valleys grass on the overburden from the old open-cast. This determined the film process known as "bleach by-pass" which de-saturates the colours and heightens the blackness of the image. Which, in turn, required the designer, Mark Tildsley, to paint the sets brighter than was normal in order to compensate for this de-saturation on the film. If you ever go to Banwen you can still see the pub painted luridly in red and green, glowing through the mist like an accidental monument to the whims of film-making.

How accidental the whole process could be in practice is perhaps best exemplified by our brief period of shooting in Canada. We were determined that for Syd's evocation of a mythical dad living in America we should have equally mythical images of the Wild West. Red-hot images of the dusty American wilderness came to mind, reminiscent of *Paris, Texas* and *Badlands*. Somehow, on our low budget, we managed to send a small crew to Alberta, Canada at the end of April 96 where we were promised a Harley Davidson to ride, a house to burn and some good weather. We had three days to shoot the sequence but when we arrived it was snowing. We had no option but to shoot anyway and that is why those sequences appear in black and white in the film. It was the only way we could think of making Canada look different from Banwen. I was at least consoled by Pierre who admitted that *La Haine* had been originally been shot in colour and only later, at the whim of the director, been converted into black and white. Proof, if it was needed, that the fate of all films can spin on a dime.

But whatever its drawbacks and accidents, low-budget film-making has its heroic aspects and that's what making *House of America* felt like to me and I think to Ed at the time, an heroic endeavour. This feeling was, no doubt, exaggerated by our own romantic notions of ourselves but also by the fact that we were operating out of Wales. After all, at that time, despite the success of films like *Trainspotting* and the emergence of a so-called "Cool Britannia" all around us, there were no films coming out of Wales at all. We couldn't help feeling that we were the first, the pioneers of a new generation. The fact that *Twin Town* quickly followed (and was released first) only added to this feeling. We knew Kevin Allen well, I had met him when we were both teenagers on The National Youth Theatre together, and when both our films ended up showing at The Sundance Film Festival the following year we felt we had arrived, together. We were like the Sex Pistols and The Clash. Surely more punks would follow where we had bravely dared to tread. But we were the first, the mighty trail-blazers!

We couldn't help ourselves, it's a Welsh disease I suppose, we felt like we were representing Wales. And Wales responded by being grateful for having any films to talk about and flattered our egos with its attentions, even if we weren't everybody's cup of tea. But looking back we were not so nasty as some people made out or as counter-culture as we liked to think. After all, upsetting the Welsh establishment is not exactly that difficult to do. Or that dangerous.

In some ways *House of America* and *Twin Town* were not the first of a new generation of films but the last of the old. Although Ed was remarkably young when he wrote the play and although his writing was muscular and modern, drawing its inspiration from American heroes like Sam Shepherd and Jack Kerouak, it was actually engaged in an argument with the past, with the Wales in which we grew up. We were at great pains while making the film to stress that *House of America* was not a complaint but a celebration and I think, that to a certain extent, we protested too much. Looking back – and hindsight is a wonderful thing – we were railing against a Wales that was already beginning to change, the Wales of our youth. Perhaps Wales is, as the oft-quoted Gwyn Alf Williams has said, always in the process of re-inventing itself. No sooner have you tried to capture it, than it is gone.

That's not to say that our film was irrelevant it's just that it was (is) talking very much from the standpoint of our own generation, from a very specific place in time. And the joke was that even if we were speaking Americanese (what Boyo calls "Yankage"!) we were most definitely engaged in an internal debate. Just as Kevin Allen and Paul Durden were in *Twin Town*, sticking two fingers up to corrupt, hypocritical Swansea and at one point literally pissing over its children, so we too were having a go at our ineffectual cultural fathers in *House of America*. No wonder, in retrospect, that the Rhondda-ati of Dai Smith's BBC refused to support the film. It was saying that all those honest-to-goodness myths of a benign, patriarchal Valleys culture were a lie and that we had in fact failed abysmally and sold ourselves down the river. This wasn't a film about the working class it was a film about Welsh white trash, about the hypocrisy at the heart of our history and education and that's what the stinking corpse in the outhouse was all about. And that's why the drugs did work.

And if all that sounds rather grand it is not meant to. It's just that what I see when I look at *House Of America* now is not necessarily what I felt while making it. I thought we were making something very modern, if not post-modern, whereas in fact we were having an argument with the past. We thought we were being really funny but looking back it seems that we were a bit, well... angry! But perception is all. You can control some of the frame, but not all of it. I remember feeling really upset by our first review in *Sight and Sound* (Liese Spencer, wherever you are, your name is carved on my heart!) which didn't even recognize the cultural context of the film. Refused to pay it any of the respect it might have a film that, say, came out of Iran or Austria or anywhere. In other words denied it any cultural specificity whatsoever and condemned it as being merely provincial.

We may not have known exactly what we were making but we certainly knew what clothes we were stealing. The melodrama was deliberate, we were more interested in borrowing from Tennessee Williams than Ken Loach to tell this particular story. Mind you, when we went to Sundance the Americans took the film at face value thinking that all Welsh people lived in houses like Clem's. And why not? They all do in Utah. To them we had made another addition to a long line of British social-realist films. To us it was totally not that. Social-realism, or "miserablism" as we called it, was the enemy. We didn't feel that we were working in the context of "British film" at all, but in a void, our own Welsh void.

I don't think that Welsh void quite exists anymore, perhaps it never did. It seems to me now that Wales is getting on with life and is less prone to arguing with itself about what it should be. Perhaps *House* was part of the process by which that happened, either as symptom or cause. But the situation was already changing as we made the film. I remember Ed commenting about Mathew Rhys who came straight out of RADA to play Boyo in our film, then went on to do a television film in his own accent, then a play at the National Theatre by Peter Gill about Cardiff (*Cardiff East*). It is like he'd inherited a different Wales to us. Compared to actors a generation older like Richard Lynch (who had played Boyo in the original play), he'd inherited a Wales that existed for real and was negotiable and pretty cool about itself. Just like the next feature film to come out of Wales after *House*, Justin Kerrigan's *Human Traffic* which didn't challenge the past at all but dealt with the whole contemporary experience of living in Cardiff and getting out of your head on ecstasy. Ecstasy as in, ex-stasis. Not staying still. Some people said it wasn't very "Welsh" but I think it was.

If *House of America* was sometimes condemned for its own ambitions, if we seemed pretentious for playing with genres we didn't own it was also a genuine attempt to say things our own way and to find words and pictures that were interesting to us then. In that sense the film is a totally genuine expression of who we were at the time and quite down to earth really. Or to be more exact, up to its knees in Welsh mud (god it was a wet shoot!). And if its bleakness of vision already belongs to another time then hopefully that at least makes it part of a collective past and an addition to a growing compendium of Welsh films. And so what if the film we ended up making was as much a product of accident as design, it was also a product of its time and place. I don't know who reads old screenplays or why but as you peruse this one at least you may get a sense of the first film we tried to make. This is where it all started – with Ed's words. It is a document fuelled by hope and steeped in naïve ambition. God it takes me back!

Marc Evans
02/02

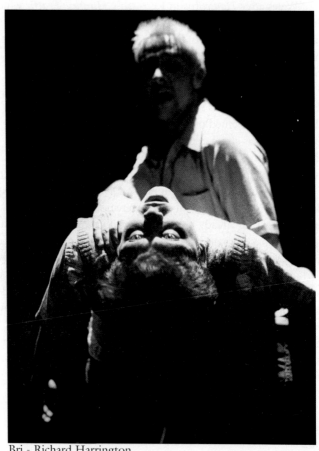

Bri - Richard Harrington
Marshall - Roger Evans

photography - Pau Ross

Gas Station Angel

"As a piece of live theatre it is stunning, great staging, flying metaphors, lots of humour and impressive performances: one of the most exciting, richest, cleverest and most theatrical productions to have come out of Wales."

The Western Mail

GAS STATION ANGEL
Premiered at Newcastle Playhouse on May 8th 1998 in a
co-production between Fiction Factory and the Royal
Court Theatre.

TOUR HISTORY
Spring/Summer 98
Brussels, Brecon, Clwyd, Cardiff and Swansea, before
opening at the Royal Court at the Ambassadors London.
Autumn 98
Berlin, Copenhagen.

Translated into German and has played in rep in
Berlin, Bremen, Hannover and Hamburg until 2002.
Spanish production planned in Bogota Columbia in
2003/4.

NOTE
Gas Station Angel was first published by Methuen in
1998. This version is the final production text. I've
kept stage directions to a minimum. It is there to be
perfomed. It moves through the real and the imagined
in a fluid way. I suppose that's all there is to say.

Cast List.

Ace: Richard Lynch
Bron: Siwan Morris
Bri: Richard Harrington
Marshall: Roger Evans
Manny: John Ogwen
Mati: Donna Edwards
Mary Anne: Valmai Jones
Gruff: Russell Gomer

Dyfrig
Keith
Mr Entertainment   } Simon Gregor
PC

Director: Ed Thomas
Producer: Mike Parker
Assistant Director: Steve Fisher
Design and Lighting: Peter Mumford
Composer: John Hardy
Assistant Design and Lighting: John Buswell
Sound Designer: Mike Beer
Production Manager: Ian Buchanan
Company Stage Manager: Maris Sharp
Deputy Stage Manager: Sandra Grieve
Costume Design: Sam Mealing

Special thanks to Neil Wallace at Offshore International,
Amsterdam.

PART ONE

ACE
I saw a woman

MANNY
Where?

ACE
Down on the beach…

MANNY
And?

ACE
She said to me…

BRON
I've seen you before.

ACE
Where?

BRON
Up on the cliff, staring out at the sea.

ACE
When?

BRON
Long time ago now. I was with my brother.

ACE
I remember. It was summer.

BRON
Yes.

ACE
August the ninth.

BRON
I can't be sure of the date.

ACE
I keep a diary. I go out at night. I write down what I see. I like to think I see everything, but I obviously don't.

BRON
No.

ACE
Because until that night I'd never seen you before.

BRON
I see.

ACE
I'd like to think I'm the night-watchman of this town but I suppose even a night watchman can't see everything.

BRON
Even night watchmen make mistakes.

ACE
They do.

BEAT.

BRON
I turned to my brother and said I can see a man.

MARSHALL
Where?

BRON
Looking down at us.

MARSHALL
Where?

BRON
There, can you see him?

MARSHALL
What's he doing out on the cliffs at this time of night?

BRON
Who knows.

MARSHALL
It can't be Bri.

BRON
No.

MARSHALL
He doesn't look like Bri.

BRON
No.

MARSHALL
I'd like it to be Bri.

BRON
And me.

MARSHALL
But it isn't.

BRON
No.

MARSHALL
Bri wouldn't stand up on the cliffs in the dark.

BRON
Unless...

MARSHALL
He wouldn't Bron, he wouldn't.

BRON
He's gone anyway.

ACE
I went home.

BRON
Maybe he's lost.

ACE
To write in my diary what I saw.

BRON
I wonder who he was.

ACE
My father was sitting at the table surrounded a sea of papers.

MANNY
-1961, -1971, -1981, -1991.

BRON
Do you know him Marshall?

MARSHALL
I know his face.

BRON
Who's his face?

MARSHALL
Ace.

BRON
Ace?

MARSHALL
Hywel Ace. He's one of the Aces of Gaerlishe.

BRON
Oh.

MARSHALL
They say their house is going to fall into the sea.

BRON
Their house?

MARSHALL
Their house.

BRON
The sea?

MARSHALL
The sea Bron, the fucking sea.

MANNY
Papers, journals, monthlies, weeklies, annuals, bi-annuals, comics, magazines and what for.

ACE
To wrap our crockery in dad, what else.

MANNY
Crockery? Crockery? What the hell do you know about crockery?

ACE
The Council will come dad.

MANNY
The Council, the Council.

ACE
They'll knock down our house.

MANNY
We'll keep an eye out for them.

ACE
They'll come with warrants.

MANNY
We'll burn them.

ACE
With eviction orders.

MANNY
We'll lock the door and won't let them in.

ACE
They'll bring JCB's!

MANNY
Over my dead body. *(BEAT)* Maybe it was the council that killed our chickens. If you see anyone from the council snooping around our chickens, you shoot first, ask questions later - capiche?

ACE
Our chickens are dead dad.

MANNY
Capiche?

ACE
Capiche dad, capiche. *(BEAT)* And then...

MARY ANNIE
Gurruga, gurruga, gurruga, no bell no lights can't see.

ACE
My mother woke up.

MARY ANNIE
Man? You there? I'm awake.

MANNY
Mmm.

MARY ANNIE
I said I was awake.

MANNY
I know.

MARY ANNIE
I haven't died.

MANNY
No.

MARY ANNIE
I'm still here.

MANNY
Yes.

BEAT.

MARY ANNIE
Man?

MANNY
I'm listening.

MARY ANNIE
What you doing?

MANNY
I'm dozing.

MARY ANNIE
Liar.

MANNY
I was dozing now I'm reading.

MARY ANNIE
You're not in your chair.

MANNY
I am.

MARY ANNIE
You're at the table.

MANNY
I'm not.

MARY ANNIE
I can tell by your voice.

MANNY
I'm in the chair.

MARY ANNIE
You moved.

MANNY
No.

MARY ANNIE
Haven't you?

MANNY
No, it's your ears.

MARY ANNIE
My external organs.

MANNY
You've got to wait for them to hear right.

MARY ANNIE
Uh?

MANNY
You've been sleeping on one and not the other.

MARY ANNIE
So?

MANNY
So the one you haven't slept on hasn't been tampered with.

MARY ANNIE
Uh?

MANNY
The one you've been sleeping on 'as been squashed... so when you unsquash it, it takes quarter of an hour to hear properly through it.

MARY ANNIE
Oh.

MANNY
That's why you thought I moved when I didn't.

MARY ANNIE
Because of my ears.

MANNY
Yes.

MARY ANNIE
The good ear was listening one way and the sleeping ear was

getting itself sorted out.

MANNY
Yes.

MARY ANNIE
It was acclimatising to the new conditions.

MANNY
Yes.

MARY ANNIE
Getting its bearings.

MANNY
Yes.

MARY ANNIE
Like us.

MANNY
We're not moving.

MARY ANNIE
We'll have to move. Man. They'll make us move.

MANNY
They can make us as much as they want but we're not moving.

MARY ANNIE
But our house will fall into the sea.

MANNY
So in to the sea it will fall then.

MARY ANNIE
But...

MANNY
We're not moving Mary Annie.

MARY ANNIE
Don't you Mary Annie me.

MANNY
I'll Mary Annie you as much as I want.

MARY ANNIE
Huh.

MANNY
Mary Annie, Mary Annie, Mary Annie.

MARY ANNIE
You never call me Wiff no more.

MANNY
Mary Annie.

MARY ANNIE
Not since the monkey's parade.

MANNY
Mary Annie, Mary Annie, Mary Annie...

MARY ANNIE
Mansell? Why don't you call me Wiff no more? Like you used to.
(BEAT) Man? I like Wiff. Wiff is who I am. Wiff is the mother of
your child. Wiff is who I am. Wiff is me. Awake. Looking up at the
moon. Full moon. Me and the fairies. Wiff and the fairies. Maybe

they'll come tonight Man? Man? *(BEAT)* Don't call me Mary Annie Man. Call me Wiff. *(BEAT)* Man? Man?

MANNY
Wiff.

MARY ANNIE
Thank you Manny, good old Manny, brave old Manny. Stop the council moving us out before our house falls into the sea.

MANNY
And?

ACE
And then we stood there in silence watching the waves come in. I watched her push a stick into a dead jellyfish. Then right out of the blue she said...

BRON
Would you like to come for a drive with me?

MANNY
A drive?

ACE
In her car.

BRON
Because I've had a shitty time of it too. Maybe you want to come for a ride with me. I got a tinted glass, Blue Marina, 1800 TC, ready to drive into the heart of Saturday night.

ACE
And I said - I'd love to.

BRON
Good. So lets drive.

ACE
And so we drove. I didn't care where. In sixteen hours forty-eight minutes she's turned my world upside down and I know in my bones things are never going to be the same again.

MANNY
Marina?

Music plays, lights and set transforms. MATI enters and turns the TV set off in her white trash world.

BRON
I was watching that.

MATI
What for? It's bloody stupid. Kicking sweetbreads blown up round the field.

BRON
What?

MATI
That's what they used to be made of innit? Rugby balls?

BRON
Bladders mam.

MATI
Uh?

BRON
Pig's bladders, not sweetbreads and anyway they're made out of

plastic now.

MATI
Shows how much I know, but it's still bloody stupid, running around after a ball in the rain, on a Saturday afternoon, bootlaces, blood, bloody bandages and all for what? For a few pints in the club on a Saturday night, looking forward to the strippers on a Sunday with her fags and her oil to pour over herself from a Windolene bottle, I know I seen them.

BRON
When?

MATI
Lorraine told me. I never been myself, it's men only. She gave it a go for a bit on a part-time basis, but the men didn't like the Windolene bottle, told her to get real baby oil in a real baby oil bottle, she packed it in after that.

BRON
Lost her bottle did she?

MATI
You'd think with all the sprogs that she's got she wouldn't find getting a baby oil bottle a problem. Five she's got, all under eight too. What did you say?

BRON
I said I'll have to remember that.

MATI
Remember what you want it's all bloody stupid, nothing makes sense to me anymore. I mean look at your father, he still drinks in the Ship and Pilot even though they've ripped the guts out of the place. All he's ever done since whatsisname modernised it is

complain. Why don't he go somewhere else innit?

The father, GRUFF enters.

GRUFF
Because the Ship's the place I've always drunk Mati, and my father did, and his father before that.

MATI
But you don't like it no more.

GRUFF
Like it? It's bastard terrible.

MATI
But they say all the furnishings are Laura Ashley.

GRUFF
Laura Ashley be buggered, it's a pub not a bastard country kitchen - pretending to be a country kitchen with flowers and curtains and fancy little alcoves with plasterboard and ply, it's all crap. And it's not even wood. It's fucking joke wood. WHO THE FUCK ARE THEY TRYING TO KID?

Enter MR ENTERTAINMENT as we go to the Ship and Pilot pub.

MR ENTERTAINMENT
If you don't like it, why don't you piss off down the road?

GRUFF
Don't worry, I'm going, I'm going. Fuck your beer, fuck your pub. FUCK YOU!

GRUFF exits.

MR ENTERTAINMENT

Miserable git, who the fuck wants people like that in the place? Pub was dying 'til I got hold of it. Old fuckers drinking three pints and pissing over the floor of the toilet. No music. No crack. TV on in the corner. Fucking dominoes with faded dots. Wonder them old fuckers could see them. Play from memory half of them did. Put a penny on the pint they go on strike, - drink stout from the bottle. Well them days are gone. Them days are fucking gone. I got the new Ship and the old Ship, not a domino in sight - new Ship for the youngsters and the dull fuckers. Bingo 6.30 to 7.30 then karaoke from eight 'til half nine. Rave disco with an extended licence 'til 1.00. Fucking lovely, fucking gorgeous, E-ed out, bottled water, bubbly water - that's when I bring it out, goes like fuck with the youngsters too, when the dull fuckers take E and whisky, shags their brains completely. But I don't care: I got Honest Mike on the door to sort out the fighting, my daughter Cindy running the fish and chip shop - we are raking it in. FUCKING RAKING IT WE ARE. MR ENTERTAINMENT THAT'S ME. But I got to go, the gambling upstairs is about to start. Call in if you're passing. We'll always keep a welcome. And remember, you'll have A FUCKING BALL. RIGHT YOU SUCKERS, POUND IN THE POT - FIVE CARD BRAG. LET'S BE HAVING YOU.

He exits.

MATI

But he keeps going there.

BRON

Habit.

MATI

Habit? Habit? 'Bout time he changed his bloody habits, cos if he's not in the Ship he's in work, bloody Ship, bloody work, between the two of them I never see him. I tell you Bron, I can't take no more, - it's all gone nuts, it's all gone crazy, nothing makes sense anymore, the world's darts don't reach all the way to the dart-board anymore.

She exits. BRON sits at a check-out counter in the supermarket.

BRON
And I suppose she's got a point too. But this town is no different to loads of other towns around the place, around the world if it comes to that, and this family's just the same too, give or take a few things. I mean we may be on the extreme side of things but the principle's the same. Secrets and lies. A fucked up past. Maybe if we faced up to the past then maybe we wouldn't find the world so confusing.

A supermarket Trolley Boy (KEITH) enters and leans close to BRON as she works.

KEITH
Everything all right check-out one?

BRON
Yes thanks, just fine.

KEITH
Good... good.

BRON
But it aint easy. I mean how do I explain my brother Bri, or my brother Marshall. Or come to that, the trolley-boy Keith?

KEITH
Flying solo tonight?

BRON
Listen Keith. When a woman takes a pack of Coco-Pops home with her at night, its a pretty sure sign that she wants to be alone.

KEITH
Bitch.

BRON
A cryptic comment is the only way to leave a nobody supermarket trolley-boy in smalltown. It preserves a woman's mystery, gives her that distance, that possibility. It makes people wonder long into their feathery beds what a girl like me is doing in a place like this. And the answer? Family.

Enter BRI.

BRI
Crack. The sound of wood snapping. It's the first thing I remember. Then nothing. Then a splash. I must have been about ten. Bron was seven and Marsh must have been about eight.

MARSHALL enters.

BRON
Has Batman got nipples?

BRI
Yes.

BRON
How do you know?

MARSHALL
Cos he's a man Bron and men have nipples.

BRON
So why can't I see them?

MARSHALL
Cos he's wearing his bat costume; if you took off his costume you'd see his nipples.

BRON
But it won't come off, he's not like Action Man, you can take off Action Man's costume, see - look.

MARSHALL
Who told you you could play with my Action Man?

BRON
I wasn't playing with him.

MARSHALL
So how do you know you can take off his costume?

BRON
Stop it Marshall. I was only... Tell him Bri, he's picking on me.

BRI
He's not.

BRON
He is. I haven't touched his action man.

BRI
So what's it doing in your hand Bron?

BRON
I was only showing you that's all.

MARSHALL
Give him here.

BRON
No.

BRI
Give him here Bron.

Snatches it from her.

BRON
Bully. I hate you Brian James. I'm never going to play with you again.

BRI
Bron ran back to the house, leaving me and Marshall talking. I was close to him then. Me and him were inseparable. That day out of the blue I grabbed his hand and cut his finger with a knife.

MARSHALL
Argghh... what you do that for?

BRI cuts his finger and joins it to his brother's.

BRI
Me and you are blood brothers now Marsh.

MARSHALL
Uh.

BRI
Means we'll always look after each other, right.

MARSHALL
Right... but we're already brothers Bri, I got your blood in me already.

BRI
It's the ritual Marsh, the ritual. And we went down to the rocks at the foot of the estuary. We made ourselves a batcave. In the roots of an old tree. The tide was coming in but we were two batmen in search of sanctuary, too busy on a mission to notice. Marsh went first, climbing into the roots of the tree. Then I heard the crack of snapping wood. Then... I saw him fall.

MARSHALL
I went under. My feet touched the bottom. I looked up, the sun streaming in through the green water. I could see Bri's red jumper. I went back up, tried to shout but nothing came out, only water, I went under again, something pulling me down, deeper and deeper. I don't remember any panic. Just peace. I looked up again. I saw a stick come through the surface.

BRI
Grab hold of it, grab hold of it...

MARSHALL
But I couldn't reach.

BRI
MARSHALL. MARSHALL...

MARSHALL
I was moving further away. I couldn't see the stick anymore and I couldn't Bri. I was on my own. In my wellingtons, trousers and a green jumper with a batman badge. I wasn't afraid. It was peaceful. Sometimes I wish I could have stayed there. Under the green water. Looking up at the sun. Floating forever and forever. Dead.

MATI enters.

BRI
Quick Mam, quick, it's Marshall. He's fallen in.

MATI
What?

BRI
In the river, he couldn't reach... HURRY MAM, HURRY, HURRY!

BRON
I never moved. I don't know why. Maybe it was shock. The next thing I can remember is jumping up and down hysterical until dad came and shook me, telling me to stop.

GRUFF enters.

GRUFF
I was just coming in. I heard Bron screaming and I saw Bri and Mati run down towards the river. By the time I got to the river everything was over.

MATI
He was floating towards the sea. On his back. He looked peaceful. I loved him. He was my son. I walked straight into the river.

BRI
But I knew Mam couldn't swim. I stood on the bank watching my mother and brother drown.

MATI
I reached him and held up his head. I don't think I panicked. I wanted to die with him. I loved him. He was my son.

BRI

Then out of nowhere two people came. Strangers I'd never seen before; a man and a woman. They dived in, pulling out my mother and brother. Mam was still breathing but Marshall was dead. The man kept shouting save the woman, save the woman, the boy's lost. The woman stopped trying to save Marshall and helped the man save Mam. I looked at Marshall lying dead on the bank. His heart had stopped beating. I could hear mam coughing and bringing up water. Then I don't know why, but I kissed him. Harder and harder, I blew air into his mouth, harder and harder, I pushed at his chest and I kissed him harder and harder and then his chest moved and I tasted water. He was alive.

GRUFF

I carried Marshall in my arms, they called the doctor and by the time he came, colour was coming back into Marsh's body. He was blue. Except round his belly button. He was going to live.

BRI

He was still unconscious but the doctors said he'd be all right. He had to give Bron an injection for shock. People came from the other houses to see if we were all right too. Mam sat with a blanket by the fire and then she said...

MATI

Where is the man and the woman?

BRI

And everyone looked round, but there was no sign of them.

MATI

Who were they and where did they come from? Bri?

BRI

I don't know Mam, I've never seen them before.

MATI
We never had a chance to thank them for what they've done.

BRI
But we never heard from them. Dad tried to find out who they were, but nobody knew.

GRUFF
Angels.

BRI
Said my father.

BRON
Fairies.

BRI
Said Bron. But nobody knew.

GRUFF
He wasn't meant to die that's all. Someone was looking after him. Marshall James is a very lucky boy.

MATI
He's a special boy.

GRUFF
Special.

BRI
And I watched them look at him in his bed. I heard them tend to him as he threw up the dregs of the river all night. He wasn't just Marshall James no more. He was special. He was Jesus. He was an angel. They told him he was. He had a future. They all thought so. Mam, Dad, Bron. Nobody said anything to me. I never made the

papers. "Strangers save mother and son in estuary drama" sa.
headline. They all forgot me. I was the angel who kissed him L
to life that night and nobody gave me the credit for it. Ti.
strangers saw it, but they disappeared. I tried to tell Dad what
happened but he just said...

GRUFF
We all know what happened Bri, now don't tell lies. Lying will get
you nowhere in this world.

BRI
So I said no more about it. He was my brother before that day.
My blood brother. And now he wasn't. He was special. And I
hated him for it. Drowning would have preserved my love for him.
Living made love impossible. It moved the goal posts. I should
have let him die. Why the fuck didn't I let you die? I lost a brother
that day and I still fucking miss him.

BRON
Things were never the same in our house after that. Marshall got
the angel treatment with milk and jaffa cakes on the settee. I
carried on trying to think everything was normal when I knew in
my bones it wasn't and Bri became the black sheep of the family,
simple as that. What foxed me was that it was our Angel Marshall,
not Bri, who axed 24 of Dyfrig-the-Farms new born lambs to
death two and a half years ago; never touched the ewes, only the
lambs. Very dark, very strange, very Welsh.

Enter DYFRIG and ACE into a Ship and Pilot disco bar.

DYFRIG
Terrible things are being done to our lambs Ace.

ACE
I know Dyfrig, I know.

DYFRIG
They're the future of the flock Ace.

ACE
I know Dyf, I know.

DYFRIG
Slaughtered and still wet they are Ace.

ACE
It's terrible Dyf, terrible.

DYFRIG
If I catch whoever's doing it Ace, I'll blow their fucking brains out with both barrels. I wouldn't ask no questions Ace.

ACE
No.

DYFRIG
I wouldn't hesitate.

ACE
No.

DYFRIG
Blam fuckin' blam. I'd watch him drop like a stone. You wouldn't know nothing about it would you Ace?

ACE
Come off it Dyf, that isn't my line. I'm an erudite fucker.

DYFRIG
Like into glue?

ACE
No Dyf.

DYFRIG
Do you sniff it, like Loctite?

ACE
No Dyfrig, it's just a word.

DYFRIG
A word, right.

ACE
Words are beautiful Dyf, they conjure up things.

DYFRIG
Like a magician?

ACE
Yeh... like take the word docile...

DYFRIG
Docile...

ACE
Don't you think that's a fucking perfect word?

DYFRIG
In what way perfect?

ACE
In what it conjures up... let it run over your tongue Dyf... d... o..
c... ile, try it. D... o... c... ile...

DYFRIG
D... o... c... ile...

ACE
What you reckon?

DYFRIG
I reckon it's alright.

ACE
Alright. Fuckin' hell Dyf, it was BEAUTIFUL.

DYFRIG
Keep your fucking voice down Ace, we don't want everyone to hear.

ACE
Why not Dyf, don't you like people to know you play with words?

DYFRIG
Only words I know.

ACE
Like what?

DYFRIG
Fuck off.

ACE
What else.

DYFRIG
Shag.

ACE
You like that Dyf.

DYFRIG
And cunt. Women's cunts. And lips and arse... and cock.

ACE
Cock.

DYFRIG
Cock and cunt.

ACE
They go together.

DYFRIG
Yeh. In and out.

ACE
That's beautiful Dyf.

DYFRIG
I know.

ACE
I can see your mind looking at the picture... you're dreaming man.
One word and all of a sudden you're there... fucking.

DYFRIG
Yeh.

ACE
In and out.

DYFRIG
Yeh.

ACE
Fast and slow.

DYFRIG
Yes Ace, yes.

ACE
Faster and faster.

DYFRIG
Yeh.

ACE
Slower and slower.

DYFRIG
Fu-uck

ACE
You're on the edge Dyf.

DYFRIG
I know man, I know.

ACE
So is she.

DYFRIG
Yeh.

ACE
She's screaming Dyf.

DYFRIG
Yeh.

ACE
And you are.

DYFRIG
Yeh.

ACE
In and out, in and out, faster and faster and faster and faster and
FASTER AND FASTER AND YOU'RE THERE DYF,
FUCKING RELEEEEAAASSSED.

*DYFRIG screams. The other people in the pub stare. Silence.
DYFRIG looks around at the shocked faces. He gets up. (PAUSE)*

DYFRIG
I am beautiful. I am fucking beautiful. *(PAUSE)* You might not be
able to see it... but I am. It's written all over my face. But nobody
can see it, only Ace. When I step out onto the street people say
there he goes. What an ugly bastard. His past is only acne and
boils. Fuck how he must have worried as a boy. Poor boy, pity
poor boy, farmer boy. Unkissable boy...but who am I now? A boy?
A farmer's boy? A man? A half man? Beast? Angel? Demon?
Member of the underworld? How will I shed rocks to become a
man in the 21st Century?.... Uh? .... Uh?.... These are the things I
think about when you all pass me in the street; when my lambs are
slaughtered. I loved my lambs. I could talk to them. They weren't
ugly. They were beautiful. I am beautiful... But none of you
notice... Only Ace. Let me get pregnant by the spunk of a fairy I
say. From the underground. The otherworld. Then you might
think me beautiful. *(PAUSE)*   Goodnight Ace.

ACE
Goodnight Dyf.

DYFRIG
Goodnight all.

MARSHALL enters. Stares at DYFRIG

MARSHALL
It was me who killed your lambs Dyf. It was me...

DYFRIG screams and exits. The James family enter.

MARSHALL
I did it 'cos I didn't fit in. Mrs Conti said. I walked into the caff, Conti's on the square. I pushed the door open, - heard the bell ring, - saw Mrs Conti look up from behind the sweets, - saw the boys watching Paul Brown playing pinball, then watching me. With his fingers still on the flipper, the silver ball hanging in time, the machine waiting for me to say something, Paul waiting for me to say something, the boys waiting for me to say something, Mrs Conti in mid sup of her sweet waiting for me to say something... I said it. "Alright Paul Brown, how's it going like?" and I slapped him on the back. The ball flew past the flippers, Paul turns and calls me a fucking wanker. Game over. He holds me up against the wall. His face is red, "you prick" he says, "you stupid fucking prick". Then he butts me. I go down. Paul walks out, the boys follow. I see them through blurred, watery eyes. My nose bleeds. Mrs Conti comes over to me with a tissue, "here", she says, "wipe your face". I wipe my face. "I'm sorry"... I say. "But I really try Mrs Conti... I really try".
"You don't fit in boy, that's your trouble. Your words is wrong. Your language. Here, wipe your face". I wipe my face. Then I went up the mountain and killed the lambs. *(BEAT)*
Why innit? Fucking why?

GRUFF
Why?

MATI
Why?

GRUFF
When he had everything going for him. How can they call him a psychopath if he's got hobbies?

MATI
Who knows.

GRUFF
I mean HE CAN TIE FUCKING FLIES. COCHABONDEES.

MATI
Maybe we spoilt him.

GRUFF
Spoilt him? He was special mun Mati, he died, then he came back to life. He was like fucking Jesus.

MATI
Don't swear.

GRUFF
He didn't come back to life to axe Dyfrig's new born lambs to death did he? - Did he?

MATI
No.

GRUFF
So, how am I ever going to show my face in the Ship from now on?

MATI
You hate the Ship.

GRUFF
I'll have to drink in the bastard Butch now. Fucking hell, fucking, fucking hell.

He exits.

MATI
And what are you looking at? It wasn't my fault. None of it is my fault.

BRI
No.

MATI
I've loved you as much as I've loved your brother. And her.

BRI
Yeh.

MATI
Wasn't me who called him an angel. It was your father.

BRI
I know. *(BEAT)* Mam?

MATI
What?

BRI
I've bought a new car.
MATI
You stupid bugger, on whose money?

BRI
It didn't cost much. I can do it up.

MATI
But we already got a car, your father's car.

BRI
I know but I wanted a car I can call my own. I'd like us to go for a drive in it, me, you, dad, Bron, Marshall, all of us.

MATI
What for?

BRI
Because I got something I want to tell you.

MATI
Tell me now.

BRI
Now isn't the time mam. I want to tell everyone the same time. And not in this house. Somewhere else.

MATI
Like where?

BRI
Somewhere.

MATI
Somewhere?

BRI
Yeh.

MATI
I'll see what your father says. I'm off to the bingo. See you after.

MATI exits.

BRON
I'll come for a drive with you Bri.

BEAT.

BRI
Why not?

BRI dishevelled and waisted, and BRON, sit in the car at an airport. Music plays.

BRON
Who's this?

BRI
Marc Bolan.

BRON
Who's he?

BRI
T. Rex... Metal Guru... seventies band, he died.

BRON
Oh.

BRI
Smashed into a tree in Putney he did... in his mini. They have vigils there on his anniversary. Like light candles and sing songs. Wonder if people will do that for me?

BRON
Why should they. You got to have done something to do that.

BRI
I know.

BRON
Like be in a band or something.

BRI
I suppose. *(BEAT)* Or disappear.

BRON
What you want to disappear for?

BRI
I don't. *(BEAT)* I just said it was an option.

BRON
Some option.

BEAT.

BRI
Come on, let's go home.

BRON
Haven't finished our cans.

BRI
We'll drink them on the way.

BRON
They'll catch you one day Bri and then you'll be fucked. No more driving.

BRI
So then fucked I'll be. Come on. Lets drive.

Lights come back up on ACE and BRON.

BRON
Two months after that they arrested him for drink-driving and he never drove that car again. Some people are born lucky, others are born to lose. That night the only thing I saw in his eyes was hate.

Lights up on a prison cell.

BRI
I'm not a sad fucking bastard. I'm not a suicide. I'm not a beam swinger. I'm not a piece of shit... I am not a piece of old rope, I aint hung, I aint fucking dead. I aint the circus, I aint the act, I aint the flying trapeze. I'm Brian Fucking James. *(BEAT)* I drive a tinted glass blue Marina 1800 TC into the heart of Saturday night you fucks.

COP
Did.

BRI
What?

COP
Did.

BRI
Uh?

COP
Drive a Marina. Blow test positive. Piss test positive, blood test positive. 3 card trick. Put an advert in the Echo, motoring. Thursdays. You're nicked. *(HE SLAMS DOOR)*

BRI sits in the cell.

BRON

And that's the last time we saw him. He walked out of the police station and disappeared into thin air. At first we thought he'd gone on walkabout and lost all track of time. I mean Bri was useless with time and he went off for a couple of weeks without telling anyone before that. Turned out he'd been to Old Trafford to watch Man. Utd. play, then the cops found him wandering around the perimeter fence of the airport and brought him home. But he was different. And Marshall was different and the house was different. Everything was different. And I was different too: two years is a long time. Some people think he's dead. *(BRI laughs)*. Some people say they've seen him. *(BRI laughs)*. Some people say he's gone with Gunn to Australia to deliver pizzas in Queensland. But nobody knows.

BRI

Nobody knows, nobody knows.

BRI exits laughing.

BRON

Dad and Marshall don't go fishing together anymore. Mam still can't work out why the world's darts don't reach the dart-board anymore, and I moved to town for my job because I didn't want people to talk anymore. *(BEAT)* Families huh?

ACE

Tell me about it. Growing up in a shrinking land next to a tantrum sea hasn't been easy. Every day I came home from school to find our house still standing was a victory. Small, but a victory is a victory.
Lights change as we go back in time to young ACE, MANNY, and MARY ANNIE at the kitchen table.

MANNY
If it carries on like this we'll lose half of Llanelli.

MARY ANNIE
Which part?

MANNY
The ugly part.

MARY ANNIE
Something good may come of it then.

ACE
Is the sea going to eat our house dad?

MANNY
One day boy, one day.

MARY ANNIE
Eat your cabbage.

ACE
On summer days when the sea was quiet I'd make up stories. Fantastic stories. Life in storyland I could control, the ongoing war against the sea and real life I couldn't.

MARY ANNIE plays a hymn on a casino.

MARY ANNIE
O pam mae dicter o Myfanwy.

MANNY
Will you stop that.

MARY ANNIE
It's Myfanwy.

MANNY
I don't care if it's Shirley bloody Bassey, it's getting on my nerves.

ACE
And besides there were the fairies to think about.

ACE
Do we go to heaven when we die Mam?

MARY ANNIE
Who knows.

ACE
Where's heaven?

MARY ANNIE
In the sky above the clouds.

ACE
And hell is under the ground?

MARY ANNIE
Perhaps.

ACE
Where the fairies live?

BEAT.

MARY ANNIE
Where they live now yes.

ACE
Is God a fairy Mam?

MARY ANNIE
No but God can be cruel.

Lights up on a graveyard where four small simple white crosses can be seen. Fairies move towards MARY ANNIE.

MARY ANNIE
He took away four little angels before you came along.

ACE
Angels?

MARY ANNIE
They would have been your brothers and sisters, but they were born with no breath. God took the breath away before they were born.

ACE
So who gave me breath mam?

MARY ANNIE
The fairies. I let them into my heart when God left me barren. You were a baby made by fairies, they came up from the underworld and put their hands on my belly. I saw them dance.

Music: we see fairies, angels and succubae dance with Mary Annie..

MARY ANNIE
Magical things can still happen in this cruel world see. You've just got to know where to look that's all.

ACE
So I believed. In stories and mysteries and magic. Stories were good. Life had the sea and the council.

The angels and succubae evaporate as MANNY enters with a letter.

MANNY
"Regrettably, I have to inform you that the demolition of your property is the only realistic solution. As I said in my letter dated March 12th, surveyors reports indicate that the cliffs fronting your property are in a dangerously unstable condition, and any anti-erosion measures taken by the council at this stage would not, and indeed could not, remedy the situation. Whilst I have every sympathy for you and your family's predicament I feel that I must endorse the decision made at council, and firmly believe we are taking the safest and most cost effective course of action. Yours sincerely, D Watkins."
Bastards.

MARY ANNIE
Revenge that's what it is.

MANNY
For what we haven't got no quarrel with the Council.

MARY ANNIE
I'm not talking about the Council... I'm talking about them.

MANNY
Who?

MARY ANNIE
Them... Them under the ground, under the sea, under our feet, digging away, having parties, wanting revenge.

ACE
Who mam?

MARY ANNIE
The bloody fairies, the tylwyth teg. Your father dug up the field where they dance, now they won't come out.

MANNY
Don't be so soft woman.

MARY ANNIE
I'm not being soft, it's not the council we got be afraid of, it's them. The Council can't do anything because it's our land, but as for the fairies... and the sea... that's a different matter.

MANNY
There are no fairies mun.

MARY ANNIE
I've seen them with my own eyes, my mother's seen them and her mother before that, they used our field, they danced on it till your father ploughed it all up, but they won't dance again til they've had their revenge on us. It's not the council we got to be afraid of, it's the fairies. They're in cahoots with the sea. *(BEAT)* I'm going to bed to wait and I'm not getting up til the fairies have had our house.

She exits.

MANNY
We got to keep an eye on her.

ACE
I know.

MANNY
In the meantime we write back to the Council telling them to bugger off and we're not moving nowhere. If they want to try and get us out they'll have to burn us out. From now on we're on a 24 hour vigil.

ACE
Vigil?

MANNY grabs a gun.

MANNY
Vigil. Anyone you see walking the hills in a suit and tie you tell me about. Capiche?

ACE
Not all the Council wear ties mun dad.

MANNY
Capiche?

ACE
Capiche Dad, Capiche.

MANNY exits.

ACE
But it didn't work. By August the ninth last year our house, that was once a farm in the country became a farm on the brink of falling in the sea. I remember the date clearly because it was the night I first saw her. I lit a spliff and watched her walk on the beach towards the Axeman-of-Smalltown; Marshall James.

MARSHALL sits with fishing rod. BRON enters with yo-yo. ACE watches.

BRON
Caught anything?

MARSHALL
Only crabs, why?

BRON
Funny.

MARSHALL
Is it?

BRON
Yeh, because you haven't thrown your line in.

MARSHALL
So?

BRON
How can you catch any fish if you don't throw your line in?

MARSHALL
Because I'm not fucking interested that's why.

BRON
So why do you do it?

MARSHALL
Because it gives me time to think, and it gets me out of that fucking house.

BRON
Maybe you should move away.

MARSHALL
To where?

BRON
Anywhere. Make a fresh start.

MARSHALL
What's the point?

BRON
What's the point staying here? *(BEAT)* Everybody thinking you're a psycho.

MARSHALL
I'm not a fucking psycho.

BRON
I don't think the lambs will agree with you.

MARSHALL
I NEVER FUCKING DID IT ALRIGHT.

BRON
So why did you confess? Blame it on Paul Brown if you never did it? Marsh?

MARSHALL
I can't.

BRON
Answer me!

MARSHALL
I CAN'T RIGHT, I FUCKING CAN'T. If you want to know the answer you'll have to ask Bri.

BRON
Bri's gone, Marsh...

MARSHALL
Not for good.

BRON
Two years is a long time.

MARSHALL
I know it's a long time, but he'll be back, he hasn't gone forever, I
know he'll be back, he's got to come back Bron, for my sake... he's
got to tell them the truth.

BRON
Tell who the truth Marsh?

MARSHALL
Everyone... he owes me, he fucking owes me Bron. I never did it.
Everything I did I did because I fucking loved him. He pulled me
out of the river, he kissed life back into my lungs, he's my brother,
my blood brother. I've got his blood in me and he's got my blood
in him. I only ever said I did it to win him back. He knows that.
SO WHY THE FUCK DID HE GO AWAY. WHY THE FUCK
DID THE BASTARD HAVE TO GO AWAY?

MARSHALL exits. Bron looks up and sees Ace.

ACE
Then she saw me. She was beautiful. An apparition. An angel. I
couldn't take my eyes off her. I always wanted to believe in the
underworld but I could never find the key, the door in the rock
that would lead me to it. But there it was in front of me all along.
It was just that I couldn't see it before. Maybe that night would be
the night that the underworld comes out into the real world and

invites it to dance.

Fade up music as a whole range of angels, demons and succubae enter the stage. ACE joins a wild masque of the underworld which builds to a climax and slowly the stage clears leaving an exhausted ACE.

ACE
Or maybe I was just stoned. *(BEAT)* I went home and watched the ants I had killed with Floret three days earlier decompose on the window sill; only bits of silvery wings remained, filtery, nearly see-through. I lit a spliff and went outside. It was hot. I sat in the water trough looking up at the sky. I'd seen what I think is an angel argue with her brother about things I couldn't hear, and I danced with the hobgoblins of fairyland *(BEAT)*. Six months later our house fell into the sea, simple as that.

BRI emerges pointing at him.

BRI
LIAR, LIAR, THROW HIM IN THE FIRE.

MARY ANNIE enters as BRI circles the stage.

MARY ANNIE
Manny? Ace? Manny? Nothing. Blackness. On my own. Wiff on her own with a bad fairy. I know you're here. You made me cry. Real tears not tiny tears. I was a summer baby with a summer memory but not anymore. You made me sad - be off with you. You hear me? Be off. Be off... *(BEAT)* I've never been afraid of the night me. I've sat in the bushes listening to good fairies in the dark, dancing. Good fairies and angels. I've given them my teeth. I've seen doors in rocks that lead to the otherworld. In the dark. On my bike. *(BEAT)* Gurruga... gurruga... gurruga... no bell, no lights... *(BEAT)* Can't see. But I'm frightened tonight... *(BEAT)* The wind, and the rain and the sea. (BEAT) Manny...! MANNY!

Lights up on MANNY soaking wet. Sound of rain and thunder increases.

MANNY
It's coming Wiff.

MARY ANNIE
I know.

MANNY
I knew it would come at night.

MARY ANNIE
But we haven't packed.

MANNY
There's no time to pack, where's Ace?

MARY ANNIE
In bed.

MANNY
Get him woken up and take what you can outside into the trailer.

MARY ANNIE
But...

MANNY
JUST DO IT MARY ANNIE.

MARY ANNIE
Mary Annie, Mary Annie, Mary Annie.

She exits. ACE enters.

ACE
It's come then.

MANNY
It's come. We were born in a shrinking land n̲
so go and get your mother and put her in the trailer.

ACE
What about you?

MANNY
I'll make sure everything's alright here then I'll be with you.

ACE
Right.

MANNY
And hurry.

ACE
I'm hurrying, I'm hurrying.

ACE exits. Clap of thunder as the storm increases.

MANNY
I knew you'd come at night. Black sea. Wild horses, wind, rain.
What made you angry? Not me. Not us. I always respected you.
Me and you were like that once. Then you had tantrums, Wiff was
right when she said the sea's gone mad, but why take it out on us?
We never walked on you, we always respected you, we've watched
you raging against the rocks, we've seen you shipwreck boats, but
we put it down to a tantrum: bear with a sore head. We knew you
were moody, but we respected your moods, we accommodated
them, we put up with them, we lived side by side with them.
Wasn't us who put oil in you, or gassed you, or fished you nearly

...less. We've pissed in you but we never shit in you. I've smoked on your back but I never threw my filters in there. Tipped ash, yes, but not butts. No filters and definitely no cigars. *(BEAT)* We never threw rubbish in as a family. Fertilized the land, that's all I did. They told me to do it. There's some chemicals to make the grass grow greener, never said it was full of shit. You've got no right to pick on me. On us. We're innocent. *(BEAT)* We were like that once. But not no more we're not. You're on the warpath. You want to take over the world. You'll only be happy when fish are drinking in here and seals clapping in here. When fucking dogfish and crabs are the dancing girls in here. *(BEAT)* But I'll still be here too. In the locker next to Davy, growing gills, growing fins, drinking and talking through bubbles. Remembering. *(BEAT)* the remembering fish, that's what they'll call me.

ACE
(O.O.V.) Dad... DAD... HURRY... HURRY.

MANNY
I'm coming... I'm coming. *(BEAT)* So rip down our house sea... do your worst. *(BEAT)* Because you'll never beat me. *(BEAT)* We'll still be here. *(BEAT)* I'll still be here. *(BEAT)* I WILL STILL BE HERE!!!

MANNY stands defiant in the rising maelstrom as it increases in ferocity. We reach blackout before the storm noise subsides.

END OF PART ONE

Gruff - Russ Gomer
Marshall - Roger Evans

GAS STATION ANGEL

PART TWO

Lights up as ACE walks on followed by MANNY.

MANNY
Marina?

ACE
A tinted glass, blue Marina, 1800 TC dad.

MANNY
And?

ACE
She said the car belonged to her brother.

MANNY
Who's her brother?

ACE
Brian. Brian James. He disappeared into thin air two years ago.

BRI enters as ACE & MANNY exit.

BRI
I went to the city where I knew no-one and no-one knew me. I changed my name. I called myself Paul Brown. What I did there nobody will ever find out. I could have been a good Angel but bad is better. My mother thinks...

Lights up on MATI and GRUFF.

MATI
He's dead Gruff.

GRUFF
Course he's not dead. What's he want to die for?

MATI
Because you never loved him.

GRUFF
Don't talk crap.

MATI
I've always loved him. After all, he's my son, just like Marshall is.

GRUFF
I don't want to talk about Marshall.

MATI
But you loved him Gruff. You loved him more than anything else in your heart. Until he shamed you. *(BEAT)* In front of all the town. That's why you drink in the Ship and Pilot.

GRUFF
I don't drink in the Ship and Pilot no more.

MATI
Exactly because you don't like the junkies coming up to you and saying hey Gruff, tell us why the angel with the jaffa cakes axed new born lambs to death on the mountains.

GRUFF
He's never an angel.

MATI
I know but that's what you called him, you called him an angel in front of Bri, you taught him to fish, you taught him how to tie flies, purple demons, cochabondees, but you never took Bri. Bri

was a fat lazy bastard who couldn't do anything to please you.

GRUFF
That's not true Mati.

MATI
It is true Gruff, he only did up that car for you and him to go for a ride in. An 1800 TC blue Marina. He only put tinted glass in it so you could go for a drive. Just you and him in the car. Talking chokes, talking fanbelts, talking father and son talk in private, behind tinted glass, away from the eyes of the town.

Mati sees Bri, walks toward him, but her hands go straight through him.

MATI
He wanted to win you back and when he'd won you back he could win his brother Marshall back, turn back the clock to how it used to be before Marshall fell in that river. A family again. Turned back the time. But you never let him, Bri was always second best, it would have been all right if he wanted me, but he knew he already had me. He wanted you and you turned away from him, and you didn't care. You didn't fucking care.

GRUFF
Shut up Mati.... SHUT UP.

MATI
Brian's dead, Gruff. You killed something in him. And he's never coming back. *(BEAT)* And now you've lost your angel too. Instead of an angel, you just got a lost boy waiting for his brother to come back. That's why he goes to the airport. But he won't be back. That son's lost for good.

MATI walks away as the lights change and come up on...

MARSHALL, sitting with his fishing rod staring at the sea.

GRUFF approaches.

GRUFF
Caught anything?

MARSHALL
No.

GRUFF
I pished on my hand.

MARSHALL
Oh.

GRUFF
It's them button up flies, don't know why your mam buys them for me. Too trendy for me. I'm a zip man. I like a zip. Always have, always will *(BEAT)* We haven't been fishing together for a long time.

MARSHALL
No.

GRUFF
We'll have to do it again.

MARHSALL
Maybe.

BEAT.

GRUFF
Where you been? *(BEAT)* Marshall?

MARSHALL
Bonin said he saw Bri at a football match. On the TV. He said he was a face in the crowd.

GRUFF
Where?

MARSHALL
Chelsea versus Arsenal in the cup.

GRUFF
Is that where you been... London?

MARSHALL
No.

GRUFF
Oh.

MARSHALL
There's no point.

GRUFF
Why not?

MARSHALL
Because Bri supported Manchester United dad. He fucking hated Arsenal.

GRUFF
Don't we all. *(BEAT)* So where you been?

MARSHALL
To the airport.

GRUFF
Heathrow?

MARSHALL
Rhoose. He liked to watch the planes take off and land.

GRUFF
And take down the numbers?

MARSHALL
No... just watch them take off and land.

GRUFF
He's a funny bugger your brother.

MARSHALL
He used to spend hours there, time would stand still for him there.

GRUFF
He's always been terrible with time. *(BEAT)* What I mean is... if time ran by his clock, trains and planes and buses would crash... everywhere.

MARSHALL
Uh?

GRUFF
Him and time. He's a law to his own.

MARSHALL
Yeh.

GRUFF
Trains and planes would crash. Because of the time zones. Everybody'd be too scared to take off.

MARSHALL
I don't follow dad.

GRUFF
Well, planes would take off on one side of the world at the same time as another eighty would take off somewhere else in the world.

MARSHALL
So?

GRUFF
So if they were running on Bri's time, and his time's all over the place, all the time zones would be all over the place too. They'd all meet in the middle and crash, none of them knowing what time it was when it happened.

MARSHALL
Because they were on Bri's time?

GRUFF
Exactly, so Pakistan would be phoning up Australia at the same time that the Poles were phoning up the Argentine asking...

MARSHALL
What happened to our planes!

GRUFF
All at the same time, but nobody would know what time it was because all the clocks would be on Bri's time so the only way they could sort it out would be...

MARSHALL
TO PHONE BRI!

GRUFF
Exactly.

MARSHALL
But he'd be out.

GRUFF
Yeh.

MARSHALL
On the razz.

GRUFF
On the town.

MARSHALL
On the nest.

GRUFF
And all the while the world would be phoning him to ask him the time.

MARSHALL
In his room. Man. Utd. clock by his bed ticking away on its own.

GRUFF
On Bri time.

MARSHALL
Bri time.

GRUFF
Not any fucking time but...

MARSHALL
Bri time.

GRUFF
Phones ringing every second, the world calling.

MARSHALL
All the dead people.

GRUFF
All the living people wanting news.

MARSHALL
But my brother is out.

GRUFF
Out.

MARSHALL
OUT.

GRUFF
The bastard.

MARSHALL
He should be ashamed of himself. He should be BASTARD
ASHAMED.

GRUFF
Yes.

MARSHALL
The least he could do was buy himself a FUCKING
ANSAMACHINE.

GRUFF
Exactly. WHAT A STUPID TWAT MY SON IS. ALL THIS PAIN BECAUSE OF HIM.

MARSHALL
Pain. Doesn't he know that people still fucking care for him.

GRUFF
That his father...

MARSHALL
And his brother still...

BOTH
FUCKING LOVE HIM!

GRUFF
So why did he fuck off? Why doesn't he keep in touch?

MARSHALL
All he's got to do is to PICK UP THE FUCKING PHONE.

GRUFF
OR WRITE A LETTER.

MARSHALL
To show that he's alive, but has he?

GRUFF
No. Because he's a FAT LAZY BASTARD AND I LOVE HIM.

MARSHALL
He pulled me out of the river. HE KISSED AIR INTO MY LUNGS.

GRUFF
So after two years of nothing, why the FUCK DOESN'T HE
RING OR PHONE OR TELL US HE'S ALIVE?

MARSHALL
THE BASTARD.

GRUFF
THE TWAT.

MARSHALL
I FUCKING HATE HIM.

GRUFF
I FUCKING HATE HIM.

Light goes up on BRON and MATI.

BRON
I FUCKING HATE HIM.

MATI
I FUCKING HATE HIM.

GRUFF
THE WHOLE OF THE ARGENTINE AND POLAND AND
PAKISTAN BASTARD HATE HIM.

BEAT.

MARSHALL
So come back Bri... come back.

GRUFF
Come back.

MATI
I love you.

BRON
I love you.

MARSHALL
I love you.

They all look at Gruff.

GRUFF
I love you.

MATI and GRUFF exit.

BRI
But I never came back

MARSHALL
And I want him back Bron. To explain. *(BEAT)* It wasn't me who killed those lambs Bron, it was Bri. It was him Paul Brown hit in Mrs Conti's caff that day, not me.

BRON
Why?

MARSHALL
Because he said. He told me to. He said...

BRI
You owe me Marsh. You fucking owe me one man.

MARSHALL
But why the fuck did you do it Bri?

BRI
Why do you think?

MARSHALL
I wouldn't have asked if I'd known Bri.

BRI
Can't you work it out for yourself?

MARSHALL
They were just lambs Bri, what the fuck have you got against lambs Bri?

BRI
Because they just happened to be there, and will you quit putting Bri at the end of all your sentences?

MARSHALL
Uh...?

BRI
Do you do it to remind yourself of who I am? Do you?

MARSHALL
No.

BRI
I PULLED YOU OUT OF THAT RIVER YOU FUCK. *(BEAT)* You don't need to put Bri at the end of your sentences. I'm Bri, normal Bri. Normal Norman, the normallest one in all of the town. *(BEAT)* I'm your brother. You aren't an angel Marsh. You're just my brother. Who I pulled out of the water. *(BEAT)* You were dead. I didn't pull you out so you could grow up and ignore me man, to put Bri at the end of your sentences. If I'd known you were going to do that I'd have left you on the bank for

dead. *(BEAT)* You owe me Marsh. You fucking owe me.

MARSHALL
So I took the rap. I took the axe one night, went up the mountain 'til I came to a farm, Gaerlishe's farm, where I saw a woman feed chickens.

MARY ANNIE enters throwing seed in the air.

MARSHALL
I waited for her to go inside until it was dark and then...

PAUSE.

BRON
What Marsh?

MARSHALL
I fucking murdered them. That's where the blood came Bron, that night in the Ship and Pilot. It wasn't lambs I murdered, it was Gaerlishe's chickens. I did it for Bri, Bron; I did it for Bri.

MARSHALL exits, ACE enters and throws a handful of feathers in the air. MARY ANNIE looks at him.

ACE
Bastards.

MARY ANNIE
Use these.

ACE
Uh?

MARY ANNIE
Gloves. Plastic gloves.

ACE
I'll be alright.

MARY ANNIE
Chickens have germs Ace. Especially dead ones. Here, take the gloves.

ACE
I'll be finished in a minute.

MARY ANNIE
What you going to do with them?

ACE
Burn them. And the shed and everything in it. Couple of hours from now, you'll never be able to tell there was ever chickens here.

MARY ANNIE
I liked the chickens. They were my responsibility. Yours and mine. You grew up feeding the chickens.

ACE
Bit of burnt earth, that's all will be left. Then it will be the end of the chicken story. No-one will ever know we ever kept chickens. If anybody asks me ever again about chickens, I'll say I don't know, we never had any. The chicken story will be over.

MARY ANNIE
So what will our story be?

ACE
We'll make up a story mam. Don't worry about that, we'll always have a story.

ACE lights a Zippo. A blaze fills the stage then recedes. MARY ANNIE exits, MANNY enters.

MANNY
The bastard, the murdering little bastard and there's me thinking…

ACE
It's over dad, in the past.

MANNY
You've changed your tune.

ACE
It's called love dad.

MANNY
Love?

ACE
Love. I think I'm in love.

MANNY
Love Ace… is a mystery.

ACE
Love dad… is an angel in a blue marina with leather upholstery.

Crash in music as the set clears and we join ACE and BRON in the car. Music plays on the radio. Bron is driving

BRON
You going to keep all that to yourself or can I have some?

He passes her the joint. She smokes.

ACE
What's Bron short for?

BRON
Bronwen.

ACE
What's it mean?

BRON
Pure One. Bron means breast, Wen means white. You have to work the rest out.

ACE
Bron also means nearly. *(BEAT)* As in bron gorffen.

BRON
Nearly finished.

ACE
Yeh. You speak Welsh?

BRON
Yeh. You?

ACE
Only when I was small. *(PAUSE)* I like Welsh.

BRON
Why?

ACE
Because it's got gaps.

BRON
What kind of gaps?

ACE
Like its not all hard and fast; like there are rules but there are still gaps... like to fill in, the meaning... you got to work the meaning out for yourself... like in English you say 'The cat sat on the mat'...

BRON
Yeh...

ACE
Well in Welsh you could say the cat sat in front of the fire... you wouldn't have to mention the mat at all. What I mean is the cat could be anywhere yet at the same time you know its on the mat in front of the fire. You got me?

BRON
Think so.

ACE
Like its got gaps. You make the pictures up in the gaps.

BRON
Like Jazz.

ACE
Bingo.

BRON
I like I like gaps.

ACE
And me.

BRON
I like things I don't understand. Only things I don't understand interest me. Why celebrate what you already know Ace?

ACE
Exactly Bron.

BRON
I mean... *(SHE STOPS THE CAR)* Toys for Christmas I've already played with should be returned to the shops.

ACE
In return for a game you've never seen before but you will never understand.

BRON
Exactly.

ACE
That's called the fucking thrill of discovery Bron.

BRON
What I don't know I like.

ACE
On the button. *(BEAT)* And imagination.

BRON
Imagination. Yeh.

ACE
A fucking fantasy world.

BRON
Yeh. To be Welsh at the end of the 20th Century you got to have

imagination Ace.

ACE
Too fucking right.

BRON
I mean. The only way to shop in Spar or Tesco's or Safeways or some shit is not to see Spar or Tesco's at all but imagine something else.

ACE
Exactly.

BRON
I mean, let's face it who ever said SHOPPING WAS BEAUTIFUL?

ACE
Not me.

BRON
Or me.

Lights change to an interior supermarket. ACE and BRON stand amongst the shoppers.

BRON
I used to work here.

ACE
Fuck.

BRON
Till two weeks ago.

ACE
Shit.

BRON
I chucked in my job and you know why?

ACE
Why?

BRON
No mystery.

The trolley-boy KEITH enters and watches BRON eat her lunch.

KEITH
You can tell what kind of a person someone is by the chocolate they eat.

BRON
Is that a fact.

KEITH
People who eat Mars bars or Snickers are filling a void in their lives, but those people who eat Turkish Delight like the exotic. *(Takes a Turkish Delight from BRON and licks it delicately.)* I see that you like the exotic check-out one.

BRON
Maybe... Why?

KEITH
Because I've been thinking.

BRON
Really?

KEITH
Really. Thinking what an exotic fuck with you would be like.

BRON
Do you think that about every woman you meet Keith?

KEITH
Most women.

BRON
But not all.

KEITH
No.

BRON
What kind of women do you not think about fucking Keith?

KEITH
Old women. Ugly women. My mother. But I'd like to fuck you. With my hand covered in oil. I'd like to put my hand on that white cotton blouse of yours. Mark it. Just on the tit. Unbutton slowly, put my filthy hand on your lacy white bra. Put my thumb in your mouth. Smudge the lipstick, then kiss it off. Then fuck you. Till your body's covered in marks. My marks, my hands. Then lick you. All of you. Clean. Back to where we started. *(BEAT)* Then I could talk to you.

BRON
Because you'd fucked me.

KEITH
Yeh... Talk and talk and fuck and fuck until it was time to fuck again. Then I'd fuck you again. And again and again.

BRON
Until you couldn't fuck or talk anymore?

KEITH
Yeh. *(BEAT)*

BRON
That sounds okay Keith.

KEITH
Yeh?

BRON
Yeh. Except. We'd have nothing to say. We'd be sitting in the same room saying nothing. We'd eat and say nothing. So we'd have to go out, to a bar, to get drunk, stare at the optics. We'd drink till we couldn't drink no more. We'd have fucked and fucked and talked and talked and drunk and drunk till we couldn't talk, drink or fuck anymore.

KEITH
Uh?

BRON
Then we'd go home Keith, and there you'd be. Fat and old. Unfuckable. With the TV on. A game-show. Holding a lottery ticket in your hand and your fingers crossed. You with your hopes pinned on a 64 million to one chance. And you'd have fuck all to say Keith. You'd have frozen in time since the last time we talked. After we fucked. You'd fucked and talked yourself into frozen time. While time all around you was moving on. Then I'd look in the mirror and I'd be as old and ugly as you. Where did it fucking go? All them fucking years. *(BEAT)* I'd listen to my body decay. I wouldn't be able to move my arms or legs or head. I would only

be able to feel my head. It would be heavy, full of all the things I dreamt about and never did. I'd feel ashamed. My face would feel as if I'd been skinned. And then I'd scream. I'd scream and scream until I couldn't scream anymore. Then I'd stare up at the moon...I'd stare and stare until Night turned into Day... Blue to Orange... Dark to Light, knowing that I'd missed the plot, the dream, the crack, the mystery. I would never wake up - and open my eyes - and see something I don't understand, a mystery I've never imagined. And I want to Keith.

KEITH
You're fucking weird check-out one.

BRON
I know. You want to fuck? Fuck the job and fuck you Keith. I got a life to live.

She pushes his trolley away as she turns to ACE.

BRON
I reckon there's a mystery, Ace, do you?

ACE
I know there is Bron.

They kiss.

ACE
And so we loaded up the car with booze and fags. We bought a tape and all the while I kept thinking, who are we anyway? Who can we ever be except...

Lights up on MANNY and MARY ANNIE standing with suitcases in their Sunday best.

MANNY
The sons and daughters of our mothers and fathers.

ACE
Exactly.

MANNY
This is our land, it grows grass, it grazes sheep.

MARY ANNIE
Do we own grass that grazes sheep?

MANNY
We used to.

MARY ANNIE
But not anymore?

MANNY
No.

MARY ANNIE
The sheep went away.

MANNY
Yes.

MARY ANNIE
Our fences go unmended.

MANNY
Yes.

MARY ANNIE
Fence-posts sit in our garden rotting.

MANNY
We never had a garden.

MARY ANNIE
Not ever?

MANNY
No.

MARY ANNIE
No border of daffodils, or pansies, or tulip, or rose?

MANNY
No.

MARY ANNIE
No garden of root vegetables or leeks?

MANNY
No.

MARY ANNIE
Cabbage?

MANNY
No.

MARY ANNIE
Peas, sprouts, kidney beans?

MANNY
None.

MARY ANNIE
Did we keep goats?

MANNY
No goats... as such. Chickens we kept.

MARY ANNIE
They were my responsibility.

MANNY
You and the boy.

MARY ANNIE
Our boy, our boy... our baby.

MANNY
Of course our baby. Would we ever dream of asking someone else's baby to tend to our chickens?

MARY ANNIE
Not ideally, no.

MANNY
Exactly. This house has been babied. Gurgles and giggles have been heard here, nappies soiled, back patted and mouth fed. Clothes have been knitted, our baby has been gloved, hatted, even balaclavad, little shoes have gathered dust in our shed.

MARY ANNIE
Little shoes?

MANNY
Grown out of as he turns into a child. Old shoes discarded in favour of wellingtons and boots.

MARY ANNIE
We should have given them away.

MANNY
Some we did. Others no doubt you forgot about.

MARY ANNIE
Forgot.

MANNY
Some things we remember about, others we forget.

MARY ANNIE
Forget.

MANNY
Not all things can be remembered Wiff, only seated memories are kept in the strongboxes of our mind.

MARY ANNIE
Funny.

MANNY
It is.

MARY ANNIE
Makes you wonder.

MANNY
It does.

MARY ANNIE
How we can keep an orderly head as we travel to nowhere.

MANNY
Nowhere.

MARY ANNIE
Place we don't know.

MANNY
Exactly.

MARY ANNIE
You and me.

MANNY
Mary Annie, Manny.

MARY ANNIE
Their house fell into the sea.

MANNY
That's why our Ace will have to fly the nest.

MARY ANNIE
To stay away from the cliffs. STAY AWAY FROM THE CLIFFS
WE'LL SHOUT TO HIM.

MANNY
And off he'll go.

MARY ANNIE
Off.

MANNY
He'll have to go.

MARY ANNIE
Mm.

MANNY
Not stay here.

MARY ANNIE
Not after what's happened.

MANNY
No.

MARY ANNIE
That's why we'll have to make up with the sea.

MANNY
Yes.

MARY ANNIE
Make up and be friends. Mop up the carpets.

MANNY
Re-build the house.

MARY ANNIE
And start again.

MANNY
Cleaned.

MARY ANNIE
We'll call back our sheep.

MANNY
And our chickens.

MARY ANNIE
And our Ace.

MANNY
Grown Ace.

MARY ANNIE
He'll cross bridges to find us.

MANNY
He will.

MARY ANNIE
We'll have to cook a bird.

MANNY
We will.

MARY ANNIE
In a pot, a big bird.

MANNY
Sit around a table.

MARY ANNIE
And talk.

MANNY
We'll have to remember to talk.

MARY ANNIE
We will.

MANNY
Remember what we talked about now.

MARY ANNIE
Now.

MANNY
Start again.

MARY ANNIE
Mm.

MARY ANNIE
Buy what we need and...

MANNY
Need what we buy.

MARY ANNIE
Exactly.

MANNY
No more. Build 'em high, sell 'em cheap.

MARY ANNIE
None.

MANNY
No more gadgets with no instructions.

MARY ANNIE
Nothing but a bed.

MANNY
A good bed.

MARY ANNIE
So that we can lie back and look at the moon.

MANNY
The half moon.

MARY ANNIE
The half lit moon. The moon that don't snore, don't burp and takes your drawers down gently. A moon with long fingers, warm fingers and clean nails.

Fairies and angels enter and create a giant bed.

MARY ANNIE
A moon you can hide under the bedclothes and watch it rise in the night. It hasn't risen yet Manny... I'm watching.

MANNY
I'm too old Wiff.

MARY ANNIE
Night time is the right time.

MANNY
I'm sixty six.

MARY ANNIE
Only one short of the devil.

MANNY
My arteries have hardened.

MARY ANNIE
Drink more whisky.

MANNY
My bones are brittle.

MARY ANNIE
Thins the blood.

MANNY
My skin is sagging.

MARY ANNIE
Fire in your belly.

MANNY
I'm shrinking.

MARY ANNIE
I know.

MANNY
I swear I've lost two inches.

MARY ANNIE
What!

MANNY
Every year I roll up my trousers, haven't you noticed?

MARY ANNIE
Size isn't everything Manny.

MANNY
No Wiff.

MARY ANNIE
No.

MANNY
Turn off the lights then and let me put your moon on my chest.

MARY ANNIE
Why not.

They kiss then snuggle under the bedclothes. They make love. Lights change. ACE and BRON sit looking down from a mountain in the car.

ACE

And I smiled and watched her drive. I didn't care where. We had the booze, we had the fags, we had the draw and I'd found a babe. We were stoned and beautiful taking time out in the country, innocent and free. And as we drove further and further and higher and higher into the night I swear I saw most of Wales spread out in front of me. Like a carpet on an uneven floor. Not even a floor just an idea of a floor. And the carpet? It wasn't fucking Axminster that's for sure, but who needed Axminster when I had all this. I could see for miles. Into England, Devon, Cornwall and beyond Cornwall, France, then Spain and right at the bottom at the far end of the horizon, I swear I can see the lights of North Africa. All of Europe spread out in front of me, of us. I turned to Bron, only a silhouette behind the wheel, only the embers of the joint showing me she was still there.

BRON

I'm still here Ace.

ACE

I never thought I'd ever see this far Bron. Maybe I'm imagining it, my head playing tricks.

BRON

If you can see it Ace, it's there. Who gives a fuck.

ACE

And she was right. As I sat in the car that night looking out from the back of beyond to the shores of North Africa, I felt in my bones that things were going to change. Maybe I can soon call myself an European. With my own language and the rudiments of another on the tip of my tongue, German, French, Spanish, Portuguese, Russian, Czech, even English. Will speaking a new language break the chains of a fucked up head? Will I be able to be who I want to be then put who I want to be back in the fucked up bit so its not fucked up no more? I hope so. *(BEAT)* But I ain't the only fucked up bastard out there. Everybody's got fucked up bits. A design flaw that only some can ever straighten out, phobias, fantasies, desires, things they don't even know they got locked up in the strongboxes of their brains. It ain't just me. I know it ain't just me. So many secrets and so little time. It ain't only me, it ain't only me. *(BEAT)* And then she said... right out of the blue...

BRON
Do you think my brother's dead?

ACE
And I said. I don't know, who's your brother?

Lights up on BRI.

BRI
August the eighth. Summer. Six months ago. I hitched back to that seaside town I used to call home. I checked into a motel in the services on the outskirts of town, the Gas Station Motel, I look in the mirror but it isn't me I see staring back at me. It's him.

GRUFF enters.

GRUFF
We all know what happened. Don't tell lies Bri. Lying will get you nowhere in this world.

BRI
Every lamb's neck I snapped was yours. I did it for you dad I did it for you... I smash a mirror. I check out. I walk along a beach until

I come to a farm. Gaerlishe. The farm where Marshall killed the chickens. For me. For Bri. The normallest one in the whole of town. I waited for dark and then...

He exits as does GRUFF. MANNY enters.

ACE
And then she told me her story. But her story reminded me of our story dad.

MANNY
We don't talk about that story anymore Ace. That story is locked up in the strongbox of our minds.

ACE
I know that but... he had a tattoo.

MANNY
That story is our secret Ace. It's family. It's a family secret.

ACE
On his arm dad, of Manchester United....

MANNY
WILL YOU SHUT UP ABOUT OUR FUCKING STORY!

Bri laughs.

BRI
Boom... boom. Fairy... Fairy... Dead... Dead.

MARY ANNIE
He's still here. I can hear him. He's still here.

She looks at him then exits. The sound of aircraft coming in to land fills the whole arena. BRON and ACE sit at the perimeter fence watching the landing plane. The noise subsides. They drink and smoke spliffs. BRI stands amongst other angels watching the action.

BRON
That's a seven four seven.

ACE
Yeh?

BRON
Cruising speed of 515 miles per hour at an altitude of between 33,000 and 37,000 feet. *(BEAT)* My brother Bri was into planes. I came with him two days before he went missing. *(BEAT)* It's his car.

ACE
It's a nice car.

BRON
He lost his licence.

ACE
That's a drag.

BRON
My mother thinks he's dead.

ACE
What do you think?

BRON
I don't know. Sometimes I think he's alive, other times...

ACE
What?

BRON
I don't know... something... in his eyes...

ACE
Maybe the Angels got him.

BRON
Uh?

ACE
The Angels and Fairies have taken him underground.

BRON
If only.

ACE
Every now and then they come up from the other world and into this world. I've seen them Bron. I've danced with them but sometimes we do bad things.

BRON
What kind of bad things... Ace?

ACE
There are good Angels and bad Angels, good Fairies and bad Fairies. Maybe Bri was a bad Angel Bron. They took him underground to a place so beautiful that your brain explodes. You can eat, drink, fuck, do whatever but you can't take anything back with you or you'll never be able to come again. Maybe Bri tried to take something back, a memento of where he'd been, thinking they won't notice but they caught him. Now he's in limbo, wandering the Earth, trying to go back to that world Bron, trying

to find the door in the rock, the key to the door, but he won't, because he fucked it all up. He had his chance and one chance he got and he blew it.

BRON
That's heavy Ace

ACE
I suppose it is. The underground parties from now on are strictly members only.

BRON
No Brian James.

ACE
No Brian James.

BRON
Because he's a fallen Angel, a bad Fairy.

ACE
Yes Bron.

BRON
That's sad Ace.

ACE
I know *(BEAT)* And I watched her. Every minute I wanted her more and more. She was an Angel, but I knew her brother was dead. And I knew how he died. I wanted to tell her but couldn't. I tried dad but couldn't. With every passing second a voice in my head kept saying tell her...

BRI
TELL HER...

ACE & BRI
Tell her, tell her, tell her, TELL HER.

ACE
But I couldn't...

MANNY
That's a secret Ace. A family secret. We've locked it away and thrown away the key. Haven't we, Ace?... Ace?

ACE
And then she said...

BRON
I want to make love until night turns into day, Ace. Blue to orange. Dark to light. I want to open my eyes to something I will never understand, to a mystery I've never imagined.

ACE
And I said I'd love to too. And so we went. To the Gas Station Motel on the outskirts of town, where she danced for me and I danced for her

Lights change to a motel room. BRON and ACE enter; they undress and make love. Lights come up into 'dawn'. BRI enters as ACE stands at the window.

BRI
Tell her, tell her, tell her...

BRON joins ACE at the window; MANNY watches.

ACE
We saw an Angel once. Me and my Father.

BRON
When?

BRI
In the middle of the night.

ACE
I woke up. I heard someone outside.

MANNY
For Christ's sake Ace, it's a family secret.

Lights change, ACE drags a bloodied BRI into the Gaerlishe living room.

MANNY
WHAT THE HELL ARE YOU DOING?

ACE
Give me a hand dad.

MANNY
Its the middle of the night!

ACE
I got a bloke here... I heard him snooping outside. I caught him red handed. Give me a hand.

MANNY
Snooping?

ACE
Yeh. He was going towards where the chicken shed was.

He drags the body to the middle of the room.

MANNY
Have you killed him?

ACE
Course I haven't killed him, just knocked him out.

MANNY
Good boy.

ACE
Is it safe to leave him here?

MANNY
Uh?

ACE
'Til he comes round?

MANNY
Who is he?

ACE
What you think?

MANNY
Do I know him?

ACE
Maybe we should put a blanket over him.

MANNY
Uh?

ACE
'Til he comes round.

MANNY
You going to leave him there?

ACE
Where else shall I put him?

MANNY
He'll be in the way there.

ACE
That's what I was asking.

MANNY
Uh?

ACE
I just asked you if I should leave him here, I just asked dad and you didn't say nothing.

MANNY
You can't leave him there.

ACE
That's what I was saying.

MANNY
You go to move him from there or he'll cause an accident. Put him in the shed.

ACE
No, he'll snoop around. I got everything all in order in my shed... all broken down into compartments, diaries labelled so that I can get to things without having to pull all the drawers and stuff out.

MANNY
So where are you going to put him?

ACE starts to drag the body into the corner.

ACE
Over here. Capiche?

MANNY
Capiche. He's better there, better there than where he was, he could have caused an accident, he's safe over there, out of harm's way.

ACE
Prowling he was see. Snooping about.

MANNY
You said.

ACE
I had to hit him.

MANNY
Mm.

ACE
Didn't mean to hurt him, not permanent, just like knock him out , teach him a lesson. He could be from the council.

MANNY
He hasn't got a tie on.

ACE
Uh?

MANNY
No tie, no suit, can't be from the council, all the council wear suits on official business, like council business, I seen them.

ACE
Well they don't all wear ties these days.

MANNY
Uh?

ACE
I seen them walking round, the hoi polloi without ties or suits.

MANNY
Where?

ACE
In the village, walking about.

MANNY
Are you sure they're on the council?

ACE
Positive, whatsisname Watkins, he's the bugger who said our house is unstable. He never wore a tie.

MANNY
The bastard.

The body makes a noise. ACE knocks him unconscious again.

MANNY
What you do that for?

ACE
I don't know.

MANNY
He was coming round.

ACE
I know… but…

MANNY
You should have let him come round.

ACE
I wasn't ready dad.

MANNY
Uh?

ACE
We haven't worked out what we're going to do with him yet.

MANNY
What's to work out?

ACE
We can't just leave him go.

MANNY
Why not can't we.

ACE
Because he'll go to the police.

MANNY
So?

ACE
He'll tell them we hit him, then we'll have the council and the police on us.

MANNY
But he was stealing our chickens.

ACE
We haven't got no chickens.

MANNY
I know, but he don't know that and you said you saw him going towards the chicken shed.

ACE
He was.

MANNY
To steal chickens.

ACE
We haven't got none dad, they're all dead.

MANNY
So what you want to hit him for?

ACE
Because I thought he was from the council, I thought he'd come to knock down our house.

MANNY
But he hasn't got a tie!

ACE
Not all the COUNCILLORS WEAR TIES DAD.

MANNY
So why did you hit him Ace?

ACE
I don't know I said.

MANNY
WHY DID YOU HIT HIM ACE?

ACE
I DON'T FUCKING KNOW ALRIGHT. I SAW HIM OUT THERE PROWLING AROUND, I PICKED UP THE FENCE POST AND HIT HIM. *(BEAT)* That's all there is to it. I saw him going towards the chicken shed. I knew it wasn't there anymore, but he didn't. Shifty he was. Look at his face. Don't he look shifty to you?

MANNY
He's out cold.

ACE
Yeh, but shifty and out cold. That's why I hit him.

MANNY
With a fence post.

ACE
Yeh.

MANNY
The ones you were going to build a fence with?

ACE
Yes.

MANNY
The ones that have been sitting out there since they came.

ACE
Two hands I got dad.

MANNY
Two winters they been out there.

ACE
My responsibility was to the chickens, anyway you were going to help me.

MANNY
I'm too old Ace.

ACE
I can't do everything dad.

MANNY
Too old and fucked.

ACE
You're not fucked.

MANNY
I am.

ACE
You're not... I NEEDED A HELPING HAND DAD.

The body moves. ACE moves to hit him. MANNY holds him back.

MANNY
No... don't.

ACE
But...

MANNY
No let him come round. Then we'll decide what to do with him.

They watch the body get to his knees. It is BRI. His face is bloodied, unshaven, confused, bedraggled: as if he's slept under the stairs for months. He looks at them then laughs demonically.

MANNY
Who are you?

BRI laughs louder, then suddenly a shot rings out from a double-barrelled shotgun held by MARY ANNIE. BRI is shot dead. But he doesn't fall, only takes off his shirt which becomes his body. BRON enters.

MARY ANNIE
He's from the otherworld. He's come to take our house. *(BEAT)* I seen him watching us. Talking fairy talk. To himself. Gibberish. Talking bad fairy talk. Nonsense. Shouting in the top field. It's where the fairies used to dance until you ploughed the field Manny. I told you they'd be angry. They put a spell on this house because they couldn't come out and dance no more. Spiteful I call it. They won't be satisfied 'til the house falls into the sea. And us with it. We'll be down there with Seithennin the drunk and Davy Jones in Cantre'r Gwaelod. *(BEAT)* I warned you Mansell. Don't go ploughing the field but you wouldn't have it. I seen them dancing there. I'm not afraid of them. He's a bad fairy. from the underworld...telling us to get out. But we're not getting out. We're staying. WE WILL STILL BE HERE! *(BEAT)* Gurruga... gurruga... gurruga... No bell... no lights... can't see... *(BEAT)*

She looks at them.

MARY ANNIE
Well, goodnight.

MARY ANNIE exits. BRON stands looking at ACE.

ACE
And then we buried him. In the black earth next to the chickens. Hoping the Angels would come, or the fairies, to take him away... *(BEAT)* It was Bri, Bron. It was Bri. *(BEAT)* I'm sorry...

BRON
So am I.

ACE
And then she drove away.

BRON exits.

MANNY
I thought we agreed Ace. To lock the door and throw away the key. We said we'd never look in there again.

ACE
I know.

MANNY
We promised ourselves for Mam's sake. And now you've gone and told the whole story. Now she'll go to the police.

ACE
No Dad.

MANNY
Why not.

ACE
Because she's an Angel.

Lights up on MATI and BRON.

BRON
Brian's dead Mam.

MATI
I know.

BRON
An Angel told me.

MATI
There's nice. What did it look like?

BRON
Like a man. In jeans and a leather jacket.

MATI
No wings then?

BRON
No.

MATI
No halo?

BRON
No.

MATI
No Wand?

BRON
No.

MATI
Just a man.

BRON
Yes.

An angel enters.

MATI
The Angel who told me had a grey suit.Made me feel better. It's the not knowing is the thing, see. Now all we got to do is wait for them to tell Marshall and your Father.

BRON
Yeh.

MATI
They've gone fishing.

BRON
Good. *(BEAT)*... Mam.

MARSHALL and GRUFF enter.

MATI
Mmmh?

BRON
I loved Brian.

MATI
And me.

MARY ANNIE and BRI enter. He looks at the other characters before putting on the shirt he dropped earlier. He knows he must die. He lies down, dies exhaling a breath.

MARY ANNIE
He's gone.

ACE
I know Mam.

MARY ANNIE
The bugger.

The stage clears leaving BRON and ACE. Fade in the sound of the sea. They stand looking at each other. Fade to black.

THE END

Ace - Richard Lynch

Gas Station Angel - 1998

FANTASTIC FICTIONS: WALES AND WELSH MEN IN THE PLAYS OF ED THOMAS

Jeni Williams

I, as much as any other person, am searching for a path, for meaning. My job as fiction-maker is to make up fiction because good fictions tell good truths. [1]

The fantastic can be seen as an art of estrangement, resisting closure, opening structures which categorise experience in the name of a 'human reality.'[2]

Two talking heads, talking bullshit in limbo [3]

In 1994 Ed Thomas collaborated with the artist Iwan Bala to create a forty-five minute installation piece, *Hiraeth/Strangers in Conversation*, in which the disembodied heads of two actors, their eyes blanked out and their faces and hair encrusted with what looks like plaster, appear out of nowhere and start to speak. There is neither action nor a recognisable plot, just 'two talking heads, talking bullshit in limbo.' The talking heads are given the names of two characters, Gwenny and Tyrone, from two of Thomas's earlier plays but they have no individual existence; their 'conversation' is interesting because of its piecemeal evocations of the earlier plays rather than because it reveals their 'humanity.' The audience is both distanced and intrigued by this strategy, seeking to trace and decode textual allusions rather than empathise with psychologically real individuals. The romance plot, that mechanism whereby the spectators are drawn to identify with the desiring characters, here appears farcical. When Tyrone attempts to seduce her - 'haven't you heard of a whirlwind romance?'[4] - Gwenny incredulously dismisses the proposition: 'Romance? In these circumstances?'.[5] Locked into conventional gender expectations he then switches to stylised accusations that she doesn't 'understand' him, while she reveals a background of madness and violation in response. Then, bizarrely, he recalls fishing a severed head that continued to talk out of the sea. This head (which is that of the mythical poet Orpheus) thus serves as a prototype for Tyrone and Gwenny. There seems to be no connection between these characters and they are only able to come to an understanding when, talking about the food and drink each yearns for from earlier, freer times, they agree on the 'heavenly' status of a safe and domestic moment: 'shortbread biscuits dunked in tea until they're soft.'[6]

Why do I start here, with this strange, generic hybrid of a piece, a fantastical sketch in which nothing happens? Thomas is hardly a traditional playwright but even for him this is an extraordinary departure from conventional theatre practice, one that violates every guideline for writing drama. Indeed, he has noted himself that he wouldn't 'be comfortable about performing it without [its] particular context'.[7] Yet, despite such reservations about its status as a free-standing work, the sketch provides a useful starting point for a consideration of Thomas's work as a whole.

Firstly, it serves as an illustration of his innovative practice and, in particular, his dismissal of the naturalistic 'well-made play' which he defines as rooted in 'certainty, built on argument, counter-argument and a message'.[8] *Hiraeth* demonstrates his preference for an art that refuses such logical progression, one that opens up debate:[9] 'I want to be taken to a landscape of imagination where I am forced to question.'[10] The 'landscape of imagination' that is *Hiraeth* demonstrates wonderfully the ways that character is created out of words inherited from the past, and how the construction of gender emerges in patterns of language and expectations rather than being intrinsic to an autonomous self. And, as a sketch, *Hiraeth* demonstrates Thomas's practice with more clarity than the developed and plotted drama. Thomas explains that he writes by starting with a landscape of alienation and blocks of dream-like, disembodied language, only later distilling this material into character and plot.[11] In *Hiraeth* the process of distillation appears deliberately suspended, the voices seemingly hanging, unfixed, in the air.

Rather than depend on conventional dramatic principles, Thomas here draws on his installation partner for alternative ways of shaping meaning. Bala's artwork places memories and images from previous work on, over and against each other to generate new pieces, producing a palimpsest which develops and highlights his recurrent themes and preoccupations. *Hiraeth* secondly, therefore, proves valuable as a palimpsest that registers Thomas's characteristic concerns. It testifies, in particular, to his fascination with storytelling, especially of forgotten or hidden stories, his interest in histories and myths of personal and cultural pasts and his perception of character as emerging out of - rather than separate from - a symbolic landscape defined by such multiple histories. Even the characteristic focus on the dysfunctional family surfaces in the transparent code of Gwenny's story of rape and mutilation. The 'stranger' who did it drives past two orphaned foals standing by a dead horse while a father and daughter, Frank and Nancy Sinatra, sing 'I love you' to each other on the car stereo.[12]

Thirdly, and finally, the sketch reveals Thomas's preoccupation with the imagination, seen as defamiliarising an audience's ordinary world in its construction of strange new alternatives. His concern with marginalised voices, especially those of Wales, is closely connected to this insistence on the transformative effects of the imagination. Thomas's theatre is political in that it aims always to elicit a response. Gwenny's words resonate throughout the drama: 'our only hope of survival is that someone out there will hear our stories and do something about it.'[13]

As a coda it is significant that the governing myth of this bizarre exploratory moment is that of Orpheus. The two stories associated with this classical myth assert the ability of art to traverse the fixed boundaries of the given world. In the first, Orpheus uses his poetry to gain admission to the underworld and, through his art, almost succeeds in summoning his beloved Eurydice back from the tomb. He fails, as he must do. She is forced to return to the grave when he confuses art for life and gazes at her directly. In the second tale, Orpheus's body is torn apart by maddened women who throw his still-singing head out to sea. In this story, the poetic voice transcends the reality principle denoted by bodily death. For any writer who writes against the tide, this is a powerful myth but it has particular resonance for a Welsh-speaking writer like Thomas who is aware of the fragility of language and seeks to create new narratives for a modern Wales.[14] In *Hiraeth*, as in the Orphic paradigm, the characters escape limbo through their voices, their survival made possible through the stories that they tell. Gwenny refuses to be a victim of her circumstances, telling Tyrone: 'At least you still have a voice. Some people I know can't talk at all. They just sit in the corner in silence. And there's nothing worse than silence when you've got something to say.'[15]

Fantastical fictions: estranging and renewing Wales

My country aint in my head Carlyle! My country is real ... I've been there ... I've been on fishing expeditions with the finest men and women you could meet in your life, film and television executives.... I SAW FISH. I SAW FISH IN THE WATER. I FUCKING SAW FISH IN THE

WATER (pp.48-49)

Although *Hiraeth* provides a good introduction to Thomas's practice and general preoccupations, his specific interest in matters Welsh is more evident in the longer plays. While he is happy to define himself as 'a Welsh writer... one who writes about his own square mile',[16] he avoids the constricting binaries of black and white, of Welsh and English, oppositions.[17] He is careful to qualify his definition by drawing on current debates and insisting on the necessity of seeing Wales as an 'imagined nation'[18] that must be ceaselessly re-imagined in its complex actuality. In *Song From A Forgotten City*, only television executives and marketing operators confuse the simplifications of outmoded stereotypes for the real thing. This section's epigraph, depicting the horrified reaction of Jackson, the media promoter in *Song From a Forgotten City*, to the suggestion that 'the only country you've got is the country in your head' demonstrates that Thomas plays dramatically with such confusion - but the drama as a whole also shows how such clichés infect and paralyse the imagination. Chasing low-grade thrillers and nostalgia coded as social realism, Jackson prefers stereotypes to a complex reality and won't even consider commissioning what he calls 'heavy art shit': 'I want bums on seats and eyes on stalks' (p.45). And, of course, the figure of Jackson speaks from within Carlyle, the writer's, head to demonstrate the internalisation of these values.

Selecting three pervasive stereotypes of the Welsh, Thomas highlights their temporal construction, pointing out that 'in the Wales of the future the coal mines will have disappeared, our ability to compete internationally on the Rugby field may or may not exist,[19] (and) the Eisteddfod may or may not exist.' The first and most powerful of these stereotypes is significantly associated not just with the Welsh Tourist Board but with the fledgling tradition of Welsh writing in English, affecting therefore not only the marketing of Wales but the imaginative choices of its writers. Jane Aaron usefully summarises the 'traditional view of what Welsh fiction had to offer'[20] in the introduction to her collection of Welsh women's short stories:

> during the 1920s and 1930s, the English-speaking voice of Wales became identified with that of the worker in the coal mines and the iron and steel industries of south Wales. Welsh novelists and short story writers characteristically wrote of and for the human communities from which they sprung, expressing and identifying with the struggles of the working class during years of economic depression and industrial strife.

Aaron goes on to point out that this tradition is strongly gendered: women were marginalised within the labour movement in ways that 'made it difficult for them to imagine themselves as suitable spokespersons for their communities.'[22]

Thomas is not alone among Welsh writers from post-industrial communities in seeking to explode stereotypes and re-imagine Wales from a perspective that focuses on the excluded - those who have lost a sense of their own agency through history - in ways that often emphasises elements of mythmaking and fantasy. During the 1980s the close-knit mining communities were devastated first by the disastrous 1983 strike and then by the massive pit closures that followed in its wake. The powerful working class movements of the past have fragmented and the social realist model of the industrial novel which once spoke for them seems now as irrelevant to men writing in Wales as it once did to women.[23]

In 1988 Thomas focused on a dysfunctional family in *House of America* to explore the suicidal fantasies of a community as much overwhelmed by another culture as by the cold winds of economics. Ten years later, in *Gas Station Angel,* fantasy is viewed more positively. Ace has made up fantastic stories since a child and explains why: 'Life in storyland I could control, the ongoing war against the sea and real life I couldn't' (p.299). Set against the reality principle embodied in male-dominated bureaucracies, it is significant that these stories derive from his mother:

> MARY ANNIE: Magical things can still happen in this cruel world see. You've just got to know where to look that's all.
> ACE: So I believed. In stories and mysteries and magic. Stories were good. Life had the sea and the council. (p.301)

The stereotypes idealised by television, heritage and tourist boards - the working class hero, the Rugby star and the Eisteddfod winner - are almost entirely male.[24] This is not surprising, given that authority is defined as masculine, that subordinated nations struggle to establish self-determination and to throw off the feminisation associated with such subordination.[25] As the industrial fiction demonstrates, the strong male stereotypes that express the 'Land of ... Fathers' simplify and normalise, asserting dignity by denying the emasculating effect of poverty and exclusion. In rejecting such simplifications and seeking to address directly the fact of marginalisation, Thomas must accept that his new mythology requires new, more complex and more fluid visions of men.

Complicating men: from the *New Wales Trilogy* to *Work, 1995-1997*

> It is the name-of-the-father that we must recognise as the support of the symbolic function, which, from the dawn of history has identified his person with the figure of the law.[26]

The symbolic father is the (ideal) embodiment of

paternal authority, the locus from which patriarchal law and language come.[27]

I'm pretty obsessed in my plays with absent fathers. I can't analyse that.[28]

As the epigraphs suggest, the absent father seems to serve as an index of a more general powerlessness. Thomas's obsession with absent fathers leads him to investigate the rivalry of fatherless sons; in psychological terms, of sons without access to the authority of the law. For Freud the family is both actually and symbolically the nurse and inhibitor of the individual voice; the paternal function is to introduce the wider public world to the child. More abstractly, for Lacan, following and developing Freud, the symbolic father (*the name-of-the-father*) provides access to the symbolic order of language and the law, that which is beyond the mother-child dyad. In wanting to develop their own stories or wanting others to hear those that already exist, Thomas's characters seek access to this symbolic order. Cora Kaplan draws on psychoanalytic theory in her meditation on the relation of imaginative writing and gender, pointing out that 'the desire to write imaginative poetry and prose was and is a demand for access to and parity within the law and myth-making groups of society'[29] and is characteristic of those groups of individuals excluded from power. Psychoanalytic criticism thus provides valuable means of relating Thomas's fascination with the absent paternal figure with his quest for a new and independent Wales.[30]

The ubiquity of absent fathers in Thomas's pressurised families thus suggests a world that lacks access to both language and law. *House of America* is the archetypal example, setting two equally, if differently, damaged brothers in conflict with each other in their relation to an absent father and present mother. The internecine violence is pronounced in the (earlier) stage version of the play where the younger, Boyo, murders his brother Sid, but that violence moves inwards in the film when Sid commits suicide. In *Flowers on a Dead Red Sea* two paranoid and competitive slaughtermen, Mock and Joe - who may be brothers - fear and struggle with an absent authority figure, Cragg. Mock crumples after hearing of his father's death, finally the death of Martin Bratton, the idealistic young man who had tried to fly 'east from the gantry' in the play of that name, indicates a lost possibility, a lost future, in a world dominated by random events. The very pervasiveness of such concern with difficult masculinity means that Katie Gramich's perceptive study of the role allocated to the mother and to 'the female in general'[31] within Thomas's claustrophobic drama, foregrounds the 'apparently rigid world of patriarchal inheritance and parricide'[32] and comments that 'the dramas are littered with dead, buried, or lost fathers, with questing sons, rival brothers'[33]. Gramich is troubled by what she sees as a reliance on 'clichéd notions of female identity: the succouring mother, the slut with a heart of gold, the dutiful but deranged daughter',[34] but suggests that through a postmodern play with stereotypes within his non-naturalistic drama, Thomas's 'habitual mockery of macho roles and behaviour'[35] serves to ironise and unsettle the clichés.

Mockery is indeed one of the dominant notes of the 'New Wales Trilogy' (*House of America, Flowers of the Dead Red Sea* and *East from the Gantry*), a series of playtexts that explore questions of alienation and cultural commodification in relation to Wales. Flowers, the central play in the Trilogy, depicts a world of shame and death where, though one slaughterman (significantly called Mock) claims that 'I WILL FIND A SOLUTION. I WILL WRESTLE FOR AN ANSWER,' and tries to stem the 'red sea' of meaningless death by emphasising his craftsmanship and limiting his daily kills.[36] The other, Joe, glories in a savage nihilism: 'I don't care about accidents. I don't care about craftsmanship, sheep, people or beasts. I care about fuck all. I JUST FEEL LIKE KILLING, THAT'S ALL'.[37] All around them rusting domestic detritus falls dangerously out of the sky - prams, microwaves, kettles. The bleak associations of men with killing and the killing with a masculine fear of what's hidden in the dark are only slightly alleviated by the memory of a woman artist who might - or might not - have loved Mock: 'she said art can save culture.'[38]

Flowers of the Dead Red Sea unsettles rather than satisfies, closing with a reference back to a culture hidden within the text, detectable in the unconscious shame Mock expresses while asleep, in the loss of his father and in the constant allusions to drowning. It emerges briefly in the anguished words that explain why Mock does not know who he is:

> Everything floats past my ears, past my lips, a million words passing, a whole language, a way of life, a people drowning, a mother, father, grandmother, grandfather, daughter, son, brother passing by.[39]

The allusion is to the flooding of Tryweryn and the culture that the artist promises to save is that of Wales, of a people evicted from their home by the demands of the free market. It is a role that Thomas accepts in his desire to reinvent Welsh identity in a new kind of Welsh theatre.[40] It also explains the play's final scene which counterpoints what seems to be the victory of naked power and a rootless, savage consumerism, with two, implicitly linked images: one of art, pictured as a woman dancing on the red sea, and one of the tenacious human subject, Mock, hanging suspended like a carcass from a hook but asserting, with dignity, in this rapacious world, the ancient Welsh claim of survival against impossible odds: 'I am still here' *(yma o hyd)*.[41]

Such beliefs in the entwined relations of art and the dignity of the human subject sit uneasily with what Gramich sees as Thomas's postmodern practice. In the postmodern world art does not function as the last refuge of human dignity in the face of the pressures of the market but is seen as an intrinsic element of consumerism. It is unsurprising therefore that Gramich reads the intertextuality of his work as an expression of 'the impossibility of tragedy in a postmodern age. He can allude to tragedy, plagiarise it, play with it irrelevantly or longingly, but he can't have it'.[42] Gramich justifies her view by claiming that Thomas's characters cannot achieve anagorisis or self-realisation because they are not conceived as free choosing agents but created out of a compulsive interplay of prior texts - more a palimpsest than a classical tragedy. However it is possible to read the failure of Thomas's characters to achieve anagorisis quite differently. One way might be to see his theatre as another kind of tragedy, more akin to the Jacobean tragedy of the misfit struggling within nets of autocratic power. This is a tragic mode that glories in intertextual references and focuses on transgression and transgressive desire, frequently within families which the authority principle is hopelessly corrupt.[43] A different approach, however, might see Thomas's writing as emerging out of a long history of silenced voices rather than out of a present of postmodern inauthenticity and loss: an approach that would explain the emphasis both on the active function of art and on the humanity of the subject. Such a view would suggest that Thomas's work be considered as more postcolonial than postmodern. Indeed Thomas's work fits perfectly into the kinds of writings that David Punter calls the 'postcolonial imaginings' not only of previously colonised nations, but of a new world order he convincingly argues is dominated by American neo-colonialism.[44] Punter, like Gramich, is concerned with the ways in which the Primal scene and Oedipal crises inform the literary texts he examines, but he also sees those texts locked into distorting histories of repression that result in the compulsive intertextuality she considers as 'postmodern.' As a Gothic scholar, Punter looks for evidence of ghosts, monsters and hauntings in the texts he studies, and believes that if there is one thing that literature tells us it is

that there is no return, no 'recourse' beyond text;
just as for the postcolonial there can be no return,
no recuperation, only a painful and already
damaged work with materials that history has left
us, distorted though those materials must inevitably
be. [45]

For a Welsh writer such as Thomas, these damaged
inheritances include the stereotypes by which both the fractured
and painful condition of negation is contained and the complicity
of the damaged subject attained. The anger and nihilism of that
inheritance is addressed most forcefully in the stage version of
House of America, the first play of the New Wales Trilogy, and
thus the first in a deliberate attempt to represent the ongoing
effects of the unspoken histories. As an investigation of the sense
of impotence felt by the communities left behind in the
impersonal march of the free market within Wales, Thomas's
fantasy seems not only to be a more 'truthful representation' of
reality [46] than social realism but to be more relevant to the lived
experience of the communities that his characters inhabit than
the nostalgic idealisations of a community spirit found in what
often passes for that mode.

New configurations can create new meanings however,
and the ordering and juxtaposition of the three plays in this
volume suggests that Thomas's concerns are changing - perhaps
indicating a more secure sense of a contemporary Welsh identity
and challenging an earlier sense of outrage and cultural
impotence. Placing *Song From A Forgotten City* first links the
'death of the [traditional] author' to his mockery of the rugby
supporter, implying that a new Wales needs a new kind of writer.
In *Song* both minor and major characters comment on the
outdated stereotype of the rugby supporter who celebrates Welsh
victory by rapturously singing in healthy all-male company. By
allowing for a kind of heroism, the screenplay of *House of
America* also testifies to changing attitudes. In the playscript of

House of America the struggle between the brothers ends with an anguished Boyo strangling a confused and frightened Sid. In the screen play, however, Sid is transformed into a more decisive figure who kills himself with an extravagant heroism, wearing the talismanic watch he removes from his father's corpse - and Boyo (now a disabled rugby player) tries to save his brother. The mockery that characterises the depiction of men in the three plays that make up the New Wales Trilogy and is reserved for an outmoded stereotype in *Song* is here suspended, allowing for a more compassionate view of the relations between men. Finally, in the last of these three plays, *Gas Station Angel*, Thomas's mockery no longer targets macho or Welsh stereotypes, but is reserved for the tacky management of the refurbished local pub or the lecherous supermarket trolley-boy, Keith. The hero, Ace, is quite different from Thomas's earlier protagonists, he does not struggle with his brothers, he has a good relationship with his father, he falls in love with an independent 'babe.' *Gas Station Angel* offers a possibility of regeneration in the coupling of Ace and Bron and their shared vision of a world that includes Europe and Africa. The absent father of the first *House of America* is conceived differently in the screen play, is ironically revised in *Song* and is missing from *Gas Station Angel* where there are two fathers. Thomas has shifted away from the debilitating legacy of the past to an engagement with the concerns of the present and this move is manifested in a more positive revision of the masculine subject. Thomas's new hero does not look back to Tryweryn but forward to a struggle with the levelling effects of globalisation, with the free trade that seeks either to obliterate local difference or to commodify them as marketable heritage. Wales thus becomes one of many small nations threatened by the monopolies of American-based multinationals. The voice of Carlyle, the hero and writer of Song expresses Thomas's intent:

> Our voices must be heard Night-Porter, we must
> play our part on the world stage. We've got to show

that the way we live, love and die means something,
that we are part of the world, not unique but
similar, universal, like small countries all over the
world. ... (p.42)

This is why Ace and Bron, the hero and heroine of the
final play in this collection, discover each other in their shared
love of things that can't be understood, their shared scorn for the
commodifications of a supermarket world. When Bron asks 'who
ever said SHOPPING WAS BEAUTIFUL?' Ace responds,
mesmerised, with 'not me' (p331).

Making things visible: Song from a Forgotten City

I'm a writer trying to escape the corridors of the
invisible who has come to the Angel to sing. (p.43)

When Thomas conjures up the world of film noir in *Song* he does
so not only to summon up a shadowy underworld of the
imagination but to critique too easy an acceptance of its tenets
and to examine its fit on the Welsh situation. The play opens in a
seedy hotel with a Night-Porter and a Bellboy finding corpse and
a cassette with a cryptic message. The action jumps back and
then moves forwards until we arrive at the murder - only to
discover it is suicide. The corpse, Carlyle, may be the 'writer' of
this drama but he struggles to control his characters. In an
extraordinary conversation he alarms the Night-Porter by
informing him that he is one of the 'minor character[s]' of a
narrative in which he has no significant role: 'You ever seen a
Welsh Night-Porter of a downtown hotel play a hero before?
(p.41). He elaborates:

the voice of the Welsh Night-Porter is invisible in
the pan national world of fiction, he and many of
his ilk will be consigned to the dustbin of the

insignificant forever (p.42)

When the Night-Porter objects that he is 'not insignificant,' Carlyle draws attention to the wider picture: 'I know that and you know that but who else in the world cares Night-Porter?' (p.41).

Thomas's concern with the value of silenced voices, with the recognition here of 'minor characters,' runs throughout his work and has already been mentioned in relation to *Hiraeth*. It is a question of 'caring.' All the characters of *Song* are damaged by their pasts and the question of 'who cares' reverberates throughout. Significantly, neither of the two women mentioned in the play, both of whom are associated with the conventional attributes of love and nurturance, actually appears. It's equally significant therefore that both have been 'cut-up' in the belly. The mother of one of the minor characters is said to have died in a car crash holding onto her bleeding belly. Carlyle sees a world 'full of dead and missing mothers.' Even his romantic dreams are tarnished by this viewpoint: 'every time you look at a full moon on a starry night there is a mother who is looking at the same moon and dying. (p.114)

In *Song,* Thomas makes Carlyle desperate to put his invisible damaged life - and the invisible lives of those like the Night-Porter - 'on the map'; but that means changing the map, redrawing the city, fantasising

> a place you never knew existed … a place where you aint treated like a piece of shit. A place where you're not fuck all squared. A place that counts on the scale of things. Is noted for something good. Is not invisible. (p.58)

Thomas is not alone in his fascination with landscape and the desire to find a space of respect and dignity in his own place. Edward Said sees this desire to discover imaginative resources at home as a defining characteristic of anti-imperialism, of cultures previously perceived only as the economic resources of another power:

> if there is anything that distinguishes the imagination of anti-imperialism, it is the primacy of the geographical in it. ... To the imagination of anti-imperialism, *our* space at home in the peripheries has been usurped and put to use by outsiders for **their** purpose. [47]

But, because this imagination can never return to a world prior to this exploitation - to do so would be to deny the historical reality of what has happened - Said is careful to point out that

> it is therefore necessary to seek out, to map, to invent, or to discover a third nature, which is not pristine and pre-historical ... but one which derives historically and abductively from the deprivations of the present.

And this is where *Song* starts: simultaneously foregrounding the old stereotypes of the Welshman, their destruction and the quest for a new sense of self and place.

The play opens in Cardiff with the Welsh Rugby team losing to the English, an event that seems to paralyse and silence every Welshman in the (real) city. The Night-Porter - that unlikely figure from *film noir* - recalls the traumatic experience of hearing about the defeat from an 'underground' place: a place that simultaneously evokes the Gothic underworld *and* the world of the Welsh miner. But this underground place is concretely and comically imagined as a toilet cubicle in the Hayes where the Night-Porter is smoking a spliff, drinking lager, eating liquorice allsorts, and looking up through the frosted glass at the street above him. The moment opens out into the space of fantasy:

> Silence for eighty minutes (PAUSE) Then shouts.
> Footsteps. Heavy footsteps. Language. Tears. The
> crowd leaves the ground. Sixty thousand capacity. I
> estimate at least ten thousand walked above me
> with the heavy tread of defeat. (p.14)

Pumping up the emotional pressure, Thomas parodies the
stereotypes mercilessly. Bellboy relates the anguish of a
disappointed fisherman:

> Who'd have said ten years ago. Or five. Or three.
> THE WHOLE WORLD IS BEATING US AT
> OUR OWN FUCKING GAME. Who'd have said.
> ... I'm fucked in the head. I'm Welsh and I'm
> fucked in the head. We're losing. (pp.16-17.)

The overwrought responses culminate in Carlyle's story of an old
barman who, faced with a silent, mourning crowd, tries to
sustain the myth of the singing Welshman:

> DO YOU WANT THEM TO THINK WE CAN'T
> SING ANYMORE? Do you? 'No' they said. 'So
> sing you fuckers, SING!' 'We don't know what to
> sing' they said. 'You sing the old songs that's what
> you sing' he said. 'How do they go?' they asked'
> 'Go? They go like they always gone. Nobody's
> changed the tune have they? Have they? Same
> tunes. Same songs.' (p.19)

The despairing barman slashes his wrists with a broken glass, the
ambulance fails to arrive and he bleeds to death... Yet this is no
tragedy, just a story, a fantasy, faintly ridiculous, that opens onto
a series of other, nested stories. When the characters ask

plaintively where 'the golden years' have gone, the rhetorical question is answered literally, locating them in commodities: 'in the shops/on video' (p.21). Lamenting that 'I was part of a nation that was fucking good at something' (p.24), the Night-Porter demonstrates the symbolism of the event as part of a widespread desire to belong to 'something good'. The rugby defeat is a recognition of the wider loss which had been hidden by earlier victories, but perhaps now recognisable in its inadequacy. Maybe the defeat can lead to new beginnings, as in Thomas's own dazzling fiction of a fictional writer's quest for a vibrant metropolis.

Carlyle is a new hero - of sorts - confused and incoherent though he is. He is ticked off, for example, by his own characters. At one point the Night-Porter warns Carlyle that if he doesn't behave he'll throw him out of the hotel: 'just because I'm a minor character doesn't mean you can go shouting at me, pointing guns at me!' (p.118). He certainly doesn't appear to understand the dialogue he has, apparently, written and the Night-Porter has to explain commonplace idiomatic phrases to him. Carlyle still doesn't seem to understand although he does get terribly, and probably drunkenly, excited at the explanation:

> slang means we're connected? ...Part of something?... Something good?... We're connected then ... connected by the way we speak? We speak the same language as dentists ... Next time I see a dentist man, I'm going to feel a connection ... me and him are going to be connected (pp.29-30).

Considering the complexity and characteristic knowing qualities of Thomas's work, it cannot be a coincidence that the name Carlyle summons up the great Victorian sage, one of whose most famous books meditated on the nature of the hero and the heroic in history.[48] *This* Carlyle however is confused by stories about his origin and his personal name - a Cumbrian city? an American car? - and couldn't be further from that learned and sophisticated cultural critic. He cannot assume that authoritative manner. No hero in the old sense, he is drunk, drugged and lives through his fantasies, weaving the narrative within which we find him, and stages, finally, the death of the omniscient Victorian narrator by shooting himself in the head. The narrative of *Song* thus seeks to decentre both stereotyped hero and traditional writer, allowing minor characters a voice and playing with the very idea of authorial control.

Song is one of the more fantastical of Thomas's texts and as Rosemary Jackson points out, 'fantasy has [always] tried to erode the pillars of society by un-doing categorical structures'[49] The structure that is 'un-done' in *Song* is that of the primary category of all, the Lacanian *name-of-the-father*. She points out then when Plato designed his ideal rational city in *The Republic* he was keen to expel

> all transgressive energies, all of those energies which have been seen to be expressed through the fantastic: eroticism, violence, madness, laughter, nightmares, dreams, blasphemy, lamentation, uncertainty, female energy, excess. ... The fantastic is thus made invisible in Plato's *Republic* and the tradition of high rationalism which it fostered.[50]

This list could provide a useful summary of the energies welcomed in Thomas's imagined city, one that brings what rationalism renders invisible into view. Jojo's transvestism and the confusion of identities involved in his sex with Carlyle (p.85) - when he wears Yvonne's skirt then he turns into Yvonne - provide the most obvious example. *This* ideal city is one addicted to excess, to the erotic energies of drugs and sex in particular, energies that appear to threaten the established order yet the play closes by revealing that this excessive mode is not outside the symbolic order of society at all but repressed in the figure of the father found at its very heart.

Carlyle describes his father being caught by his mother in full drag: 'her clothes, her underwear, wig, make-up, the whole jamboree' (p.121). In an earlier version of *Song* the father dies of shame and Thomas allocates the wife the function of reasserting her husband's normative masculinity by undressing him, putting him to bed and telling the doctor that he died 'on the job'. In this version, however, things are very different:

> She said he made a noise. Like an animal noise. Like a wounded animal. In a trap. She said his face looked as if it was melting. [PAUSE] she'd never seen a man look so ashamed.

It is a quite extraordinary passage: as the transgressive father becomes visible he drops the binoculars and hence loses the ability to see (the scopophilic masculine gaze deemed so important in film criticism, particularly of *film noir*), simultaneously losing access to language and, even, the very solidity of his physical self. In every way he thus loses his position as the stabilising phallic centre of the symbolic order. This loss is no tragedy however but a release into pleasure. Refusing the social role of policing gender norms - 'what the fuck did he think she was going to do?' - the mother responds erotically: 'she undressed him and took him to bed.'

In line with the Gothic elements of *film noir*, both the cosy familiar image of Wales and the solid, masculine stereotypes associated with it have fallen apart to reveal an uncanny space of excess and desire. Here there is no safe place: the action flickers between a hotel and an unheated squat that the spaced-out Carlyle thinks is a hotel; Rosie's home has been burgled and the women have been 'cut-up'. Without a city in reality, Thomas conjures one out of a mixture of *noir* elements pasted over a culture defined by silence and loss: 'a whole tradition vanished in front of our eyes ... singing, dancing, winning at rugby' (p.119). Though *Song* seems to exist purely in the imagination of its drunk, drugged and decentred author, it sets out the desire for the good place, a place that is simultaneously a metropolis and a place of nurturance and respect, an ideal home where men don't have to assume mastery -

> Like friends. A whole feast of friends. A giant family ... a sparkling room where we all go to laugh ... celebrations and success punctuated by ... by laughing (p.99)

- for a place where a new country might be born in the Angel Hotel.

Chasing a dream: House of America

> All his life he knew he could have been something,
> but something happened when he was young that
> stopped the real man from ever showing himself. ...
> He saw his pappy die (p.223)

Where *Song From A Forgotten City* exists in a no-man's world without proper families or homes, *House of America* gives us both - only to defamiliarise them, disqualifying them from being the desired sites of security and laughter. Each is as fragile as the house of cards that serves as a leitmotif throughout. For, of all Thomas's plays, *House of America* focuses the most on the absent father and in both playscript and screen play the home is envisioned as the site of Oedipal tensions that cannot be resolved in his absence. The three adult children of the dysfunctional Lewis family are locked in an incestuous embrace with their mad mother, unable to function in the world outside, excluded from any assumption of authority in their exclusion from the public space of work. Two of the children are fixated on a consuming fantasy of the missing father as a figure of plenitude, a drifter who has escaped the tedium of ordinary life in the mode of Kerouac's *On the Road*. This is a dangerous fantasy however: below the lawless glamour, the drifter does not challenge the status quo but merely inverts its terms, accepting a position of powerlessness. Jonathan Culler warns of 'the power of the reality principle to transform its enemies to its mirror image,'[51] a valid point in the light of Sid and Gwenny's uncritical acceptance of the American Dream. Culler goes on to insist that 'we assert fantasy's responsibility to resist before we accept Yeats's formula: "In dreams begin responsibilities".'[52]

In the stage play Sid, who instigates the appalling charade, knows from the start that Kerouac did not find freedom on the road but 'went half-mad in 1967, and died in [his] mother's arms'.[53] In the screenplay however Thomas removes this passage, changing both the relations between the siblings and the dramatic tensions by making Sid see his father die. The addition of scenes set in the ruined house that forms the father's tomb, with Sid sitting alone, weaving fantasies that idealise his dead father and fighting off memories of his mother burning bloodstained clothing, creates a sense of unbearable isolation. Early scenes of familial intimacy are thus rendered as much of a charade as the fantasy of Jack and Joyce. Boyo's attempt to rescue Sid at the end of the film thus grants the understanding Sid craved for throughout his life and finally, in death, allows him dignity - a message emphasised by the director's choice of a pieta-like composition for the shot of Boyo cradling Sid's corpse.

This change makes Sid a far more empathetic character. The fantasy about his father in America is explicable psychologically as the only way he can cope with his obscene burden and the powerful elaborations of rootlessness and loss to which he gives himself up signify his subliminal rejection of a maternal space perceived as threatening. This change alters the meaning of the joint fantasy with Gwenny too; both seeking to protect his sister and desperate for a vanished intimacy he offers her the fantasy that has enabled him to cope. But Gwenny translates it into a fantasy to serve her own needs. Thomas makes Gwenny more like her mother in her demand for love and desire for a family, for something to make sense of the world around her in which she is always left behind, left out. Her response to the situation is therefore to overvalue the father she cannot remember and associate him with the all-powerful location of America.[54] She becomes pregnant seeking to create a family in her father's image.

Kerouac romanticised himself as the active travelling hero of his fictions but Sid and Gwenny are stuck at home and consume Kerouac's as alien, second-hand fantasies using them as scripts to obliterate themselves and turn into other people.[55] By assuming American accents and idioms they literally lose their own (Welsh) voices, identifying with a man whom they believe ran off with a 'floozy.' Gwenny reveals the association of Kerouac and father when she links the year of her parents' wedding with Kerouac and Jonson's first meeting (pp.114-15). This identification is more than a personal proclivity: Mam's words reveal it to be part of a cycle of generational repetition - 'why does [Sid] have to wear your father's clothes? ... Reminds me of her [the floozy] she does. ... Gwenny.' (pp.188-89) - that is part of the wider, dysfunctional culture of small countries everywhere who have lost what Thomas calls their 'sustaining myths' and look to America for their replacements. Thomas sees the American Dream as an 'exportable myth ...of freedom and equality [which] is wrapped in crass commercialism.'[56] This absent father thus offers no escape to the problems of a culture under siege but, by promoting the desire for access to the symbolic order of another society and another law, signals instead a seductive cultural death. The abandoned house, the '*House of America*' where Sid creates his fantasies, in line with this, is a house of death. That Sid identifies so strongly with the father he saw die demonstrates the impossibility of escape through such a dream. If anything else is needed to show the way that Kerouac's mythology serves as a 'mirror image' and inversion of the reality principle for a small Welsh community - and hence as negation of its power to resist the domination of the powerful American corporation - it is Sid gazing into the mirror at his own reflection and murmuring 'R.I.P.' (p.204).

There are at least four houses in *House of America* but none of them serves the central function of the house as sheltering space, as home.[57] The first is the American ranch in Banwen which has its uncanny double in the imaginary ranch in America: both are reflected in the derelict house where the father is buried and, symbolically, in the house of cards that cannot be made to stand up with any stability unless through the pretence of Sid's glue of lies. In this unstable world of doubles and inversions the desire for a stable and nurturing home is rendered impossible, outside the law of the given world. Like the men, the women of the Lewis family are condemned to transgressive repetitions, first to commit crimes within the family (murder, incest) and then to go mad. The film concludes with them together in the imaginary home that is the "House of America", a place now revealed also as the place of madness, accepting jointly that America, the place of death, is where the beloved live.

Although the idealisation of America can be traced back over the past twenty years or so - after all the Lewis house is called 'the ranch' - it is the arrival of the open cast that triggers the catastrophe by making the two sons aware of their own impotence as social agents. The decision to make the open cast operators American makes the film of *House of America* more than a tragedy of deindustrialisation; through the depiction of an American domination of both culture and economics, it becomes one of neo-colonialism. Thomas links the two directly: 'the Dream is still a global phenomenon and America is eminently successful at exporting crap all over the world - Mickey Mouse, McDonalds and KFC.'[58] In offering local employment, the open cast offers the slim possibility of access to the world that counts, the world where things happen (Boyo's friend Cat gets a decent second-hand car and drives to Swansea for example!) but it employs so very few people that it creates an even greater sense of exclusion than before: 'it's all Mickey Mouse' says Sid, 'small time, fourth division, second class toys ' (p.141). The Michigan Mining Company marks the return of the coal industry to a mining community in a new, yet more rapacious form. As in *Song* there is an intense desire to make this place mean something, be the good place, but it's here curdled by the self-disgust of those who feel left behind in the global stakes. Sid bitterly refuses to believe that anything good could come out of Wales:

> It don't matter if Cale came from fucking Banwen, he's living in New York now, and I bet you that's where he'll stay. Huh, can you imagine Lou Reed

walking around Banwen? Alright Lou? How's it
going wus, like on the wild side? Not cool enough
for him, no way, probably never even heard of
Wales. (p.134)

House of America seems to bear out Said's contention
that postcolonial writing seeks to establish the homeland as a
complex space defined through memory and imagination, history
and mythology - not an economic resource for somewhere else.
But the ecological devastation caused by the open cast, a form of
mining that tears the land apart, reduces it to precisely that: a
place without landmarks, history, stories, uninhabitable, a pure
resource. Michigan Mining employs labourers, not miners,
atomised servants of the corporate machine not 'comrades'
working together. Open cast mining thus serves as a perfect
metaphor for the pitiless workings of the global market which,
according to Punter, seeks to:

> abolish difference altogether; against the force of
> the apparently unalterable facts of geography and
> history, the two great putative salvations of our
> national and regional differences, free trade needs a
> world in which all is essentially the same, a terrain
> from which bodies have been conveniently
> removed.[59]

Yet bodies have a habit of asserting themselves and two
in particular haunt *House of America*. The corpse of the father,
signifying abandonment, treachery and the lost possibilities of
the past, is buried in the ruined house while the drugged, too-
fertile body of the daughter, signifies the monstrous future of the
decaying community through its incestuous pregnancy. This
place with lies instead of history has become what Punter calls 'a
hysterically empty space',[60] where the body takes the place of
speech and is condemned to sterile repetitions, where madness

takes over.

House of America brilliantly explores the way that globalisation works as destructively on the cultural imagination as on the economic sphere. The free trade economy must encourage dissatisfaction if it is to expand its markets, must build on the ceaseless stimulation of desire for the unattainable. Robert Young adapts Deleuze and Guattari's concept of 'the desiring machine' for his analysis of how such a distorted economy of desire is drawn to the forbidden, an attraction that leads to the 'unlimited and ungovernable fertility of "unnatural unions".'[61] The sexual union of Sid and Gwenny in the maternal bed is an unholy example, its transgression amplified in a room historically and metaphorically splashed with the father's blood.

Where Sid and Gwenny identify with their absent father, Boyo, as his name suggests, is rooted in the family and identifies with their mother. Indeed Sid mocks him as a 'Mammy's boy' (p.195). Yet, although hostile to the father he believes has abandoned them, he is as frustrated as his brother and desperately wants a traditional pursuit to prove his masculinity. In the stage play Thomas makes him translate Brando's famous 'I could have been somebody' into lost work possibilities, rejecting Sid's dreams: 'I could have been a boxer, or a farmer, or a miner, or I don't know. Something real, something to get your teeth into, not lies, lies, actors, films'.[62] The screen play associates him more closely with Wales and a home-grown escape: 'I could have played rugby for Banwen, for Cardiff, the World, the fucking lot, not sit in and watch bastard films, lies, fucking cloud cuckoo buckoo!'(p.147).

The brothers respond differently when their social impotence is confirmed by the savage beating they receive in the fight with the Americans. Sid drives off into fantasy but Boyo continues to try to operate in the social world. He becomes increasingly isolated as his family slides into madness and then his local pub, the only place of friendship and security left, is spoiled for him by the invasion of the Michigan men. In her meticulous study of the way that torture unpicks the entwined construction of self and world, Elaine Scarry shows how frequently it works by inverting the basic securities that enable both elements to come into being. Her analysis demonstrates the power of Thomas's writing is for it describes exactly what happens to Boyo when his place of protection becomes a place of pain and he is ridiculed and isolated:

> The domestic act of protecting becomes an act of hurting and in hurting, the object becomes what it is not, an expression of individual contraction … when it is the very essence of these objects to express the most expansive potential of the human being, his ability to project himself out of his private, isolating needs into a concrete, objectified, and therefore shareable world.[63]

Self-hating and hysterical, Boyo attempts to destroy that which has turned from an expansive 'shareable world' to 'an expression of individual contraction,' revealing its contamination by smashing up the toilets and thus ensuring his own expulsion from the pub's residual security.

In the microcosm of Wales that is the Lewis household, the lost father is connected to the wider loss of social possibilities of regeneration. Anna-Marie Taylor's comment that in 'Edward Thomas's crazed Lewis family cooped up in their *House of America* [we see] south Wales gone mad in its post-industrial decline'[64] summarises perfectly the relation of the dysfunctional family to the wider cultural trauma. Many aspects of that 'crazed family' reappear in the families of *Gas Station Angel*: the rivalrous brothers and a lonely sister, the mad mother who kills a man, a house sliding into ruin and the possibility that a murdered corpse will be revealed when it finally collapses and, in this case, falls into the sea. But the differences are profound. *Gas Station Angel* is not a tragedy like *House of America* but a romance, a form that stresses continuity. Rather than focusing on an inevitable cultural dislocation dramatised through unresolved Oedipal crisis it seeks an expansive multi-lingual world that recognises the failures of the past and moves on. After all, as the father and son of the Ace family agree we cannot escape the past and: 'who can we ever be except / the sons and daughters of our fathers and mothers' (p.335).

Imagining a future: Gas Station Angel

> This town is no different to loads of other towns around the place, around the world if it comes to that, and this family's just the same too, give or take a few things. I mean we may be on the extreme side of things but the principle's the same. Secrets and lies. A fucked up past. Maybe if we faced up to the past then maybe we wouldn't find the world so confusing (p.274)

In *Gas Station Angel* the savage concentration with which Thomas focuses on the single, twisted family as both site and expression of destruction has vanished and he gives us two families instead, families secretly linked by a hidden violence but which move towards a more positive association by the close. This play is far more interested in cultural survival than in the endgame of cultural trauma and its form - the romance - looks forward rather than back. And although this is not a play marked by absent fathers it is deeply interested in the kind of man that may be produced in a future dominated by a homogenising free market. By focusing on two families instead of one the father figure no longer functions as an archetype - and along with this shift both fathers are present in their particularity. The effect of this deconstruction of the father figure breaks the gravitational pull of a strong centre, and releases minor male voices otherwise repressed into the margins of the plot. There are three of them (all played by the same actor in the 1998 performance[65]): Mr Entertainment, Keith the trolley-boy and Dyfrig, the farmer's boy. The first two are parodies of the master and slave mentalities generated by the enterprise culture. They speak a language of power which fixes the world around them into neat categories for exploitative purposes. Mr Entertainment is the voice of the entrepreneur who seeks to undermine any local distinctiveness in the promotion of a homogenised 'leisure industry:' 'Miserable git, who the fuck wants people like that in the place. Pub was dying 'til I got hold of it' (p.274); Keith is one of the victims of such thinking, brainwashed by advertising clichés: 'You can tell the kind of person someone is by the chocolate they eat' (p.332). Thomas is coruscating about both. The figure of Dyfrig however, whose voice I will discuss in more detail later, is given a passionate interior monologue, breaking out of the loutish stereotype imposed by a powerful outside on an inarticulate farm boy, a stereotype that is constructed in order to dismiss both him and his world as peripheral to the interests and values of its appraising eye. Dyfrig's voice is a powerful critique of the price paid for a supermarket future but he cannot speak from within its discourse. He turns instead to fantasy to express his desire as that excluded from a rational centre. Knowing he is accounted ugly, he cries out 'let me get pregnant by the spunk of a fairy I say. From the underground. The otherworld. Then you might think me beautiful.' (p.290). Dyfrig's impassioned voice demonstrates why, in the end, Thomas turns to magical realism in *Gas Station Angel*.

House of America draws on a range of what Thomas calls 'global myths.'[66] Primary amongst these are the valorisation of the freely choosing individual of the American Dream and the appropriation and analysis of Greek tragedy by Freudian psychoanalysis as a way of understanding the identity of an individual constructed in that frame. Closely following these two narratives of society and self comes the inevitable movement of individual protagonists towards catastrophe characteristic of both classical and Jacobean tragedy. All three stress the alienation of the isolated individual in a socio-symbolic order dominated by a punitive law, with an authoritative core translatable into Lacan's *name-of-the-father*.

The global status of these narratives reflects the central values of the dominant order - even as their familiarity ensured a wide audience for Thomas's first play. Yet this very accessibility poses problems for the dramatist who refuses the values they express, or who wishes to revalue the voices that they marginalise (the inarticulate, the powerless, the ugly, the rural: Dyfrig). Thomas claims that *House of America* not only demonstrates that, 'you can't buy the American Dream of a shelf and call it Welsh,' but also that 'you've got to make up your own heroes, your own contemporary mythology.'[67] This is what Thomas tries to do in *Gas Station Angel* where he turns from the American cult and culture of the individual to alternative models in the angels and fairies of old Welsh stories and European folklore, 'the myths and stories that sustain us at home.'[68]

The play starts with a stark memory: 'I saw a woman' (p.258). This tantalising statement is made in the simple past of the archetypal fairytale and settles the audience to listen to a story. In its brevity - no place, no time, no description, just boy meets girl - the statement suggests the romance plot and stimulates curiosity about its development. Thomas himself notes this as a new departure, commenting, almost with surprise, that: 'I am, after seven years as a fiction maker, writing good heterosexual sex.'[69] The change is framed by a relationship of mutual interest and understanding between a son, Hywel Ace, and his father, given the revealing name of Manny or Man. Like the audience Manny listens to his son's story and voices our questions: 'Where?' he asks, then, encouragingly, 'And...?' (p.258). The closeness of the relationship between father and son is reflected in the way that Ace puts similar questions to Bron. 'Where?' he says, and 'When?' The problems of the Ace family are clearly not those of the absent father but are to do with the past and how it connects with the present.

In *Gas Station Angel* the past is the stimulus to the act of writing, related to memory from the start. Ace can remember when he first saw Bron because he wrote it down: 'August the ninth. ...I keep a diary. I go out at night. I write down what I see' (p.259). But, as with any history, there are hidden narratives which he is not supposed to record. We discover much later that Ace's love narrative displaces one of violence: the day when Ace and Bron see each other for the first time is the day after Bron's brother Bri was killed by Ace's mother, Mary Annie, and the family has decided jointly to cover it up. Ace's desire to keep watch is part of that repressed sense of responsibility. He likes to think of himself as 'the night-watchman of this town' (p.259) though he admits that there are some things that he doesn't see: 'I like to think I see everything, but I obviously don't.' Ace is dominated by his memories and unable to stay in the present: 'So many secrets...' (p.347)

In *Gas Station Angel* the voices flicker in conversation, jumping around in time and across space: Ace speaks now to his father in their house about Bron, now to Bron by the sea; and Bron speaks now to Ace and now to her brother Marshall with whom she saw - and is now discussing - Ace for the first time. Rather than focusing on the individual trajectory of a single voice at the expense of the others Thomas creates a polyphonic texture that quickly builds a community of voices.[70] And even though the characters are only talking, the layers of intercut memories produce a sense of activity and movement, memories that bubble up and enact themselves before our eyes rather than speaking from any fixed place or present.

The play's elliptical dialogue moves back and forth in time like the meanderings of the unconscious mind itself, sliding between past and present, an impression marked all the more by its unfixed rural setting. This is the archetypal space of dreams, found in the pastoral world of the Shakespearean comedy or late romance, a space in which the politics that cause tragedy can be resolved. The events of *Gas Station Angel* take place on the uncertain boundary between land and sea, in an overground threatened by underground forces, caught between life and death. As Gramich points out 'most of [Thomas's] characters are precariously poised in besieged "last places", on the edge, on the frontier'.[71] But, because the playworld is in constant flux, there is the possibility of change. When the younger James brother, Marshall, drowns as a child, he is brought back to life, 'like,' his father says, 'fucking Jesus' (p.291). We expect heroic death when, at the end of part one, we see Manny about to be overwhelmed by the sea, standing erect within the battered house, repeating the ancient Welsh phrase that signifies defiant survival: 'we'll still be here (BEAT) I'll still be here. (BEAT) I WILL STILL BE HERE!!!' (p.311). In part two, however, he turns up with his wife, Mary Annie, discussing mopping up carpets, rebuilding the house and starting again (pp.340-341). As here, much of the play undermines the idealisation of the unmoved hero, undercutting the major narratives that promote that figure. Rebuilding their home Mary Annie and Manny decide that 'we'll buy what we need'/' 'and need what we buy' (p.341). What they need is a place to have - and make - love: a bed.

Like his father, Manny, Ace is no doomed hero who will die fighting impossible odds but a lover, a man who will form something out of the rubble of the past: 'I sat in the car that night looking out from the back of beyond to the shores of North Africa, I felt in my bones that things were going to change' (p.347). This transposition of Hollywood cliché into a Europe seen from Wales, decentres the received map, just as rewriting the hero does, and both refuse the deterministic histories of commercial exploitation (Hollywood, the supermarket) and the obsessive geometries of the given world order with its separate nations defined by separate languages. Ace dreams:

> maybe I can soon call myself a European. With my
> own language and the rudiments of another on the
> tip of my tongue, German, French, Spanish,
> Portuguese, Russion, Czech, even English.

With this change comes his release from the isolation of the
alienated individual: 'I aint the only fucked up bastard out there.
Everybody's got fucked up bits. ... it aint just me. I know it aint
just me.'

Ace turns, like his mother to the old stories of the
underworld as a way of expressing what the modern life does not
allow. Describing his meeting with Bron he describes something
fresh coming into his world, something that he can believe in:

> She was beautiful. An apparition. An angel. I
> couldn't take my eyes off her. I always wanted to
> believe in the underworld but I could never find the
> key, the door in the rock that would lead me to it.
> But there it was in front of me all along. It was just
> that I couldn't see it before. Maybe that night
> would be the night the underworld comes out into
> the real world and invites it to dance (p.307).

Though being Thomas, Ace is given the get-out of 'or maybe I
was just stoned.'

What Ace rejects is represented by Keith. Every thought
that Keith, the trolley-boy, has about the world has been
processed through the market. He assesses Bron as an 'exotic
fuck' (p.334) but even his fantasies of fucking her are rooted in
an ideology of domination, framed by the soft-porn format of
top-shelf magazines. He has neither the imagination nor the
language to think of anything different and his thinking would
be the same wherever he lived. Bron draws attention to the way
that Keith's underlying passivity replicates the values of the
market when she imagines him as 'fat and old. Unfuckable. With

the TV on. ... Holding a lottery ticket in your hand and your fingers crossed' (p.335).

That Thomas focuses on relationships as a means of ideological critique implies that Keith represents more than the commodification of desire by the market but also the denial of its complications: families, home, love. Bron stresses its utter sterility: nothing to say or do, just two lonely people watching TV. 'Keith' therefore figures more than a deadening future. Like the market whose language he speaks, he has no respect for anything outside of himself. The link is made by Manny in the final scene of part one when he stands shouting at the sea in the classic fairy tale manner:

> what made you angry? Not me. Not us. I always respected you. Me and you were like that once. Then you had tantrums. Wiff was right when she said the sea's gone mad, but why take it out on us? (p.310)

He insists that the reason that the sea is rising up against the land - and there is always a reason in fairy tales - is because of the exploitative values of the market. Manny's defence is that he never knowingly polluted the sea but only followed instructions: 'fertilized the land, that's all I did. They told me to do it. There's some chemicals to make the grass grow greener, never said it was full of shit.' Fantasy here is a better teller of truth than the discourse that reproduces its own values in the name of fact for the fate of the Aces' home clearly denotes the price paid for exploitation of the land, not just within Wales but throughout the world. As in the other texts in this collection, the trope of Wales serves to draw attention to the necessity that difference be respected, that we listen to the stories of the margins.

The story of the James brothers is a different example of the price paid for a such lack of respect. Briefly, Bri's action in saving Marshall's life is not recognised by his father who ignores him and favours his brother. Desperate to win his father's love, Bri buys a car. The strategy fails and he not only loses his licence but hacks Dyfrig's lambs to death. He defines himself through negation: 'I'm not a sad fucking bastard. I'm not a suicide. I'm not a beam swinger. I'm not a piece of shit' (p.296). He disappears. Later in the play he gazes into a mirror only to see his father's face reflected back and, thinking of the slaughtered lambs, mutters that he did it 'for you' (p.348). What he remembers is his father accusing him of lies. Too late, his mother, Mati explains what he needed: 'talking chokes, talking fanbelts, talking father and son talk in private, behind tinted glass, away from the eyes of the town' (p.314).

This bald summary makes Bri's story seem a near-replica of Sid's but, unlike that of Sid, it is never allowed to become tragic. Thomas evokes the love-affair of the doomed hero with his absent/distant father in order to displace it firmly from the centre and allow other narratives, other voices that space. The voices of Mr Entertainment, Keith and Dyfrig are far more striking because they speak the present. Bri's story, told in the past tense by others, and by Bri himself, has lost its immediacy: it is only being recalled in memory as a backdrop to the events that happen before our eyes. Slipping back and forth through time and space, the magical realist narrative depicts him on stage throughout the play interacting unseen with the living characters, and Bri becomes a character who just happens to be dead.

Like Sid, Bri yearns to drive away into the distance: a desire that expresses both characters' attempt to become 'men' in the old sense. But Bri is no hero and this play leaves that kind of man behind - after all, he does choose to return. Punter's intelligent reading of postcolonial fiction proves useful again when he stresses the pervasive trope of the journey in such writing, and points out 'the notion that there are further places to go, the myth of the freedom of the transient who feels he has choices as to how to proceed along the road'[72] is pure illusion. There is no simple way out.

Because it is a trope closely connected with the impotent dreams of the man who wishes to have choices, freedom, respect, but who cannot change what or where he is, the journey is a trope that lends itself to the tragic mode. In *House of America* it is clearly associated with the lost father's escape from home. Sid and Gwenny loll drunkenly in the bathroom singing Kerouac's song to the road. And, of course, Sid initiates it:

> SID: Home in Missoula, home in Truckee...
> GWENNY: Home in Oplousas ain't no home for me.
> SID: Home in old Medora...
> GWENNY: Home in Wounded Knee...
> SID: Home in ... what is it?
> GWENNY: Ogallalla...
> BOTH: Home I'll never be ... (p.194)

Gas Station Angel is more honest about what this rejection of home really means. If, like Sid, Bri dreams of losing himself in travel, as his mother points out, he really bought the tinted glass blue Marina 1800 TC because he wanted his father and his family: 'He wanted to win you back and when he'd won you back he wanted to win his brother Marshall back' (p.314).

By giving Bri's car to his sister, Bron, Thomas revises the trope. Bron does not want to run away: she stays where she is because she loves her family. Bron takes Ace on a very different kind of journey in that car, one that stresses pleasure in the trip itself, seeking to see differently from the place that is home rather than leave it behind. And Bron - not Ace - draws Thomas's twin concerns with imagination and Welsh identity together when she claims that 'to be Welsh at the end of the twentieth century you got to have imagination' (p.331).

Thomas gives one of the most powerful voices in the drama to Bron. As Gramich has rightly pointed out, the depiction of women in the earlier work is characterised by cliché.

But, unlike these women - absent in *Flowers* and *Song,* suffering in *Hiraeth*, grieving a lost beloved in *East from the Gantry* and insane in *House of America* - Bron is questioning and imaginative, interested in language and ideas. She is given the strongest refutation of utilitarian thinking: 'I like things I don't understand. Only things I don't understand interest me. Why celebrate what you already know Ace?' (p.330). She walks out of her job in the supermarket in protest at its lack of stimulus. Her response to Keith's unsophisticated overture reveals a clearer sense of what the marketing and commodification of sex implies: an appropriation and denial of the real living body in a mechanistic fantasy of repetitive fucking. She imagines herself physically ageing:

> I'd listen to my body decay. I wouldn't be able to move my arms or legs or head. I would only be able to feel my head. It would be heavy, full of all the things I dreamt about and never did. I'd feel ashamed. My face would feel skinned. And then I'd scream. I'd scream and scream until I couldn't scream anymore .... Knowing that I'd missed the plot, the dream, the crack, the mystery. I would never wake up - and open my eyes - and see something I don't understand, a mystery I've never imagined . (p.329)

In this play Thomas gives Bron the voice of possibility. Like Gwenny, she comes from a dysfunctional family but, unlike Gwenny, who is still a confused child, Bron knows what she wants and she refuses to be the victim of her past. She instigates change at every level of the plot, initiating the conversation with Ace ('I've seen you before'), offering 'out of the blue' to take him for a drive in her car because she too has had 'a shitty time' (p.270). When they talk in the mountain he can recall a little Welsh from his childhood but she still speaks it. Welsh is seen as the least utilitarian of languages and hence the most closely associated with the imagination. A brilliantly conceived - and very stoned - discussion about the language and its characteristic 'gaps' conveys the sense of two people reaching over the 'gaps' between them in an attempt to connect beyond language (p.329). This understanding, not the mechanised fucking generated by Deleuze and Guattari's 'desiring machine,' is what allows the complex body to resurface, the self to be happy with where and what it is. It is because of this ability to connect that Ace is able to walk away from the debilitating effects of his past. Despite his father's panicking commands -

> We don't talk about that story anymore Ace. That story is locked up in the strongbox of our minds. ... That story is our secret Ace, It's family. It's a family secret. ... WILL YOU SHUT UP ABOUT OUR FUCKING STORY! ... For Christ's sake Ace, it's a family secret (pp.348-53)

- he tells Bron the truth about her brother's death. As with *Gas Station Angel* as a whole, Ace refuses the language of authority and turns to his mother's tales of the underground to convey the story: 'every now and then [the fairies] come up from the other world and into this world. ... I've danced with them but sometimes we do bad things' (p.351). Bron responds in the same register: 'no Brian James .... Because he's a fallen Angel, a bad Fairy.' This recourse to fantasy may appear whimsical but I think that Thomas here attempts to find a language of the emotions that has not been - as in psychoanalysis itself - appropriated by the voices of the powerful. He looks for this language in the native stories of the land itself, reimagined as a space of fantasy, its history turned into the underground mazes of its folk tales.[73] It is unsurprising therefore that he should turn to what has traditionally been defined as the terrain of the 'feminine' (the imagination, the unconscious, the body, human relationships - all excluded from the rational centre associated with authority) in order to reject a tragic model of masculinity and find a new way of imagining Wales. Ace's ability to trust Bron may come from his close relationship with his father but it is her imagination that enables him to see the possibility of change. This is the crucial difference between Thomas's fantasising hero and the old destructive myths of absent fathers which lead to the lonely, tragic self-determination of the James brothers.

I close by looking more closely at the extraordinary speech given to a very minor character. Dyfrig, the farmer boy speaks to the audience:

> I am beautiful. I am fucking beautiful. (PAUSE) You might not be able to see it ... but I am. It's written all over my face. But nobody can see it, only Ace. When I step out onto the street people say there he goes. What an ugly bastard. His past is only acne and boils. Fuck how he must have worried as a boy. Poor boy, pity poor boy, farmer boy. Unkissable boy ... but who am I now? A boy? A farmer's boy? A man? A half man? Beast? Angel? Demon? Member of the underworld? How will I shed rocks to become a man in the 21st century? ... Uh? ... Uh? ... These are the things I think about when you all pass me on the street; when my lambs are slaughtered. (p.289)

This is the voice of the excluded. And what he rejects so passionately is the stereotype of the loutish farmworker. Dyfrig is sensitive and anguished in his desire for recognition and attention. He recognises that only Ace, an artist and dreamer like so many of Thomas's new heroes, cares enough to see below the simple surface. Dyfrig's voice is the answer to that of Mr Entertainment, a plea for the development of a different kind of masculine vision within Wales. It is interesting that Thomas's strategic allocation of attention to such peripheral voices attracted the censure of *The Independent* critic Dominic Cavendish who did not seem to understand it. Already uncomfortable about the play's 'whimsy,' he complained that 'the play's main problem is that, for all their dreams of flight, Ace and Bron never stand out from the rest of the crazy talking town.'[74] Yet, the point is surely not that they are the special ones, the only ones who want extraordinary things, but that, in a random world where houses fall into the sea and drowned boys are brought back to life, their voices are part of a woven texture of stories that challenge the idea of the 'chosen one,' of the fixed and favoured centre. In this play Ace and Bron happen to be 'lucky' in their ability to see - and dream - further than the rest.

Jeni Williams
Swansea Oct 2002

NOTES

1 Not much of a dream then is it?' Interview with Hazel Walford Davies, in Hazel Walford Davies (ed.), *State of Play: Four Playwrights of Wales*, (Llandysul: Gomer, 1998), p.118.

2 Rosemary Jackson, *Fantasy: the Literature of Subversion*, (London: Routledge, 1981), p.313.

3 Ed Thomas, *Hiraeth/Strangers in Conversation*, collected in Phil Clark (ed.), *Act One Wales: Thirteen One Act Plays*, (Bridgend: Seren, 1997), p.175.

4 *Ibid*, p.170.

5 *Ibid*.

6 *Ibid*, p.181.

7 Not much of a dream then is it?' p.124.

8 *Ibid*.

9 Although focused on the novel, Rosemary Jackson's seminal discussion of fantasy literature is equally pertinent to theatre - and especially to the rule of the 'three unities' of its classical form: 'fantasies from the late eighteenth century onwards attempt to undermine dominant philosophical and epistemological orders. They subvert and interrogate nominal unities of time, space and character, as well as questioning the possibility, or honesty, of fictional re-presentation of those unities,' (Jackson, p.313)

10 Quoted in Heike Roms, 'Edward Thomas: a Profile,' in *State of Play*, p.188.

11 See Thomas's description of his writing practice in 'Not much of a dream,' (p.120).

12 *Hiraeth*, p.177.

13 *Ibid*, p.178.

14 'I want a Wales at ease with itself and rejoicing in its natural eclecticism ... with a myriad of sustainable myths,' 'Not much of a dream', (p.117).

15 *Ibid*, p.175.

16 'Not much of a dream', p.126.

17 In this Thomas avoids the reactionary essentialism Cynthia Cockburn considers 'designed to shore up differences and inequalities, to sustain dominations. It operates through stereotypes that fix identity in eternal dualisms.' (Cockburn, *The Space Between Us: Negotiating Gender and National Identities in Conflict*, (London: Zed Books, 1998), p.13).

18 See the influential work of Eric Hobsbawm in, for example, Nations and Nationalism since 1780: *Programme, Myth, Reality, Cambridge:* CUP, 1992; Hobsbawm specifically analyses the textuality of the national myth in 'The Nation as Invented Tradition,' in John Hutchinson & Anthony D.Smith (eds.), *Nationalism*, (Oxford: Oxford UP, 1994), pp.76-83. Benedict

Anderson is a second hugely influential figure, who roots the development of the nation in the narratives that emerged with the development of print culture, *Imagined Communities*, London & NY: Verso, 1991. Homi K.Bhabha is a third, more modern voice: see 'Narrating the Nation' in Bhabha (ed.) *Nation and Narration*, London: Routledge, 1990. He develops his thesis in *The Location of Culture*, London: Routledge; 1994.

19 'Not much of a dream,' p.117.

20 Jane Aaron (ed.), Introduction to *A View across the Valley: Short stories by women from Wales*, *c.1850-195*0, (Dinas Powys: Honno Classics, 1999), p.x.

21 *Ibid*.

22 *Ibid*, p.xi.

23 See for example, Tredegar-born Christopher Meredith's novel of deindustrialisation, *Shifts* (Bridgend: Seren, 1988) which appeared in the same year as *House of America*. Like Thomas, Meredith depicts the destabilisation of traditional masculinities, explodes the idealisation of the drifter - and turns to a rediscovery of marginalised histories.

24 The first woman to win the Chair was at the 2001 Eisteddfod at Denbigh. Interestingly, Meredid Hopkins's *awdl* celebrated a new, female topic: pregnancy.

25 Matthew Arnold argues seriously for the femininity of 'the Celts:' 'no doubt the sensibility of the Celtic nature, its nervous exaltation, have something feminine in them, and the Celt is thus peculiarly disposed to feel the spell of the feminine idiosyncrasy; he has an affinity to it; he is not far from its secret.' 'On the Study of Celtic Literature' (1866), *On the Study of Celtic Literature and On Translating Homer*. London: Macmillan, 1893.

26 Jacques Lacan, *Écrits. A Selection*, (London: Tavistock, 1977), p.67.

27 Elisabeth Grosz, *Jacques Lacan: A Feminist Introduction*, (London: Routledge, 1990) p.72.

28 'Not much of a dream,' p.119.

29 Cora Kaplan, 'Literature and Gender', in Kaplan, *Sea Changes: Essays on Culture and Feminism*, (London: Verso, 1986), p.71.

30 Thomas discusses his work primarily in relation to his position as a Welsh writer and it is this that forms the focus of my essay. I wish to avoid the reduction of writing to personal expression and hence avoid discussion of Thomas's biography.

31 Gramich, '*Geography, Intertextuality, and the Lost Mother*', in State of Play, p.159.

32 *Ibid*.

33 *Ibid*.

34 *Ibid*, p.172.

35 *Ibid*.

36 Ed Thomas, *Flowers of the Dead Red Sea* in Thomas, *Three Plays*, (Bridgend: Seren), 1988,

p.162.

37 *Ibid*, p.156.

38 *Ibid*, p.142.

39 *Ibid*, pp.134-35.

40 In a 1997 interview with *The Observer* Thomas commented on the prospects of Welsh devolution, declaring that we are 'free to make up, re-invent, redefine our own versions of Wales, all three million different definitions if necessary, because the Wales I know is bilingual, multi-cultural, pro-European, messed up, screwed up and ludicrously represented in the British Press.' Quoted in Roms, 'Profile,' p.186.

41 *Flowers*, p.166.

42 Gramich, p.164.

43 Examples might include John Webster, *The White Devil* (1612), Thomas Middleton, *The Changeling* (1622) or, (under the doomed rule of Charles I) John Ford,'*Tis Pity She's a Whore* (1630).

44 David Punter, *Postcolonial Imaginings: Fictions of a New World Order*, (Edinburgh: Edinburgh University Press, 2000) p.3.

45 *Ibid*, p.10.

46 Heike Roms, 'Caught in the Act: On the Theatricality of Identity and Politics in the Dramatic Works of Edward Thomas', in *State of Play*, p.133.

47 Edward Said, *Nationalism, Colonialism, and Literature*, (Derry: Field Day Theatre Company, 1988) p.12. (Italics in original).

48 Thomas Carlyle, *On Heroes, Hero-Worship and the Heroic in History* (1841).

49 Jackson, p.176.

50 Ibid, p.177.

51 Jonathan Culler, 'Literary Fantasy,' *Cambridge Review*, 95 (1973), p.33.

52 *Ibid*.

53 Edward Thomas, *House of America* in Thomas, *Three Plays*, p.75.

54 Freud's wonderful discussion of family romances sheds light on Sid and Gwenny's joint fantasy of an ideal father. He claims that 'the whole effort at replacing the real father by a superior one is only an expression of the child's longing for the happy, vanished days when his father seemed to him the noblest and strongest of men and his mother the dearest and loveliest of women. He is turning away from the father whom he knows today to the father in whom he believed in the earlier years of his childhood; and his phantasy is no more than the expression of a regret that those happy days are gone.' Sigmund Freud, 'Family Romances' (1909), in vol 7, Penguin Freud Library, *On Sexuality,* compil./ed. Angela Richards (Harmondsworth: Penguin

1991 [Pelican, 1977]) pp.224-5).

55 See Heike Roms's sophisticated analysis of this process in 'Caught in the Act,' esp.pp.134-37.

56 'Not much of a dream,' p.116.

57 I quote Elaine Scarry's wonderful summary of how the structure of the house enables it to become the place of safety that is the home: 'the room, the simplest form of shelter, expresses the most benign potential of human life. It is, on the one hand, an enlargement of the body: it keeps warm and safe the individual it houses in the same way the body encloses and protects the individual within; like the body, its walls put boundaries around the self preventing undifferentiated contact with the world, yet in its windows and doors, crude versions of the senses, it enables the self to move out into the world and allows that world to enter. But while the room is a magnification of the body, it is simultaneously a miniaturisation of the world of civilisation. .... the walls are also, throughout all this, independent objects, objects which stand apart from and free of the body, objects which realize the human being's impulse to project himself out into a space beyond the boundaries of the body in acts of making, either physical or verbal, that once multiplied, collected, and shared are called civilisation.' (*The Body in Pain: the Making and Unmaking of the World*, (Oxford: Oxford University Press, 1985), pp.38-39.)

58 'Not much of a dream,' p.116.

59 Punter, p,123.

60 *Ibid*, p.124.

61 Robert Young, *Colonial Desire: Hybridity in Theory, Culture and Race*, (London: Routledge, 1995), p.98.

62 *House of America*, in Thomas, *Three Plays*, p. 37.

63 Scarry, p.41.

64 Anna-Marie Taylor, 'Welsh Theatre and the World,' in Anna-Marie Taylor (ed.) *Staging Wales: Welsh Theatre, 1979-1997*, (Cardiff: University of Wales Press, 1997), p.112.

65 Simon Gregor.

66 'Not much of a dream,' p.116.

67 Quoted by Caroline Hitt, review of *Gas Station Angel* in *The Western Mail*, 16/5/1998 (collected in State of Play, p.241)

68 'Not much of a dream,' p.116. Thomas is not alone in this interest in myths to explore what is left out of the dominant narratives of the West. It is a well established pattern in much postcolonial writing. See for example, the contrasting attention to the function of myths, legends and dreams in Wilson Harris, *The Womb of Space: the Cross-Cultural Imagination* (Westport Conn.: Greenwood Press, 1983) and Jean Franco, 'Beyond Ethnocentrism: Gender,

Power and the third-World Intelligentsia,' (in Cary Nelson and Lawrence Grossberg (eds), *Marxism and the Interpretation of Culture*, Basingstoke: Macmillan, 1988).

69 'Not much of a dream,' p.126.

70 Familiar in dramas as diverse as television soaps or Dylan Thomas's 'play for voices,' *Under Milk Wood*.

71 Gramich, p.167.

72 Punter, p.83.

73 Said notes that the quests for an 'authentic' language of nation, 'a more congenial national origin than that produced by colonial history, for a new pantheon of heroes, myths and religions, [is similarly] enabled by the land.' (*Nationalism, Colonialism, and Literature*, p.13.)

74 Review of *Gas Station Angel* in *The Independent*, 11/6/1998. (Collected in *State of Play*, p.243-44.)

Production Reviews

House of America

Coal the dole and heaps of soul. *House of America* is an honest triumph.
NME

Terrific….achingly well acted for those who like their meat raw.
Daily Telegraph

This is a universal soul-mate for anyone who has experienced the angst of an untrendy upbringing in a drab place. Mesmerising.
Buzz

Song From a Forgotten City

Stunning performances but it is the words from a machine gun volley which steal the show. Roller coaster of emotions, simultaneously shocking, touching and funny.
The Western Mail

A grand slam triumph, buzzing steaming dialogue delivered to a spellbound audience.
Sunday Times

Unsentimental, urban, madly imaginative and lyrical…brilliant.
The Independent

Gas Station Angel

Thomas has a wonderful ear, his rich anecdotal writing creates a whole world out of a handful of characters. His direction is impeccable and his actors work for him with well-deserved devotion.

Sunday Times

Gas Station Angel is entirely Thomas, lock stock and barrel....part cartoon cut out, part grand quignol, part latter day soap beaten into bizarre shapes it is Wales, and it's mythological fairy-lands turned upside down. His writing carries unmistakable verve and originality. A tremendous ensemble.

Glasgow Herald

The message will speak to universal audiences, thanks largely to a script with a longer shelf life than most of today's new plays... Thomas paints a moving picture of love at a time of abject despair... his writing, in a brutal, authentic language, remains persuasive.

The Stage,

The most amazing play I've ever seen... incredibly exciting, vibrant, funny and challenging... A tour de force exploration into what it means to be human (and Welsh) in the late 20th century... outstanding performances... the direction was truly inspired... a joy to watch.

South Wales Echo

As a piece of live theatre it is stunning... Great staging, flying metaphors, lots of humour, impressive performances... one of the most exciting, richest, cleverest and most theatrical productions to have come out of Wales for some time.

Western Mail,

Theatre junkies should check out *Gas Station Angel*...
dark, strange and very Welsh, as one of the characters
puts it. Funny, stirring, and original
The Independent

Richly indigestible melange of myths and moods... sit
back and enjoy.
The Daily Mail

A rollercoaster ride between different locations,
lives and states of being... quite wonderful...
Thomas's colourful, rhythmic use of language... a
beguiling and unique poetry... Thomas directs his own
piece with outstanding brio coupled with extreme
tenderness, presenting a production which is as
delicately moving as it is robustly funny... The cast
perform with an energy and wit... Absorbing,
enchanting and observant, this will leave even the
most cynical with a confirmed belief in fairies.
What's On In London

This surreal approach makes for powerful theatre...
rich and strange, unexpectedly funny and peppered with
great one-liners...Thomas at his fizzingly inventive best..
The Financial Times

A wild and whirling talent... The production
itself... makes good use of the space. Richard Lynch
plays Ace with skill, Siwan Morris is a sexily
appealing Bron, and Richard Harrington makes his mark
as the blond, bolting Bri.
The Guardian

Ed Thomas
photography: jo mazelis